D0805575

The All-Volunteer Force

and American Society

The publication of this volume
is sponsored by
the White Burkett Miller Center
of Public Affairs,
University of Virginia

The All-Volunteer Force and American Society

Edited by John B. Keeley

University Press of Virginia
Charlottesville

THE UNIVERSITY PRESS OF VIRGINIA
Copyright © 1978 by the Rector and Visitors
of the University of Virginia

First published 1978

Library of Congress Cataloging in Publication Data

Main entry under title:

The All-volunteer force and American society.

1. United States—Armed Forces—Addresses, essays, lectures.
2. Military service, Voluntary—Addresses, essays, lectures. 3. Sociology, Military—United States—Addresses, essays, lectures.
I. Keeley, John B., 1929-
UA23.A59   355.2'2   78-18420   ISBN 0-8139-0762-4

Printed in the United States of America

355.22
A41

79-3185

Contents

Foreword

This book, a collection of related essays, is the result of
two years of intensive study, observation, and consultation.
Its subject is one of vital importance to the United States--
the effectiveness of our system of recruiting, training,
retaining, and organizing our armed forces. The study has
timely practical significance. In a broader sense, it
furnishes food for thought to those interested--and they
are many--in the optimal utilization, with freedom, of our
relatively diminishing human resources.

No panaceas are offered, no severe indictments made.
This volume delineates and defines, from several perspectives, issues which the American public and its government
cannot afford to neglect.

The concept of "solutions" of major national and
international problems is, in my view, a simplistic notion,
ill adapted to the essential nature of human development in
social and political matters. The authors of this volume
have wisely avoided the temptation to offer specific solutions. Instead, they have opened vistas and suggested
directions for change which are valuable and persuasive,
if not always identical.

Starting with a well-informed view of the American
military forces under the all-volunteer system, the book
offers comparisons with the British system (the United
Kingdom has had much longer experience with volunteer forces),
moves on to consideration of possible improvements in our
present system, and finally without advocating radical
departures at this time, suggests changes which may become
necessary in the future.

The move from conscription to the all-volunteer system
in the United States was basically dictated by political
forces arising from the Vietnam War. In my view, the major
attitudinal danger resulting from our experience in Vietnam
was a resurgence of isolationism--a danger which fortunately
has been perceived and avoided by the American people. As

a nation, we have, it is true, become more wary of foreign military involvement, but we have sensibly refused to reject our unavoidable role as a major power in the world.

After nearly five years of experience with the all-volunteer system, the condition of our armed forces is drawing, and deserves to draw, increasing public scrutiny. Some facts are obvious: growing difficulty, in the Army especially, of initial recruitment; greatly increased personnel costs; high rates of attrition (or in the reverse, low rates of reenlistment after training). These all have their consequences in terms of money, management, and force effectiveness. But it is rather in the realm of the intangibles--the human factors involved in the problem of maintaining large, highly trained forces in peacetime--where this book presents its most valuable and enduring insights.

One notices, from time to time, flare-ups of public interest in certain decisions regarding our armed forces, usually involving dramatic and highly technical equipment. The B-1 bomber and the cruise missile are recent cases in point. But a layman is rarely called upon to think about the people, the men and women of the armed forces, whose performance is crucial to the success or failure of any weaponry. It may well be that the area where public enlightment and debate are most needed, and most effective, is not in the field of technical equipment but rather in that of human relations, involving in particular morale, leadership, training, command systems, and military-civilian interactions. In this respect, this book has a good sense of priorities.

The tools of the President in dealing with other nations are diplomacy, national consensus and will, and finally the armed forces, indirectly or directly applied. The Miller Center has sponsored this study in the conviction that there has been a disproportionate amount of time and effort devoted to the technological and management aspects of our military establishment, at the expense of the human and social aspects, and ultimately at the expense of our nation's security and power. This volume, by its insistence that no military establishment can perform above and beyond the competence of its personnel, opens new perspectives. Experts on weaponry and management are not hard to find, and they certainly have much to contribute. The authors of these essays have concentrated on the areas in which they have special competence, through experience and study within the military services and as civilians. The editor is a distinguished combat soldier and scholar. His insights, together with those of the other contributors, have led to a volume unusual in its focus and findings.

It may be that all studies on military subjects suffer
in public estimation from the widespread American view that
military forces are a necessary evil. That view, I think,
is comparable to the view that hospitals, or rescue squads,
are necessary evils. We certainly do not want their services, when needed, to be inferior. As citizens, we try
to see to it that they are not. Public attention to the
problems inherent in the all-volunteer system is needed
now. This educational book deserves to be read.

                        Frederick E. Nolting, Jr.
                        University of Virginia

Preface

The title of this collection of essays, The All-Volunteer
Force and American Society, is not intended to indicate
the scope of these studies. Indeed, it would require a
number of volumes to encompass the complex interrelation-
ships between our society and its military forces. Rather,
the title was selected to emphasize the fact that there is
a close, vital, truly organic relationship between our
society and its military forces.

The nation's military establishment will inevitably
atrophy if it is neglected. Even if not neglected, these
forces will become something other, something less, than
what is needed for our national security if the fundamental
character and needs of these forces as human organizations
are misunderstood or ignored. It is probably in this latter
sense that our military forces suffer the most. Notwithstanding perhaps the longest and most active public debate
in our history about the condition of our military establishment, it appears either that the wrong issues are being
debated or at least that some of the most fundamental
issues are being neglected.

Surely the thoughtful citizen could be justifiably
puzzled concerning the status of the all-volunteer force.
On the one hand he hears glowing affirmation of its
success from the generals and service and defense secretaries. On the other hand he reads of the highest
desertion rate in the U.S. Navy's history and of an attrition rate of nearly 40% of all soldiers and sailors before
the completion of their first terms of enlistment. He may
also have some questions about the racial mix of the Army,
with over a quarter of its members black, and he may be
disturbed about the increasing evidence that women will
shortly be permitted into combat roles. Somehow the image
of women participating in the ferocity of combat doesn't
come across convincingly.

Our thoughtful citizen is right to be concerned. The
all-volunteer force has serious problems which raise
questions concerning its present vitality and its future

viability. The problems of the all-volunteer force stem
from a variety of causes: the manner in which conscription
was ended, the changing nature of war and its complex
technological dimensions, the kinds of inducements used to
enlist people, the employment of management techniques which
inevitably tend to emphasize efficient peacetime forces at
the cost of wartime effectiveness, questionable strategic
premises, especially regarding the role of reserve forces,
and, most sadly, lack of understanding of what motivates
people, not merely to join the military but to become
members of an organization whose ultimate demand is a
personal sacrifice to a greater good; squad, platoon,
company, ship, squadron, country. Certain of these issues
have been ignored in the debates on the AVF.

Perhaps the best explanation for the less than complete
consideration of the issues is that the rostrum of debate
over policy decisions concerning the all-volunteer force
has been held almost exclusively by the economists and their
pragmatic offspring--the business school graduates. The
preeminence of economic considerations in evaluating the
all-volunteer force is noted in the latest major study on
the subject, Military Manpower and the All-Volunteer Force,
by Richard V. L. Cooper of the Rand Corporation. Cooper
states:

> Thus, partly because of the nature of the issues that
> made up the 1960s debate and partly because of the
> style with which the social scientists approached
> their analyses of the military, the noneconomic social
> sciences were a relatively minor part of the draft
> debate. Perhaps one of the greatest shortcomings of
> the draft debate, then, was the failure to develop an
> effective dialogue between the economic profession and
> the social scientists on the draft and the alternatives
> to do it. (p. 39)

This shortcoming still persists, for Cooper is an
economist and his extensive analysis is by his own admission
largely economic.

Each of the contributing authors to this volume is
deeply concerned that policymakers look beyond the statistical indices of success or failure of the volunteer force,
beyond the concepts of free-market solutions, beyond "cost
effectiveness" as the lodestone of military management.
The success or failure of our military forces is defined
ultimately in the crucible of war. Whatever these forces
have in organizational efficiency and the latest weaponry,
they will fail if they are not animated by pride, self-
respect, and identity of self and organization. The
vitality of spirit of our military forces has suffered in
recent years, and it is not likely to be enhanced by the

continued evaluation of their contribution to the nation in free-market equivalents.

Professor Moskos in addressing these issues has stated the crux of the matter in the conclusion to his essay: "It may be that we are coming to a realization that many of the things we need as a nation we can never afford to buy. If we are going to have them, we must give them to ourselves."

In exercising the editor's prerogative of having the last word, I should like to give a summary impression of the significance of the essays comprising this volume.

Professor Snyder has evaluated the improbability of present military personnel-procurement policies meeting future force requirements in an era of shrinking manpower resources. His analysis, with several interesting suggestions for rationalizing conflicting national manpower programs, emphasizes the need to establish a set of national manpower priorities and the tailoring of the many current manpower programs in support of these priorities.

Professor Moskos paints the profile of the current Army enlisted force. He has convincingly demonstrated that today's Army fails by a wide margin to approach the national youth profile in racial mix, education, marital status, and economic background. He has identified several attitudinal problem areas among young soldiers which have a potential for serious difficulties for the Army in the future. The most complex, pervasive, and potentially corrosive attitudinal problem he addresses is the growing transformation of the Army (along with the other services) from a profession or calling to an organization which is becoming increasingly occupational in its values.

Professor Harries-Jenkins's essay on the British experience in maintaining volunteer forces is especially thought provoking. Without gainsaying the fact that each nation's military forces are sui generis, there are parallels in the efforts of both countries to maintain force levels through the manipulation of benefits and conditions of service. The British experience should dim our hopes of finding financial and managerial solutions to military manpower problems.

Mrs. Landrum has in her essay cut through much of the confusion which clutters consideration of the use of women in the armed forces. Accepting the value and right of women to serve in the armed forces, and without defining the limits of this service, she raises issues which indicate that the best interests of all will be served by a methodical and gradual integration of women into the armed

forces, rather than by a pell-mell recruitment of women
into organizations uncertain of how to employ them effectively.

The essay by the editor raises the question of whether
United States reserve forces as presently organized are
relevant to the strategic needs of the nation. The political sensitivity of the reserves has prevented the needed
assessment of new functions and organizations for these
forces. Alternative concepts for training, organizing,
and utilizing reserve forces are suggested.

Robert Leider's "Muddling Through" is possibly the
most emphatic and most coherent exposition of the fundamental, myriad, and complex changes occurring in the military since the end of conscription. He suggests that the
military in its desire to "succeed," to again become acceptable to society and to eliminate the hostility
engendered by Vietnam, may have compromised much of its
traditional ethos, with severe consequences to those unique
spiritual qualities which are essential to its organizational effectiveness in time of war. Mr. Leider also
presents several provocative insights into the changing
functional nature of military organizations and suggests
that these changes provide, indeed demand, new ways of
allocating manpower.

The realization that the United States has the requirement to maintain large and expensive military forces
for the indefinite future can be wearisome and even distasteful to a nation which for most of its history has
not had to shoulder this kind of burden. But now we, and
our children and probably their children, must accept this
burden. We can accept these responsibilities cheerfully
with the conviction that the safety of the nation and our
way of life merits commitment and sacrifice. But in the
absence of this straightforward acceptance, we can tem-
porize with our responsibilities. We can blur the external threats to our national interests. We can describe
our defense goals in such amorphous terms as "sufficiency"
and "parity." We can make military service more appealing
through increased emphasis on its vocational aspects and by
diluting the discipline and values of military organizations, by making the military more like "us."

Democracies seldom do anything exactly right, or in
a particularly timely fashion, but we believe that given
an awareness of challenges to its fundamental well-being,
our system has the capacity to meet them better than any
other form of government. This collection of essays is
intended to stimulate a greater awareness of the breadth
and depth of the problems inherent in our defense forces,
now and in the future. Without this awareness, we as a

nation are not likely to be true to our responsibilities
and, thus, we will fail ourselves.

John B. Keeley

Acknowledgments

The editor of a book such as this one owes much to many
people. His problem is knowing where to start and where
to stop, for surely more people have contributed than can
be recognized.

     The editor is particularly grateful to the contribu-
tors to this volume. They have provided many insights,
have been generous in their comments, and have made the
process of bringing this together a most pleasant and
intellectually profitable activity. Morris Janowitz of
the University of Chicago has provided encouragement and
guidance to countless scholars and others who have shown
interest in exploring the dark forests of our military
institutions. He has been unstintingly generous to me and
I thank him. Thanks are also due to H. Maxwell Potter,
Robert L. Goldich, and John R. Brinkerhoff for their
criticisms and their insights, which they have generously
shared. Craig Mense and Stuart Darling, former research
associates of the Miller Center, are thanked for their
research which helped to establish the directions and
parameters of this study. Ellen Stern, the secretary of
the Inter-University Seminar on Armed Forces and Society,
has helped in countless small ways that add up to a great
deal. Shirley Kingsbury and Kate Wiencek, secretaries at
the Miller Center, are thanked for all of the innumerable
tasks which must be done and redone if such a book is to
be completed. Lastly, my deepest appreciation must be
given to Frederick E. Nolting, Jr., director of the Miller
Center, whose patience and encouragement have been an
inspiration. This work would not have come to pass with-
our his interest and efforts.

MILITARY PERSONNEL-PROCUREMENT POLICIES

ASSUMPTIONS--TRENDS--CONTEXT

William P. Snyder

After four years of relative success with voluntary recruitment, the armed forces are beginning to have trouble
obtaining a sufficient number of volunteers of appropriate
quality to meet military manpower requirements. Demographic trends projected for the 1980s seem certain to make
maintenance of desired force and quality levels even more
difficult. Two broad alternatives--a military draft
and a national service scheme--are now being discussed
as possible solutions to the question of how the United
States should obtain personnel for its armed forces.

    Opinion on the issue is sharply divided. A February
1977 national sample indicates substantial opposition to
a draft--54% oppose, only 35% favor, and 10% have no opinion.[1] One-year national service, an unsatisfactory solution to military needs, fares somewhat better: in a
December 1976 survey 62% favored such an approach, as
compared to 33% opposed and 5% with no opinion.[2] While
a decision on the issue is probably unnecessary for several
years, this division of public attitudes suggests that a
solution to the military manpower problem will be difficult
and divisive. My purpose in this essay is to discuss sev-

Note: I am indebted to John B. Keeley and two colleagues
at Texas A&M, Mary Lenn Miller and Roger Beaumont, for
helpful comments on an initial draft.
    [1]The Gallup Opinion Index, no. 142 (May 1977), p. 16.
    [2]Ibid., no. 139 (February 1977) p. 8.

eral major trends that will serve to shape the issue over
the next few years and to speculate on the political
context in which the issue might be addressed. First,
however, some background comments on the experience with
the all volunteer force may be useful.

The Context of the All-Volunteer Experience

An accepted premise of a decade ago was that both the
defense budget and military manpower levels could be reduced sharply after the Vietnam War had ended. The size of
this "peace dividend" was not precisely defined--some early
projections were as high as $40 billion; later, more real-
istic estimates were as low as $3 to $4 billion[3]--but the
underlying assumption was that a peace settlement would
release resources to meet deferred social needs, growing
educational requirements, and pressing urban problems.
     Although the "peace dividend" predicted for the post-
Vietnam era was consumed by rapid inflation early in the
1970s, the early years of this decade did see a major
realignment of federal spending priorities. In FY 1970,
defense expenditures amounted to 8.3% of GNP, as compared
to 6.2% for social and welfare programs. By FY 1977,
federal spending on social and welfare programs had
increased to 10.0% of GNP while the share of GNP devoted
to defense had fallen to 5.5%.[4] The current level of
defense spending can be contrasted with defense outlays
of 9.2% of GNP in the period 1958-64 and 8.5% of GNP
during the peak years (FY 1966-71) of the Vietnam War.[5]
Military manpower levels also declined; from a high of 3.55
million in mid-1968, military strength dropped to about
2.1 million in 1974, the lowest level since the 1947-49
period and roughly 400,000 below the number of personnel
in uniform in the period between the Korean and Vietnam
wars. The number of civilians employed by the Defense Department dropped to 995,000 by the end of 1976, about 10%
below the average number employed in the pre-Vietnam era.[6]

[3]Murray L. Weidenbaum, "Vietnam Peace and the Budget,"
Nation's Business, August 1969, p. 78. Also see the Economist, October 19, 1968, p. 39, and Newsweek, September 8,
1969, p. 28.
     [4]Computed from Office of Management and Budget, The
Budget of the United States Government, Fiscal Year 1978
(Washington, D.C.: USGPO, 1977), Tables 21 and 22, pp.
435-6. Current budget documents now lump most welfare and
grant payments under the category "Payments for Individuals."
     [5]Ibid.
     [6]Department of Defense, Selected Manpower Statistics,
May 1977, pp. 20 and 68. Direct hire only.

The President's Commission on an All-Volunteer Armed Force, which prepared its report in 1969 and early 1970, concentrated mainly on manpower supply, civilian substitution, and equity issues, giving little attention to the question of defense manpower requirements.[7] In recommending an end to the draft, the commission asserted that a volunteer system could meet defense requirements under thre three-million level.[8] Acceptance of the commission's recommendations by the President and the Congress was obviously influenced by the strong opposition to the draft that mounted after 1965. But expectations of a "peace dividend" undoubtedly contributed to the generally favorable response accorded the committee's recommendations, as well as to strong congressional support of the legislative proposals regarding military pay and service facilities developed by the Nixon administration to facilitate the transition to an all-volunteer force.

Foreign policy initiatives during this period confirmed expectations that defense manpower requirements would be sharply lower after Vietnam. The Nixon Doctrine projected a lessened U.S. role in the defense of other nations, and thereby rationalized a reduction in overseas troop deployments, particularly in the Pacific area. The Nixon visit to Peking created a new framework for U.S. relations with the People's Republic of China and the Soviet Union. Force structure planning, which had been based on the assumption of 2½ wars, now assumed 1½ wars-- a major war in Europe and a small contingency in Asia or elsewhere. The doctrine of nuclear sufficiency established a new basis for strategic force planning and set the stage for the equivalence posture later accepted in the SALT I and Vladivostok Accords. Thus, as the services moved from reliance on the draft to an all-volunteer force, the redefinition of U.S. strategic interests moved in an essentially compatible direction. Congressional refusal in mid-decade to extend further assistance to South Vietnam and military aid to Angola confirmed this redefinition of America's strategic interests and thereby avoided an early challenge to the concept of an all-volunteer force.

Although initially skeptical of the all-volunteer proposal, the armed services recruited agressively and obtained a sufficient number of new enlistees to meet service strength authorizations. The quality of new accessions was also satisfactory--especially in the Air Force and Navy

---

[7]Report of the President's Commission on an All-Volunteer Armed Force (Washington, D.C.: USGPO, 1970), pp. 35-47, 23-33.
    [8]Ibid., pp. 7-8.

--and higher in some respects than the personnel provided by the draft. Public confidence in military institutions improved significantly after 1973, which undoubtedly contributed to early service recruiting success. Similarly, high levels of unemployment, particularly among teenagers, provided an additional incentive for young men to visit military recruiting stations.

Voluntary recruiting has enjoyed less success in recent months. The Army and Marine Corps have had some difficulties in maintaining authorized active-duty strength levels. The reserve components are over 100,000 below authorized strength. The quality of active force enlistees appears to be declining slightly; in the reserves, quality has dropped sharply. The number of black Americans in the enlisted force is also a concern to some. The Army is the least representative of the services--its share of black Americans is double that of the general population and some Army combat units are as much as 40% black.[9] Attrition among new enlistees has also risen sharply in recent months, resulting in excessive personnel turnover in many units.[10] Finally, the cost of manpower in the all-volunteer force is high: According to some projections, military and civilian personnel costs, now about 58% of the defense budget, will exceed 65% by FY 1980.[11]

While conceding that the all-volunteer force was an early success after 1973, some observers have become concerned by these recent developments. A number have suggested an early return to the draft or to some form of national service. Predictions that voluntary recruitment will be unable to meet service manpower requirements in the 1980s generally assume that defense requirements will remain essentially stable over the coming decade. Similarly, advocates of the all-volunteer force seem to assume that future recruiting shortfalls can be offset by improved efficiency in the ways in which military personnel are utilized or by the enlistment of more women.[12]

The assumptions underlying these policy proposals need careful examination. Trends in three areas seem particularly relevant to future decisions on military manpower policies:

[9]U.S. Congress, Senate, Committee on Armed Services. Achieving America's Goals: National Service or the All-Volunteer Armed Force? by William R. King, Committee Print, Study (Washington, D.C.: USGPO, 1977), pp. 11-18. Hereafter King Report.
[10]Ibid., pp. 25.
[11]Ibid., pp. 19.
[12]Interview with Senators Sam Nunn (D., Georgia) and William Proxmire (D., Wisconsin), U.S. News and World Report, February 14, 1977, pp. 59 ff.

1. Defense personnel requirements--how will they be affected by changes in international political and military relationships? Specifically, what are the implications of the continuing Soviet arms buildup?

2. Can significant personnel economies be achieved in the U.S. armed forces through civilian substitution, headquarters and staff reductions, and increased productivity among military personnel?

3. The number of young Americans in the 17-21 age group decreases by roughly 14% between now and the mid-1980s. Will the educational and employment opportunities afforded members of this age cohort change and, if so, with what impact on voluntary recruitment?

Beyond examining trends in these areas, it will be useful to speculate on the likely political context in which the issues must be addressed: Are the most frequently advanced alternatives to the all-volunteer force-- a draft or a national service scheme--effective and politically realizable solutions to the problem? If not, what steps might be taken to ease the severity of the manpower procurement crisis of the 1980s? It is to these questions that we now turn.

Military Requirements in the 1980s

Of the several broad trends affecting the future of the all-volunteer force, the most crucial is the evolving strategic relationship between the United States and the Soviet Union. As Charles Burton Marshall notes in a recent essay: "The relationship between the United States and the Soviet Union . . . will continue to set the great strategic frame. A multiplicity of political forces unrelated in origin to that relationship will contend on the world scene, but the United States-Soviet stragetic equation--and how it is viewed by the principals and by others, however aligned--will have pervasive effects on the interplay of these forces."[13] The central importance of the U.S.-Soviet military balance is suggested by the fact that about 60% of worldwide military expenditures are made by the United States and the Soviet Union. When the outlays of major allies in NATO and the Warsaw Pact are included, the share increases to over 80%. The U.S. and U.S.S.R. are, not unexpectedly, the major military arsenals, producing about three-fourths of all

[13]Charles Burton Marshall, "National Security: Thoughts on the Intangibles," in James R. Schlesinger, ed., Defending America (New York: Basic Books, 1977), p. 82.

military equipment sold abroad.[14] Thus any analysis of
future U.S. (or even Soviet) military requirements can
reasonably begin with an overview of the U.S.-Soviet
military balance.

That balance has been the object of controversy for
several years. Recently, however, there has emerged
general agreement among knowledgeable American and foreign
analysts over the scope of the Soviet military buildup.
This large-scale buildup has extended to all elements
of the Soviet military establishment, as follows:

1. Strategic forces have been improved through the
development, testing, and deployment of four new land-
based ICBM systems, two new sea-based missile systems, and
the Backfire bomber. A major research and development
effort supports these and further improvements in strategic forces.

2. Conventional forces have been strengthened through
the integration of additional personnel and the acquisition of more modern fighting vehicles, tactical air
defense systems, antitank weapons, and chemical warfare
defenses.

3. The Soviet Navy has been expanded and modernized;
new ship types carrying antiship cruise missiles provide
the Soviets with an extended "blue water" capability.

4. An already high quality air defense system is
being strengthened.

5. Additional mobility forces have been acquired.[15]

The extent of this buildup is suggested by Soviet budget
increases of recent years: From 1965 through 1974
Soviet military expenditures doubled, an annual increase
of almost 8% per year.[16] Recent estimates place the current Soviet defense budget at about $150 billion.[17]

[14]See U.S. Arms Control and Disarmament Agency, World
Military Expenditures and Arms Transfers, 1965-1974, (Washington, D.C.: USGPO, 1976), pp. 14-17, 46, 50, 54, 69, 71.
    [15]For a convenient summary of these developments, see
U.S., Congress, Senate, Committee on Armed Services. United States/Soviet Military Balance: A Frame of Reference
for Congress, by Congressional Research Service, Committee
Print, Study (Washington, D.C.: USGPO, 1976). For a brief
although pessimistic narrative summary, see Edward N. Luttwak, "Defense Reconsidered," Commentary, March 1977, pp.
51-58.
    [16]United States/Soviet Military Balance, p. 46.
    [17]See Donald H. Rumsfeld, Annual Defense Department
Report, FY 1978, January 17, 1977 (Washington, D.C.: USGPO,

Because the Soviets have relatively low manpower costs, the
amounts available for research and development and new
procurement exceed comparable U.S. expenditures by
substantial margins.[18]

The organization, doctrine, and equipment of Soviet
and American military forces differ in important ways.
These dissimilarities stem from contrasting historical
experiences, technological and industrial inequalities,
and differing policy choices over time. The force structure asymmetries that result make direct comparisons of
capabilities difficult. In terms of Soviet strategic
capabilities, however, the gains of recent years have
been impressive. As measured by several indices of
strategic force effectiveness, the Soviets have achieved
parity with or an advantage over the United States during
the last decade. American forces continue to have greater
reliability and warhead accuracy--but U.S. leads in these
categories are diminishing. One prominent analyst,
Paul Nitze, argues that the Soviet advantage is greater
than indicated by conventional measures of strategic
capabilities; in the event of a nuclear exchange, he
suggests the Soviets would enjoy marked superiority
against the surviving United States' force.[19]

While there is substantial agreement on the scope of
the Soviet buildup, controversy continues as to the motives
underlying the Soviet effort. Early in this decade it
was assumed that the Soviets were striving for strategic
parity; once achieved, the argument continued, the Soviet
buildup would end. Substantial parity has been achieved,
yet the buildup continues. A number of analysts have
therefore concluded that the Soviets seek clear strategic
superiority. Two related subjects, estimates of the rate
of the Soviet buildup and the nature of Soviet strategic
doctrine, have recently become the object of debate--the
one in the "team A - team B" exercise of 1976; the second
in Professor Richard Pipes's provocative article "Why the

1977), p. 7. For a brief discussion of the difficulties
involved in estimating Soviet defense expenditures, see
"Soviet Defense Expenditures," The Military Balance, 1976-
1977 (London: International Institute of Strategic Studies,
1976), pp. 109-10.
    [18]United States/Soviet Military Balance, p. 17.
    [19]Paul H. Nitze, "Nuclear Strategy: Detente and
American Survial," in Schlesinger, Defending America,
p. 102. Also see "Measuring the Strategic Nuclear Balance," The Military Balance, 1976-1977, pp. 106-8.

Soviet Union Thinks It Could Fight and Win a Nuclear
War."[20]

Soviet strategic force improvements coupled with
persuasive arguments that Soviet leaders will not settle
for equality have led a number of analysts to conclude
that the strategic balance is shifting against the United
States. While both the Ford and Carter administrations
have attested to the adequacy of U.S. defenses, the public
seems increasingly concerned about this issue.[21] That
congressional attitudes are shifting is suggested by the
recent resolution expressing disapproval of the administration's proposal to withdraw U.S. forces from Korea and
by efforts to restore B-1 prototype funding. The forma-
tion in 1976 of the Committee on the Present Danger, a
bipartisan group of prominent citizens who regard the
present situation with concern, is further evidence of
changing elite perceptions of the strategic balance.[22]

Arms limitations agreements have established ceilings
on the number of strategic delivery vehicles and multi-
ple warheads each side may have. Whatever their consequences for the arms race, the agreements have focused
public attention on the relative size of the two strategic
forces. Consequently, reductions in strategic force capabilities are acceptable only on the basis of mutual
and equivalent reductions. Put another way, deterrence
is now assumed to require, at a minimum, strategic forces
roughly equal in size to those of the Soviet Union. Any
reductions in U.S. strategic forces through the mechanism
of future SALT agreements must therefore be accompanied
by what are perceived as equal reductions by the Soviet
Union. Arms control proposals incorporating balanced re-

[20]See David Binder, "New CIA Estimate Finds Soviet
Seeks Superiority in Arms," New York Times, December 26,
1976, pp. 1 ff.; William T. Lee, "Understanding the Soviet
Military Threat: How CIA Estimates Went Astray," Agenda
Paper no. 6, National Strategy Information Center (New
York: 1977); and Richard Pipes, "Why the Soviet Union Thinks
It Could Fight and Win a Nuclear War," Commentary, July
1977, pp. 21-34.
[21]For a brief discussion of changing public attitudes
towards defense, see Luttwak, "Defense Reconsidered,"
pp. 51-52.
[22]The Committee's initial policy statement reads, in
part: "Our country is in a period of danger, and the danger is increasing. Unless decisive steps are taken to a-
lert the nation, and to change the course of its policy,
our economic and military capability will become inadequate
to assure peace with security". ("Common Sense and the Common Danger, A Policy Statement by the Committee on the Present Danger," n.d. (November 1976)).

ductions advanced early in 1977 by the Carter administration apparently found little favor with the Soviets.[23] Moreover, President Carter's decision to reject the B-1 bomber in favor of air- and sea-launched cruise missiles has, in the view of some analysts, raised new issues likely to make subsequent agreements more difficult to achieve.[24] In the event that some modest reduction becomes possible, however, the budgetary and manpower savings will be limited: strategic forces account for only about 5% of defense manpower and roughly 10% of the current U.S. defense spending.

Existing arms control agreements do not limit qualitative improvements in strategic forces. Indeed, one effect of quantitative restrictions may be to stimulate qualitative competition. In any event, technological upgrading that serves to reduce vulnerability, to improve control, and to enhance credibility--either by improving existing systems or through development of more advanced systems--have every prospect of continuing. This further limits the possibility of savings--in fact, the cost of keeping up with the Soviet Union will put great pressure on programed budget ceilings.

Excluding the U.S. and the Soviet Union, the only nuclear power seriously concerned with expanding and upgrading its nuclear forces is the People's Republic of China. Currently the PRC's nuclear capabilities are limited--in particular, it lacks a modern, long-range delivery system.[25] While estimates of the rate at which the Chinese buildup will occur are highly speculative, any expansion in the PRC's strategic capability is likely to be regarded as relatively more threatening by its northern neighbor, the Soviet Union, than by the United States. The Soviet Union may therefore be increasingly reluctant to accept further limitations on its strategic forces. An expansion of PRC strategic capabilities might also threaten U.S. interests in the Pacific.

The proliferation of nuclear weapons proceeds apace-- five nations now have nuclear weapons; India recently tested a nuclear device; and a dozen or more other governments have the necessary know-how and industrial resources to build nuclear weapons within a relatively short period of time. With rising petroleum prices, nuclear power gen-

[23]For a summary of developments in the ongoing SALT negotiations, see Richard Burg, "All about the Talks on Limiting Strategic Arms," New York Times, October 23, 1977, p.3.
[24]Alexander R. Vershbow, "The Cruise Missile: The End of Arms Control?" Foreign Affairs, October 1976, pp. 133 ff.
[25]See "China," The Military Balance, 1977-1978 (London: International Institute of Strategic Studies, 1977), pp. 52-54.

eration has become more competitive and may be expected
to increase the availability of nuclear materials and re-
processing facilities. This diffusion of nuclear materials
and technology increases the likelihood that one or more
of the "threshold" nations will soon acquire nuclear
weapons. As nuclear proliferation proceeds among the
threshold nations, safety, control, and security considerations may be expected to receive less attention than
they deserve.[26] The result is higher odds of a nuclear ac-
cident, the potential use of nuclear weapons by terrorist
or radical groups, or a nuclear exchange in the local and
regional wars of the 1980s.

Nuclear proliferation is unlikely to threaten U.S.
security directly; rather, the danger is greater instability and uncertainty in relations among second- and third-
level powers. Given the extent of superpower interest
in local and regional issues, however, both the United
States and the Soviet Union are likely to become deeply
involved should other nations or groups employ nuclear
weapons. Paradoxically, this development suggests a
requirement not only for improved intelligence capabilities but also for additional U.S. conventional and mobility forces to maintain a presence in threatened areas, to
aid in reestablishing order, and to conduct relief and
peacekeeping activities.

In the decade after World War II the United States
entered into alliance relationships on a global basis.
In each instance, these alliances assumed fundamental
antagonisms between the Western and communist blocs,
and were designed to deal with security and political
issues arising from ideological and other differences.
The first and most important of these alliances, the
North Atlantic Treaty Organization, was also intended to
promote political stability in Western Europe by creating
a framework in which West Germany could regain its sover-
eignty and economic viability. Other alliances had similar if less ambitious objectives in other regions of the
world.

While the process has been largely informal, the
alliance relationships created after World War II have
been reevaluated and reconsidered in the years since
Vietnam. One alliance--SEATO--has effectively lapsed;
another--the mutual defense treaty with South Korea--is
undergoing some modification; and the defense treaty with
the Republic of China seems a likely candidate for revoca-
tion. The remaining Cold War alliances, despite sharply

[26]Stockholm International Peace Research Institute,
The Nuclear Age (Cambridge, Mass.: MIT Press, 1974),
pp. 46-95.

changed political and security needs and new perspectives
on national interests, have been judged of continuing
importance, not only by the United States but by its
alliance partners as well. In at least four cases--NATO,
the Rio Pact, ANZUS, and the informal but durable relationship with Israel--the American commitment has been clearly
reaffirmed.

The alliances to which the United States is a party
create major national obligations. Two types of military
requirements flow therefrom: First, the alliances involve nuclear guarantees extended by the United States to
signatory countries. The validity of these guarantees
has long been questioned in many quarters abroad; were
U.S. strategic forces to fall below the level of "rough
equivalence" with those of the Soviet Union, it is unlikely that these guarantees will have much credibility.
Moreover, any erosion in the credibility of U.S. nuclear
guarantees carries an additional risk--increased incentives for national nuclear forces. Both these relationships underline the importance of maintaining U.S. strategic forces at levels perceived as generally comparable
to those of the Soviet Union.

Second, existing alliance arrangements create requirements for conventional military forces. Conventional
forces are designed to deter, or to defend at lower levels
of destruction; their availability makes unnecessary an
immediate escalation to nuclear weapons; and they provide
defensive capabilities which can be employed in a variety
of circumstances. Conventional forces are also visible
symbols of U.S. nuclear guarantees and of the broader
alliance relationships of which they are a part.

The conventional capabilities needed to maintain the
credibility and effectiveness of our alliance relationships
vary widely--ground, air, and naval forces in the case of
NATO; naval and air forces, at least, for Pacific and
Latin American allies. Currently, about one-third of all
U.S. general purpose forces are deployed abroad; most
Army and Air Force general purpose formations stationed
in the United States are configured for rapid deployment
to reinforce units stationed abroad. Overseas deployments
in the NATO area have increased slightly in recent years;
deployments in the Pacific, in contrast, have been reduced. Return of units to the U.S. does not necessarily
mean a reduction in overall force levels; the planned
Korean troop withdrawal, for example, does not so far
involve a corresponding reduction in the number of Army
divisions.

The current balance of conventional capabilities finds
the Soviet with substantially larger ground and tactical

air forces; the United States possesses larger and better
naval and mobility forces, and a qualitatively superior
air force. As indicated above, over the last decade the
Soviets have strengthened and modernized their ground
forces and have reduced the U.S. advantage in air, naval,
and mobility capabilities. In the NATO area, where the
conventional balance is most critical, the Warsaw Pact
has numerically larger forces and has achieved marked
superiority over NATO in terms of tanks, fighting vehicles,
and artillery.[27]   Moreover, Warsaw Pact general purpose
capabilities are less affected by problems of mallocation
and logistical vulnerabilities than are NATO forces.
These circumstances are a major concern to the Carter
administration, which recently initiated a "NATO improvement program" designed to increase NATO capabilities vis-a-
vis the Warsaw Pact at an initial cost of some $600
million per year.[28]

Alliance commitments also create continuing requirements for mobility forces. Forward deployed units in
NATO or in the Pacific are admittedly insufficient to
halt conventional attacks of the scope possible, particularly in Europe. To achieve the military stalemate
essential for possible political negotiations--and to
avoid the danger of escalation implicit in a quick defeat--
rapid deployment of reserve units from the U.S. is essential. Early availability of logistical support for
American and allied units is equally critical. NATO
and Korea present the severest requirements for U.S.
mobility forces. With respect to Israel, whose needs
thus far have been confined to emergency resupply
during brief periods, the problem is difficult less
because of the tonnages involved than because of the
uncertainty regarding overflight rights in Western
Europe and the Mediterranean. Most other contingencies
present lesser problems--assuming, of course, they do not
occur simultaneously. In any event, it is clear that the
United States will require large, modern mobility forces
throughout the 1980s.

The growing dependence of the United States on
petroleum imports coupled with an apparent inability to
address this issue satisfactorily creates complex security
problems for the United States. An interruption in the
petroleum supply would have severe and immediate effects
on the American economy. Military capabilities would be
less affected--at least in the short run--since the
forces could rely on existing stocks or even diversions

[27]For a comparison, see "The Theater Balance between
NATO and the Warsaw Pact," The Military Balance, 1977-1978,
pp. 102-11.
[28]Benjamin F. Schemmer, "Pentagon Moves Forward with
New Initiatives for NATO," Armed Forces Journal, September
1977, pp. 30 ff.

from civilian supplies. A sustained military effort,
however, would be virtually impossible during a lengthy
oil embargo. In these circumstances, additional naval
forces would be useful in two ways: First, naval forces
showing the flag might strengthen political and economic
actions taken to deter a boycott; second, by making it
more difficult and costly to sever tanker routes, naval
forces would reduce somewhat the possibilities of interruption of oil imports during a war. Thus, a modest increase
in the number of sea control ships might contribute to
our security; insurance against any interruption of the
sea lanes involved is out of the question.

The circumstances described above--maintenance of the
strategic balance with the Soviet Union, the obligations
to other nations created by continuation of our alliance
relationships, and the problems that stem from nuclear
proliferation and energy imports--would seem to require
military forces at least as large as those now maintained
by the United States. Beyond that, U.S. defense requirements may be expected to remain sensitive to Soviet actions. Put another way, the number and kind of military
forces the United States will want in the 1980s depends
importantly on the kinds of forces the Soviet Union de-
cides to maintain. If the Soviets continue to spend heavily on defense, which the record of the past decade would
seem to suggest, and regardless of the basis for such
action, the possibility of reductions in U.S. force levels
during the next decade will diminish further. For the
U.S. to maintain its security and to continue its role as
a superpower over the next decade will require military
capabilities equal to or greater than those presently
available.

Manpower Utilization in the Armed Forces
Illusions and Realities

Present military capabilities are achieved by a mixed
force of uniformed and civilian personnel. To what extent
can easy-to-obtain civil service employees be substituted
for hard-to-recruit military personnel? Similarly, can
less essential service activities--those that contribute
little to overall combat effectiveness--be eliminated,
with the subsequent transfer of released military personnel to combat units, thereby achieving a higher "tooth
to tail" ratio? Finally, what are the possibilities of
improving productivity among military personnel? Given
the approximately 20% decline over the next decade in the
number of young men in the 17-21 year age cohort (see below), actions in any or all of these areas would ease recruiting problems in the years ahead. It is therefore
important to determine the extent to which significant

economies in military manpower can be achieved through
actions involving substitution, elimination, or productivity increases.

Major technological advances in military weaponry
have occurred since the end of World War II. Strategic
forces utilize weapons systems not available three
decades ago--nuclear submarine and long-range ballistic
missiles are examples. The warheads carried by strategic
missiles are as much as 100 times more powerful than
those exploded in 1945 at Hiroshima and Nagasaki. Developments in strategic weapons, however, have tended to
obscure equally important changes in conventional weapons
since World War II. Most ground combat forces and their
logistical support are now mechanized and can move rapidly
over a large battle area. The effective range of conventional weapons has increased sharply--artillery weapons by
half; tank weapons three to four fold. Precision-guided
munitions, both surface and air, have improved accuracy
by a factor of ten. More powerful and accurate weapons
with higher rates of fire and longer range have increased
lethality substantially: An artillery battery, firing
currently available ammunition, has three times the
effectiveness of its World War II counterpart.[29] Similar
trends are evident in conventional air and naval weapons.
The new A-10 close support aircraft, for example, carries
an ordnance load thirty times greater than the World War II
P-47 fighter, with double the operating range and time it
can spend in the target area.[30]

Improvements in the range, accuracy, and power of
modern conventional weapons have several consequences.
First, the political implications of military forces and
weapons have increased. It is quite understandable why
high-level political leaders have come to regard control
of operating forces as an important, even critical, part
of their overall responsibilities. Modern communications
equipment, which permits voice contact with operating
military forces, facilitates detailed management of
military operations. Second, combat elements are increasingly dependent upon target acquisition and surveillance
operations to provide up-to-the-minute intelligence on
enemy forces. Third, survival of military forces in the
battle area requires wide dispersion of operating units,
both laterally and in depth throughout the battle area.

[29]For a brief discussion of technological advances in
conventional weaponry, see Department of the Army, FM 100-5,
Operations (Washington, D.C. 1976) pp. 2-1 - 2-32. Hereafter FM 100-5.
    [30]Ibid., pp. 2-20.

More centralized control, the collection and dissemination
of intelligence information, and the extension of the spa-
tial dimensions of warfare require, in turn, complex
communications systems. This relatively new dimension
in warfare--generally termed "C^3," for command, control,
and communications--is of growing importance, consuming
about 4% of recent U.S. defense budgets.[31] An integral
part of C^3 is the need for larger military staffs at all
levels of the chain of command to plan, coordinate, and
control military operations.

Recent wars involving conventional military forces
equipped with modern weapons and communications systems
have been exceptionally intense. The consumption rate of
supplies by such forces is substantially higher than the
rates of comparably sized units in similar engagements in
the past. Equipment losses of engaged forces are similarly high: In twenty-four days of combat in the 1967 and
1973 Arab-Israeli wars, Egyptian forces lost about 2,000
tanks, and over 500 combat aircraft. Israeli losses were
less severe, but nevertheless exceptionally high as compared to the losses experienced in earlier wars.[32] Sustained combat operations among modern military forces
therefore demand larger maintenance, supply, and transportation capabilities, plus an expanded logistical
control system to plan and coordinate support for combat
forces.

The defense strategies of the superpowers as well as
those of less powerful regional protagonists seek to deter
the outbreak of war. A central element in all deterrence
relationships, strategic or conventional, is the immediate
availability of combat-ready forces. Since the efficient
operation of combat elements depends heavily on C^3, intelligence, and logistical capabilities, it is essential that
both types of units have the same level of training and

[31]Donald G. Brennan,"Command and Control," in Francis
P. Hoeber and William Schneider, Jr., eds., _Arms, Men, and_
Military Budgets: Issues for Fiscal Year 1978 (New York:
Crane, Russak & Company, 1977), pp. 332 ff. Also see Davis
B. Bobrow, "Communications, Command and Control: The
Nerves of Intervention," in Ellen P. Stern, ed., _The Limits_
of Military Intervention (Beverly Hills: Sage, 1977) pp.
101-20.
[32]The Arab-Israel wars have stimulated extensive com-
mentary on the implications of modern conventional warfare.
For interesting and useful analyses, see Trevor N. Depuy,
Elusive Victory; the Arab-Israeli Wars, 1947-1974 (Indiana-
polis: Bobbs Merril, 1977), the Insight Team of the London
Sunday _Times_, The Yom Kippur War (New York: Doubleday 1974);
and Anthony N. Cardesman, "How Much Is Too Much?" _Armed_
Forces Journal, October 1977, pp. 32-39.

readiness. Indeed, many support units require more
extensive and rigorous training and higher quality personnel than do combat units.

    The importance of communications, intelligence, and
logistical capabilities to modern combat operations is
clearly recognized by current military doctrine. Enemy
units and facilities performing these functions are
assigned high priorities in weapons use and target planning, just below major tactical units.[33] Because of
the fluidity of modern combat, C^3, intelligence, and
logistical units are expected to provide their own
local security or even to undertake combat operations
on occasion. As a consequence, the age-old distinction
between "front-line" and "rear-area" units has been largely eliminated. Not only have the risks of death and in-
jury been equalized--a fact often overlooked because
U.S. forces in Vietnam enjoyed a total air power monopoly
--but the relative importance of these different types of
units to the immediate outcome of the battle has been
altered.

    Modern conventional warfare is thus characterized by
the following: Greater destructive power is being applied
over increasingly larger areas. The efficient application
of military power over an extended period of time requires
substantially larger C^3, intelligence, and logistical
elements than was the case in the past. The share of the
total force directly engaging an enemy has declined,
while the portion involved in controlling the battle and
supporting it logistically has increased. Put another
way, technological developments have been shifting the
"tooth-tail" ratio in favor of the "tail." In a larger
sense, the "tooth-tail" concept has become increasingly
irrelevant. Both elements are equally essential in
combat operations--any degradation of control and support
capabilities implies a near immediate loss in effectiveness of combat elements.

    The implications of these technological and doctrinal
trends in terms of elimination, substitution, and productivity actions vary sharply, depending on the functions of
the units involved. Functionally, military units and defense activities can be divided into four general categories, as follows:

    1. Deployed units. Tactical and support units sta-
tioned overseas or deployed at sea, including C^3 and logistical elements, and configured for combat operations in or

[33]FM 100-5, pp. 4-5 - 4-6, 11-11.

near their location.

2. Reinforcing units. Tactical, service, and related c^3 and logistical units available as reinforcements for deployed U.S. units or for use in other areas. Most units in this category are stationed in the United States, Hawaii, or Okinawa.

3. Training Base. The units and activities that carry on the training and educational activities undertaken by the armed forces.

4. Support activities. Installations and activities that provide logistical, administrative, and other services for the rest of the force. Most support functions are undertaken at large fixed installations located in the United States, although some intelligence and military advisory activities are conducted abroad.[34]

A rough estimate of the number of uniformed and civilian personnel involved in each of the four general functional categories indicated above is contained in Table 1.

Table 1. Functional distribution of military and civilian personnel number (percentage)

Category	Military (%)*	Civilian#(%)*	Total (%)*
Deployed units	450,000 (22)	60,000 (6)	510,000 (17)
Reinforcing units	705,000 (34)	70,000 (7)	775,000 (25)
Training base	370,000 (18)	80,000 (8)	450,000 (15)
Support activites	445,000 (21)	755,000 (76)	1,200,000 (39)
Other**	105,000 (5)	30,000 (3)	135,000 (4)
	2,075,000	995,000	3,070,000

Sources: Estimated from Department of Defense, Manpower Requirements Report for FY 1978, March 1977, pp. II-20 to II-22; Secretary of Defense Donald H. Rumsfeld, Annual Defense Department Report, FY 1977, January 27, 1976, p. 232; Department of Defense, Military Manpower Training Report for FY 1976, March 1975, p. ix; Department of Defense, Selected Manpower Statistics, May 1977, p. 81-85; and Department of Defense Fact Sheet 559-77, December 6, 1977.
    * Percentages rounded.
    # Direct Hire.
    ** Military: transients, patients, prisoners, and cadets; civilian: students and disadvantaged youth.

[34] The conventional approach, a carry-over from sociological comparison of large civilian and military organizations, is to analyze skill or occupational classifications, with these military positions that duplicate skills found

In deployed units, the opportunities for personnel
economies or for civilian substitution are limited. As
noted above, C^3, headquarters, and logistical activities
are essential to the success of combat units. In addition, all units in this category must be ready to undertake operations on short notice.

Much of the same argument applies to reinforcing
units. If they are to perform their assigned missions--
rapid deployment overseas followed by early commitment to
combat operations--these units must be similar in design
and composition to deployed units. The potential for
manpower economies or civilian substitution in this portion
of the force is limited for the same reasons as in deployed
units.

Since the training base would remain in the United
States during an emergency, it affords greater opportunities for manpower economies and civilian substitution.
Even here, however, the potential is limited. First,
half to two-thirds of the training base consists of personnel undergoing training, mostly basic recruit training.
Although many military skills have counterparts in the
civilian economy, new recruits are for the most part
untrained in any skill. Physical conditioning and ac-
climatization, which require long periods, are also
essential. Second, many training activities are best
accomplished by military personnel. This is particularly
the case in those training activities involving uniquely
military skills, the inculcation of discipline, and the
socialization of enlistees to military life. Third,
U.S. naval and military forces are technology intensive--
sophisticated weapons and equipment are substituted for
manpower. Operation and maintenance of this equipment
demands high technical skills which can be acquired only
through long training. Similarly, the need for personnel

in the civilian work force open to civilian substitution.
Although useful in some respects, this approach fails on
two counts. First, the same skills are found in many
types of military organizations. Cooks, clerks, and
drivers, for instance, are found in rifle companies and
large military headquarters. Civilian substitution may
be acceptable in the headquarters, but is unacceptable
in the rifle company. Second, it is increasingly difficult to assign a specific level of personal risk (and
risk, if not the only difference, is a fundamental distinction between civilian and military) to a particular
skill. A weather forecaster at an airbase may now face
as much risk as the pilots that he briefs. The approach
employed here assumes that each category involves a
roughly equal level of personal risk, regardless of the
specific task an individual performs.

with an awareness of the political and social implications
of modern warfare justifies the extensive educational
programs of the mid-career and senior level military
schools. Fourth, the services are reluctant to further
civilianize the training base--it provides a small pool
of readily available and well-trained personnel who can
meet expanded training requirements or replace combat
losses in the early days of a crisis. Finally, the
services have recently achieved substantial economies
in their training programs through the adoption of per-
formance-based training techniques.[35] Additional manpower economies and further civilian substitution are
perhaps possible in the training base, but the bulk of
the training workload will continue to require military
personnel.

As Table 1 indicates, most civil servants employed
by the services and DOD are involved in support activities.
The same is true of other categories of civilian employees
--indirect hires (i.e., foreign nationals employed overseas) and contract hires. As a result, efforts to improve
efficiency in this element of the stateside force, to the
extent they are successful, will result in the saving of
civilian, not military, positions. While some uniformed
military personnel are involved in stateside support activities, the potential for civilianization in this element
has also largely been realized. The most recent effort
to substitute civilian for military personnel occurred
in the period 1973-76, when some 48,000 military positions
--mostly in support activities--were converted to civilian
positions.[36]

Although further economies in military manpower may
be possible, deployed and reinforcing units and the training base afford few opportunities without an offsetting
loss of readiness and combat effectiveness. The extent
to which civilian substitution is possible is also relatively limited. Opportunities for civilian substitution
in the support category are also restricted: First, many
of the women in uniform serve in support activities. Pend-
ing a change in the policies and laws prohibiting assignment of women to combat units or to ships, and a demonstration of their interest in and suitability for such service,

[35]For a brief summary of recent training developments
in the Army, see Donn A. Starry (General, USA), "Putting It
All Together at TRADOC," Army, October 1977, pp. 42-43.
Similar changes have occurred in the other services.
[36]Secretary of Defense James R. Schlesinger, Annual
Defense Department Report, FY 1976 and FY 1977, February 5,
1975 (Washington, D.C.: USGPO, 1975), p. V-7.

women will of necessity occupy billets that might otherwise
be filled by civilian employees. Increasing the number of
women in the services will, therefore, make civilianization more difficult. Second, as indicated above, substantial conversion of military billets to civilian
positions has already been accomplished. The extent of
this conversion is suggested by the ratio of civilian
employees to military personnel (see Chart 1), now
substantially higher than at any time in the recent past.[37]
In short, the opportunities for civilian substitution
have largely been realized; future civilianization efforts
are almost certain to involve fewer people than in the
past--and be more difficult to achieve.

Beyond these considerations, the opportunities for
civilian substitution within that portion of the force
located in the United States are restricted for other
reasons. One such restriction is the "rotation base."
Rotation of personnel between assignments in the United
States and overseas is desirable both to equalize hardships
among service personnel and to avoid social and political
isolation within particular segments of the armed forces.
Present personnel policies not only limit the duration of
overseas assignments but provide stateside assignments
between overseas tours. For these policies to be carried
out, however, the services must have a "rotation base"--
units and activities in the United States to which military
personnel can be assigned between overseas tours.

Maintenance of a rotation base presents little difficulty for the skill specialties found in combat units--
these personnel can rotate between deployed units overseas
and reinforcing units in the United States. Moreover, some
of the time that career military personnel spend in the
United States is consumed in activities which have no counterpart overseas--assignments to military schools or to
major headquarters such as the Pentagon. Much greater
difficulty is experienced, however, with the job specialties common to logistical, support, and in C^3 activities.
Overseas, for the reasons indicated, these activities
need to be performed by military personnel; although they
could reasonably be accomplished by civilian employees
in the United States, some of these positions must be

[37]In addition to its extensive efforts to civilianize
positions, the Department of Defense has greatly expanded
its use of contract labor to perform routine housekeeping
tasks. Contract personnel now number about 450,000, as compared to 220,000 in 1964. See Richard V. L. Cooper, Military Manpower and the All-Volunteer Force (R-1450-ARPA)
(Santa Monica, Calif.: Rand Corporation, 1977), p. 294.

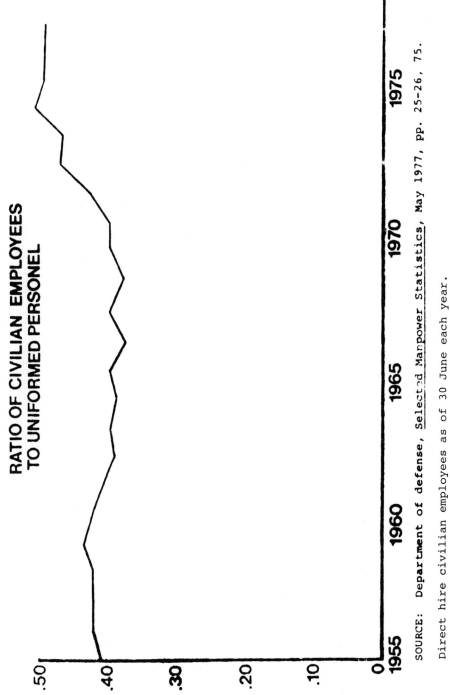

CHART I

**RATIO OF CIVILIAN EMPLOYEES
TO UNIFORMED PERSONEL**

SOURCE: Department of defense, Selected Manpower Statistics, May 1977, pp. 25-26, 75.

Direct hire civilian employees as of 30 June each year.

reserved for military personnel. Hence, the need to
provide relevant career-enhancing assignments for military personnel between overseas tours limits the extent
to which stateside support tasks can be converted to
civilian employees. Put another way, military personnel
policies relating to the frequency and length of overseas
assignment, desirable for equity and other reasons,
restrict the extent of civilian substitution.

Efficiency is to some extent constrained by the
location and size of military facilities. Consolidation
of stateside activities at large installations contributes to greater efficiency in local overhead functions,
and closing of many small bases is justified on these
grounds. Base-closure decisions, however, are intimately
linked with local economic conditions and have proved
to be intensely political in character. Rationalization
of the base structure thus hinges in part on considerations
outside the purview of the services or the Department of
Defense. Notwithstanding the difficulties involved,
the services have closed or earmarked for closure some
216 smaller facilities;[38] the Carter administration is
expected to add additional facilities to this list in the
near future. Studies now underway on joint, or cross,
service utilization of major facilities may identify additional bases for closure.[39] Yet, as was the case with
civilian substitution, base-consolidation opportunities
have largely been exploited; further rationalization of
the base structure, while not impossible, will clearly
be more difficult to achieve.

Companion actions to the civilianization and base-
closure programs are the Nunn Amendment and the recent
"headquarters review." Under the Nunn Amendment the
services were authorized to create new combat units in
Europe, using military positions taken from headquarters
and service units. The conversion involved 18,000
positions; twelve new battalion-sized combat units were
formed and personnel levels in other tactical units were
increased.[40]

[38]Schlesinger, _Annual Defense Department Report, FY
1976 and FY 1977_, p. VI-2, and Rumsfeld, _Annual Defense
Department Report, FY 1977_, pp. 240-41.
   [39]Schlesinger, _Annual Defense Department Report, FY
1976 and FY 1977_, p. Vi-2.
   [40]The Nunn Amendment is PL 93-365. Because of the critical tasks that would fall to headquarters and service units in the early days of a NATO crisis, many senior officers
were less than enthusiastic about the conversion. For a
report on the conversion, see Rumsfeld, _Annual Defense Department Report, FY 1977_, pp. 231-32.

The headquarters review, designed to reduce duplication and
layering between the Pentagon and subordinate headquarters, eliminated a total of 23,000 civilian and military
positions. The military positions freed by this review
are being used to create additional combat elements,
including three new divisions in the Army and several new
squadrons in the Air Force.[41] The scale of this conversion is suggested by the drop in the number of personnel
at the Pentagon: a reduction of 22% and 26%, respectively,
in the number of military and civilian employees over the
last nine years.[42] In view of the interest of political
leaders in control of operating forces and the general
importance of C^3 activities, however, one must conclude
that additional manpower economies through actions of
this sort are limited.

There is some potential for improving the productivity of military personnel by means of changes in other
military personnel policies. The military pay system
involves large "in-kind" and "fringe" benefits; in the
eyes of many critics, it fails to promote efficiency in
terms of personnel retention and effectiveness. The present military retirement system permits essentially un-
controlled retirement, often at an early age. Assignment
policies may also fail to serve the interests of efficiency. These issues have been studied extensively in recent
years.[43] Proposals for change have met with strong opposition. Service personnel, by and large, are adamantly
opposed, viewing each proposal as threatening to what is
regarded as an increasingly marginal life-style. The
concern of active-duty personnel is shared by retired
personnel, who regard efforts to rationalize compensation
policies as an attack on benefits earned through earlier
service.[44] Perceptions by many active-duty and retired
personnel that their sacrifices for the nation's security,
especially their service during the Vietnam War, are
deprecated or distorted have contributed to a general
skepticism within the military community about any
change in personnel policies. The service associations,
joined by retired, reserve, and veterans groups, have, thus
far, been effective in blocking changes in these policies.
Unfortunately, the focus of discussion on military compensation has been primarily on the issues of compensation for

[41]Schlesinger, Annual Defense Department Report, FY
1976 and FY 197T, p. V-3.
    [42]See Department of Defense, Selected Manpower Statis-
tics, May 1977, p. 12
    [43]See Defense Manpower Commission, Defense Manpower:
The Keystone of National Security, Report to the President
and Congress (Washington, D.C.: USGPO, 1976).
    [44]See the Retired Officer Magazine.

career personnel. Little thought has been given to
making military compensation more attractive to potential enlistees. Studies of these complex issues continue;
significant economies or improvements in effectiveness
seem unlikely.

To summarize, technological developments have dramatically altered the character of modern warfare. The
increased range and destructive power of modern weapons
heighten political interest in controlling operating
forces and equalize risks among different types of
military units. In addition, a relatively greater share
of the overall force is now required to control, coordinate,
and support combat elements. These developments mean
that economies in military manpower can often be achieved
only by acceptance of some loss in readiness or effectiveness. They also restrict civilian substitution largely
to support activities. In recent years the armed forces
have shifted military personnel from headquarters and
service activities to combat formations; approximately
50,000 military positions have been converted to civilian
ones. As a result of these and other actions, the services have become relatively more efficient in their use
of military manpower. Further economies are possible,
but they will be limited and difficult to achieve.

Demographic Trends and Alternative Youth Opportunities

Demographic trends apparently received little attention during the Gates Commission's deliberations or in President
Nixon's decision to accept the Commission's recommendations.[45] In terms of prospects for voluntary enlistment,
however, the timing could hardly have been better. When
the transition from the draft to the all-volunteer force
began in 1971, the number of 17- to 21-year-old males, who
constitute virtually all new enlisted accessions, totaled
about 9.5 million. The pool has grown steadily larger and
will number 10.8 million in 1978, an increase of 14%
in the first seven years of the all-volunteer experience.

Demographic trends are clearly unfavorable for military
recruiting in the years ahead. Beginning in 1979, as
Chart 2 indicates, the number of males aged 17-21 declines
each year. By 1986 the 17- to 21-year-old male cohort will
be slightly smaller than it was in 1971, when the transition to an all-volunteer force began. The decline continues until 1994; at that time the cohort will include only

[45]The only reference to demographic trends occurs in
chapter 9. See Report of the President's Commission on an
All-Volunteer Armed Force, p. 116.

CHART II

Male Population, Age 17-21, 1970-2000

Population (X 1000)

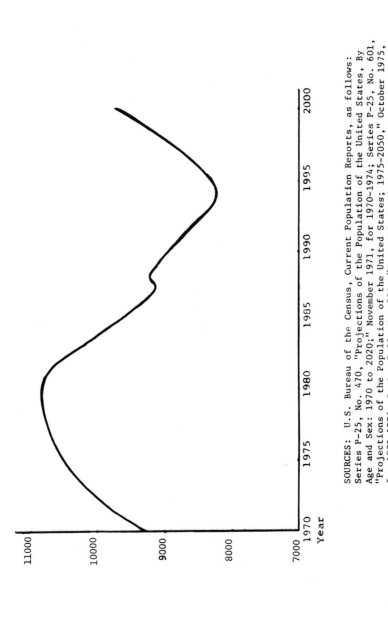

SOURCES: U.S. Bureau of the Census, Current Population Reports, as follows:
Series P-25, No. 470, "Projections of the Population of the United States, By
Age and Sex: 1970 to 2020;" November 1971, for 1970-1974; Series P-25, No. 601,
"Projections of the Population of the United States; 1975-2050," October 1975,
for 1975-1976: Series P-25, No. 704, "Projections of the Population of the
United States; 1977-2050," July 1977, for 1977-2000.

8.2 million males, 24% below present (1978) levels and
14% lower than the 1971 level. After 1994, the cohort
increases slowly in size; not until 1999, however, does it
return to the 1970 level. The demographic pattern, in
short, is adverse over a long period; it contributes to
a problem that extends over a generation and is not easily
amenable to temporary or expedient solutions.

Major segments of the 17- to 21-year-old male cohort
are either not eligible for or not interested in military
service. Presently, about 50% of all 17- to 21-year-old
males are disqualified for service because of physical,
mental, or emotional disabilities. Another 20% consists
of college and university students who, while qualified,
have clearly defined interests other than military service. Veterans and men already serving in the active
forces or reserve components account for some 15% of the
cohort. Those 17- to 21-year-old males remaining, roughly
15% of the cohort, constitute an identifiable recruiting
pool that provides the bulk of new enlisted accessions.
About 1.1 million, or 70%, of the 1.6 million males currently in the recruiting pool are high school graduates.[46]

If recent experience is a guide, it will become
increasingly difficult in the face of this demographic
pattern for the armed forces to maintain authorized
strength levels in the active and reserve components.
Currently, the active forces require about 400,000 nonprior
service accessions annually; the reserve components need
another 100,000. Assuming that female accessions levels
remain stable, this means that about 30% of all males
qualified and otherwise available must now be recruited for
military service. If requirements remain at the 500,000
level and continue to come from the small (15%) segment of
the male cohort identified as the recruiting pool, then by
1986 military recruiters will need to enlist   33% of the
males in the pool. By 1994, when the recruiting pool
drops to its lowest level, the services will need 38%
of the males in the pool.

The recruiting problem can be depicted in yet another
way. Assume that requirements remain the same and that
the services are unable to increase the share accessioned
above the current level of three of ten, a not unreasonable
assumption since the Army and Marine Corps are now experiencing some problems in obtaining enough new recruits.
By 1986 the shortfall would be about 80,000; by 1994 the
shortage would be roughly 130,000. If this shortfall

[46]See Harold G. Moore (Lt. General, USA), "Sustaining
the Volunteer Army," Defense Management Journal, October
1976, p. 11.

in male accessions is filled by women, about 16% of all
accessions in 1986 will be women; by 1994, under the same
assumptions, women would provide about 26% of all new accessions. Both accessions levels imply a larger number of
women in the active force than currently projected by the
services or suggested by most of the recent studies dealing with the utilization of women in the armed forces.[47]

Demographic trends influence two other major dimensions of the all-volunteer force. First, as the 17- to
21-year-old male cohort declines in size and the services
attempt to recruit a larger share of the manpower pool,
maintaining authorized strength levels will necessarily
involve accepting more recruits of lower ability. Second,
the services will become increasingly unrepresentative in
racial makeup. Black Americans now constitute about 11.6%
of the total population but roughly 16.6% of the enlisted
force. However, the disparity is likely to increase in
the years ahead. The reason is that the percentage of
blacks in the recruiting pool is not only higher but is
increasing faster than in the population as a whole.
Table 2 indicates the extent of disparity between the
recruiting pool and the general population. Given the
already high attraction of military service for young
black males, the armed forces may be expected to be even
less representative in the future.

Table 2. Black Representativeness (%)

	1977	1980	1983	1986	1989	1992	1995	1998
Recruiting Pool	13.0	13.4	14.0	14.4	14.7	15.3	15.1	14.5
Total Population	11.6	11.8	11.9	12.1	12.2	12.3	12.4	12.5
Difference	1.4	1.6	2.1	2.3	2.5	3.0	2.7	2.0

Source: U.S. Bureau of the Census, Current Population Reports,
Series P-25, No. 704, "Projections of the Population of the
United States: 1977-2050 (Washington: USGPO, 1977), pp. 37-58.

[47]See Office of the Assistant Secretary of Defense
(Manpower, Reserve Affairs, and Logistics), Background
Study: Use of Women in the Military, May 1977, pp. 29,
B-6, C-12, and D-4. A recent Brookings study suggests
that women could fill up the 540,000 enlisted positions,
a somewhat higher level than projected here. See Martin Binkin and Shirley J. Bach, Women and the Military
(Washington, D.C.: Brookings Institution, 1977),
pp. 98-101.

The demographic trends described above have implications for activities other than military recruiting--higher
education is particularly affected by changes in the number
of young men and women. Enrollment in post-secondary
educational institutions amounted to about 10 million in
1976, of which some 7.2 million are full-time students.
Of all full-time students, some 5.2 million, or 72%, are
in the 18- to 24-year-old cohort.[48] Special education
activities--cooperative, community, and extension programs
designed to meet the needs of groups beyond college age--
may well grow in importance over the years; but young
people are, and will remain, the basic raw material of
American higher education.

The prospect of a sharp decline in student enrollment
comes after two decades of unprecedented growth in higher
education. The decline in enrollment may be greater than
the demographic trends suggest: (1) the cost of attending
college is increasing; and (2) college appears to be
becoming relatively less attractive to high school graduates, particularly to male graduates.[49] Moreover, until
recently more high school graduates were electing to attend
two-year institutions, which further weakens enrollment
levels at four-year institutions.[50] Enrollment declines,
of course, foreshadow more difficult issues for American
higher education, including faculty and program termina-
tions.

As the dimensions of the enrollment problem have become clearer, college admissions officers, particularly
those at private institutions, have expanded and intensified student-recruiting activities. Initially many of
the recruiting programs were "excessive and misguided";[51]
more recently they demonstrate increasing sophistication--
indeed, some have been designed by major advertising agencies.[52] Anxious to avoid the implication that recruiting
is "selling," college officials, following Peter Drucker,
now speak of "marketing" their institutions.[53] Marketing

[48]U.S., Bureau of the Census, Current Population Rep-
orts, Ser. P-20, no. 309, "School Enrollment--Social and
Economic Characteristics of Students: October 1976" (Advance
Report), (Washington, D.C.: USGPO, 1977) pp. 1-3, 5, 8.
    [49]Ibid., p. 6.
    [50]Ibid., p. 3.
    [51]Philip Kotler, "Applying Marketing Theory to College
Admissions," A Role for Marketing in College Admissions
(New York: College Entrance Examination Board, 1976) p. 55.
    [52]See "Colleges Turn to Pros as Enrollments Decline,"
Advertising Age, July 9, 1973, p. 34.
    [53]See College and University, 50, no. 4 (Summer 1975),
p. 340.

must begin "in the offices of the president and the board
of trustees";[54] institutions must "actively search for
exciting and relevant new programs to enrich the schools'
operations and attractiveness."[55] The growing importance
attached to student recruiting is suggested by several
developments: Panel discussions on recruiting have been
presented at recent annual meetings of the American Association of Collegiate Registrars and Admissions Officers
(AACRAO). Recruiting was the subject of a national colloquium in 1976; papers presented at that colloquium, including one by a senior associate of a major national
public relations firm, were recently published by the
College Entrance Examination Board.[56] Finally, "marketing"
costs have risen sharply in recent years; by one estimate,
college and universities now spend about $100 per high
school student[57]--about one-tenth the amount spent by the
armed forces for each new accession.

Teenagers about to graduate from high school are
bombarded with recruiting materials from the armed forces
and from colleges and universities. Although each focuses
on different segments of the teenage population, both the
services and higher education, for quite different reasons,
are keenly interested in the high school graduate of
moderate ability. As higher education expands its recruiting activities to bolster enrollment levels, the armed
forces will almost certainly encounter stiffer competition
for male high school graduates, the backbone of the present
enlisted force.

Beyond intensified competition from higher education,
military recruiting may become increasingly difficult for
another reason--federal jobs programs. The linkage between
recruiting and jobs programs is unemployment in the civilian work force. The expiration of induction authority in
1973 occurred at a time of moderately high unemployment.
A mild recession in 1974 and 1975 increased the unemployment rate; currently it stands at about 7% in the civilian
work force but is almost 20% among teenagers.[58] Economists
and manpower specialists agree that the high unemployment
level of recent years has facilitated military recruitment.
By one estimate, each percentage point increase in unem-

[54]Kotler, "Applying Marketing Theory," p. 57.
[55]Ibid., p. 60.
[56]See A Role for Marketing in College Admissions, and
Howard Getzer and Al Ries, "The Positioning Era: A Marketing Strategy in the 1980's," pp. 73 ff.
[57]Ibid., p. 76
[58]See Mary Eisner Eccles, "Jobs Programs: How Well Do
They Work?" Congressional Quarterly, 35, no. 8 (February
19, 1977), 305.

ployment brings a corresponding increase in the number of
moderate to high quality volunteers.[59]

Persistent high unemployment, especially severe in
major urban areas, has prompted a range of federal actions.
The major federal initiatives designed to attack unemployment now include: (1) $2.5 billion per year for public
service jobs under Title VI of the 1973 Comprehensive
Employment and Training Act (CETA); (2) an emergency public
works program funded at $2 billion in 1976; (3) $1.25
billion in "countercyclical" aid to states and cities
in 1976; and (4) over $900 million per year for work
experience and training activities under Title I of CETA.[60]
There are, in addition, 12 federal employment, training, or
service programs aimed especially at teenagers. In 1976,
some 1.6 million young American participated in these
programs.[61]

The Carter administration, at the urging of black
and urban leaders, has devised a broad strategy which it
hopes will be more effective in attacking the unemployment problem.[62] The major elements in the Carter plan
include a general tax reduction, designed to stimulate
job creation in the private sector; an expansion from
320,000 to 725,000 in the number of public service jobs
under CETA; and increased funding of the emergency public
works program.[63] The programs targeted at teenagers will
also be expanded--Job Corps positions, for example, would
be doubled from 22,000 to 44,000. Finally, as part of its
welfare-reform proposal, the administration envisages
creation of 1.4 million public jobs for welfare recipients
and low income persons.[64] Whether this strategy will
achieve the national goals--an unemployment level of 4%
overall, with a rate of 3% among workers aged 20 and over--
recently announced in the revised Humphrey-Hawkins Bill
is uncertain.[65]

[59]Richard V. L. Cooper, Military Manpower and the
All-Volunteer Force, p. 187.
[60]See Eccles, "Jobs Program," pp. 302-7.
[61]For a convenient summary, see King Report, pp. 113-17.
[62]See Walter S. Mossberg, "Black Jobless Problem Still
Haunts President despite New Programs," Wall Street Journal, November 28, 1977, pp. 1 ff.
[63]Eccles, "Jobs Programs," pp. 306-7.
[64]See "The Welfare Package--1.4 Million Jobs, 1.4
Million Questions," National Journal, November 12, 1977,
pp. 1764-68.
[65]See Mary Eisner Eccles, "Backers Defend Revised Humphrey-Hawkins Bill," Congessional Quarterly, 35, no. 48
(November 26, 1977), 2475-76.

Public service jobs programs of the type enacted in
recent years are regarded by many observers as relatively
inefficient in terms of reducing unemployment. In some
respects, public service and public works jobs programs
have become revenue-sharing mechanisms under which state
and city agencies use CETA and other federal funds to keep
already employed persons on the payroll.[66] Moreover,
except for the Jobs Corps and other youth programs,
the major federal actions, particularly CETA and the
public works programs, aim at segments of the population
of little interest to military recruiters. Yet any
reduction in unemployment, by whatever mechanism, is
certain to put some teenagers to work. In addition,
more talented teenagers are likely to be attracted by the
vocational training opportunities afforded by the Jobs
Corps and the Apprenticeship and National On-The-Job
Training programs. Thus, employment opportunities open
to teenagers--because of a greater number of jobs in the
private sector or through the federal government's job-
creation programs--are almost certain to grow over the
next few years.

Long-term demographic trends are unfavorable for
military recruiting--by 1986, the number of 17- to 21-year-
old males will decline 14% from the present level; the
decline continues until 1994. Higher education is also
affected, and colleges and universities are strengthen-
ing student-recruiting activities. In response to high
levels of unemployment, federal jobs and yough training
programs have also been expanded. Further expansion
of these programs has been proposed by the Carter administration. As a result, teenagers will be afforded improved
educational, employment, and jobs training opportunities.
As the recruiting pool declines in size and the opportunities open to young men and women increases, military recruiting may be expected to become more difficult.

The Political Context of the Personnel-Procurement Policy Issue

The emerging crisis in military personnel-procurement policies stems in part from a change in supply--the size of the
17- to 21-year-old male cohort declines between 1978 and
1994 and is relatively low until the turn of the century.
But the implications of this shift in manpower supply are
magnified by other developments: First, competition for
these males will intensify as higher education and jobs
training programs will provide increasingly attractive alternatives to military service. Second, military manpower
requirements are sensitive to developments in international

[66]Eccles, "Jobs Programs," pp. 305-6.

affairs, particularly to Soviet defense policies. The
continuing Soviet arms buildup suggests that reductions
are unlikely in the near future--indeed, a modest increase
may be indicated. Finally, while some savings in military
manpower remain to be achieved, the opportunities afforded
by economy actions, civilian substitution, and productivity increases have already been substantially exploited.
As these trends converge in the 1980s, military personnel
procurement can be expected to become a difficult public
policy issue.

In a recent interview with U.S. News and World Report,
Senator Sam Nunn noted that "the volunteer force came about
not on the basis of good analysis but on the basis of a
political decision that was made by the executive branch--
and, I must say, endorsed by Congress--that would buy
time for Vietnam, cool the campuses, take the political
heat off. I think it has been a real national mistake."[67]
Senator Nunn's judgment is disputed by many observers; his
observation is nevertheless a useful reminder that any
change in military personnel-procurement policies will be
made by political leaders acting in some political context.
If the problem is defined by the trends described above,
the political context in which it must be addressed will,
in all likelihood, involve two other complex issues. One
concerns the structure and mission of the reserve components; the second the status and rights of women in American society.

To date, voluntary recruitment has a mixed record--
reasonably successful in meeting active force recruitments;
less successful in terms of meeting the needs of the
reserve components. As competition for manpower inten-
sifies over the next few years, the reserve forces are
likely to fare poorly as compared to the active forces.
Consequently, any proposal involving a military draft or
a national service scheme will, of necessity, rest in part
on personnel shortages in the reserve components.

The ability of major portions of the reserves, as
presently organized and equipped, to contribute usefully
in the event of a crisis is increasingly questioned.
Reserve units, even those earmarked for early deployment,
are unlikely to be available soon enough to be of assistance in the most important crisis--a war in Europe. Administrative processing and unit exercises are necessary
before deployment can take place; recent estimates indicate
that many units would require several months to achieve
the desired level of combat readiness.[68] The central prob-

[67]February 14, 1977, p. 60.
[68]See Kenneth H. Bacon, "Achilles' Heel?" Wall Street
Journal, August 9, 1977, pp. 1 ff.

lem is the lack of training time. Even if reserve units
have all of their personnel, most of them would not achieve
the required readiness level soon enough to contribute in
an emergency. The situation in the Individual Ready
Reserves (IRR)--a pool of individuals available to replace
losses in active and reserve units--is different but even
less satisfactory.[69] Individuals in the IRR are readily
available, but most are poorly trained. Hence the dilemma:
organized reserve units are partially trained, but not
ready for early deployment; individual reservists are
readily available but not adequately trained. With
some exceptions, such as the Air National Guard, neither
reserve units nor individual reservists are likely to be
able to contribute usefully to the central defense
problem, a major war in Europe.[70]

    Draft or national service proposals which are justi-
fied even in part by manpower shortages in the reserves
therefore involve broader issues of reserve force mission,
structure, and training. Even if fully manned, critics
will contend, reserve forces will be of only marginal
value in the most important crisis. What is needed is
not a new method of manpower procurement but a reorganization of the reserve components, a reorganization that
meshes reserve organization with realistic missions and
manpower availability. Reserve reorganization--difficult
because of the involvement of the states and of historic
attitudes regarding the role of citizen forces--therefore
becomes a precondition to a change in manpower-procurement
policies. Indeed, some proponents of reserve reorganization
might welcome a modest crisis in personnel procurement in
the hope that it would create a political climate favorable to such a reorganization.

    The second issue to which military personnel-recruit-
ment policy is closely linked is the status and rights of
women in American society. While this issue has many
dimensions, the public barometer reflecting its status
is the Equal Rights Amendment. ERA has been ratified by
35 states of the 38 total required. Some ERA proponents
are debating legislative proposals which would extend the
ratification period from 1979 to 1987.

    If the Equal Rights Amendment is approved, passage of

[69]Ibid. The IRR currently enrolls only about 150,000
reservists, as compared to some 975,000 in 1972.
    [70]For a useful summary of the problems of the reserve
components, from which I have drawn heavily, see Roy A.
Werner, "The Other Military: U.S. Reserve Components." Paper
presented at Annual Meeting of Inter-University Seminar on
Armed Forces and Society, Chicago, October 20-22, 1977.

a military draft or national service scheme would raise a
difficult political issue: Women would almost certainly
be subject to compulsory military service (although not
necessarily a combat role). While much of the public
supports equal rights for women, this support does not
extend to compulsory military service.[71] At the very
least, then, a draft or national service proposal would
involve a divisive, volatile issue of broad public concern
--a decision many in Congress would prefer to avoid or
defer.

Failure of the Equal Rights Amendment does not
necessarily sever the relationship between the role of
women and military personnel-procurement policies. Any
serious proposal to institute a draft or national service
will have opposition; it is reasonable to believe that
opponents will, if only for tactical reasons, argue that a
draft or national service should, "in fairness," apply
equally to women. The dilemma facing individual members
of Congress is clearly not as severe as it would be if
ERA is approved; yet the question of fairness will be
both hard to avoid and difficult to face.

Fairness and equity have other dimensions. They are
achieved only if all serve. Yet military needs can be
met by a small share of the total number of young people
available. Since only a few will be needed, will deferments and exemptions be permitted? The Vietnam era
saw strenuous objections to the inequities created by
deferments and exemptions. Even service in the reserve
components, in lieu of the active forces, and deferment
to permit participation in officer training programs were
regarded by some as inequitable. Without such exemptions,
however, opposition to compulsory service can be expected
from religious organizations, higher education, and the
social classes of Americans most likely to attend higher
education--politically efficacious institutions and individuals.

For the reasons noted above, existing personnel-
procurement policies are unlikely to meet the personnel
requirements of the armed forces in the future. Yet the
most widely proposed solutions to this problem are politically suspect because of their relationship with other difficult issues. Moreover, draft or national service proposals may face opposition on still other grounds. First,

[71]Not only is the public opposed to a draft, but it
is against national service for women, 51% to 40%. The
18-24 age group that would be affected by compulsory service is more strongly opposed. See The Gallup Opinion Index, no. 139 (February 1977) and no. 142 (May 1977).

national service has been viewed favorably because it
promises a solution to the military recruiting problem
and simultaneously makes possible realization of other
socially desirable activities through an acceptable mechanism, i.e., everyone serves. But the core of the problem
is a shortage of young Americans willing to serve in the
military; a solution that requires all 17- to 21-year-olds
to participate in activities which, while desirable, are
not currently regarded as sufficiently important to warrant
support by the federal government, makes little sense.[72]
In this regard, national service proposals would have a
particularly severe impact upon higher education--or
necessitate a complex and ultimately unacceptable system
of exemptions and deferments.

Second, a return to compulsory service might have some
undesirable consequences for the armed forces. In all
likelihood compulsory service would mean a shorter period
of service than present-day volunteers now provide. First-
term enlistees now serve three years or more; the maximum
period of service with a draft would probably be eighteen
to twenty-four months and national service from twelve to
eighteen months. While the quality of draftees might be
somewhat higher than that of the volunteers available in
the 1980s, quality may not in itself offset the loss of
effectiveness that can be achieved through longer terms of
service. And while a draft might provide a fully
manned reserve, barring a major reorganization, the net
improvement in military effectiveness is likely to be small.
Compulsory service might therefore serve to reduce the overall effectiveness of the active forces, particularly of
the Army and Marine Corps, with little or no offsetting
gain in reserve force capabilities.

However difficult the military personnel-procurement
crisis of the 1980s, the most widely advocated solutions--
a military draft or a national service scheme--present
formidable, perhaps insurmountable, political difficulties.
Personal-procurement policies are inextricably linked to
other complex issues: the mission and structure of the
reserve components and the role and status of women in
American life. In the absence of educational and other
deferments, equally controversial issues, institutions of
higher education and agencies sponsoring vocational train-

[72]Public support for national service, while favorable,
has declined over the past decade. See The Gallup Opinion
Index, no. 139 (February 1977), p. 18. The cost of national service scheme is also likely to be a major stumbling
block.

ing activities can be expected to regard a draft or national services as contrary to their interests.

Given the scenario outlined above, the main question is: What should be done to alleviate the worst effects of the impending supply shortage? Leadership must rest with the Department of Defense; many of the actions it is now considering are relevant. But three warrant special attention:

1. A change in the "mix" of the enlisted force should be considered. Currently, enlistees in their first term of service constitute about 60% of the enlisted force. An increase in the share of second-term and career enlistees would allow a reduction in the number of new accessions required each year. The personnel costs of, say, a force with only 50% first-term enlistees would be higher; a reduction in training costs might offset some of the higher personnel costs. [73]

2. Efforts to increase the number of women in the armed forces should continue, as recommended in the recent Department of Defense study "Use ofWomen in the Military." That study concludes that the young women currently in the armed forces are serving effectively. It also recommends that the Department of Defense seek a change in the law prohibiting women from serving on Navy ships. More important, perhaps, is that DOD explore further the as yet unanswered questions regarding "flexibility, response to uncertainty, readiness, and deployability . . . . (that result from) having more women in the military who are precluded from combat service." [74] However, more careful analysis of the supply of women volunteers is required. [75]

3. Efforts to improve the structure and effectiveness of the reserve components should continue. A starting

[73]For a discussion of the "mix" issue, see Cooper, Military Manpower and the All-Volunteer Force, pp. 303-19.
[74]Assistant Secretary of Defense (Manpower, Reserve Affairs, and Logistics), May 1977, pp. iii-iv.
[75]Available evidence suggests that women are less interested in military service than men, although not dramatically so. See Jerald G. Bachman, John D. Blair, and David R. Segal. The All-Volunteer Force: A Study of Ideology in the Military (Ann Arbor: University of Michigan Press, 1977). However, women in the military do not seem especially interested in nontraditional jobs--75% of enlisted women now occupy clerical, health care, communications, and intelligence positions. See Binkin and Bach, Women in the Military, p. 19.

point for such efforts is the realization that, because
of training-time constraints, most reserve units cannot
achieve the degree of readiness required for early deployment. Thus, other approaches must be explored. Two that
might be considered are: (1) mobilization assignments
for selected enlisted and officer retirees, which would
permit early transfer of active duty personnel in training
base and support activities to combat units; and (2)
proficiency-maintenance training for individual reservists
in hard-to-acquire skill areas expected to be in critical
demand during the early days of a crisis.

4. At the present time roughly four of every ten
young Americans are disqualified from military service
because of physical or other disabilities. Remedial
medical treatment and more effective matching of physical
skills with military jobs might serve to increase the
number of qualified applicants. In addition, uniform
physical standards may be unnecessary given the range of
tasks which people in uniform now perform.

5. As the 17- to 21-year-old cohort decreases in
size, the competition for these young Americans will
increase. Some coordinating mechanism is required to
insure that the manpower needs and policies of the private
sector, higher education, the armed forces, and federal
agencies are addressed in a timely and coherent way.
This task was performed informally in the period after
the Korean War by the Selective Service System, which
"channeled" the nation's youth into desired directions
through changes in classification and deferment policies.[76]
An interagency commission would be an appropriate vehicle
to coordinate federal policies and programs in the years
ahead.

6. In the last year or so, attrition (i.e., early
separation, before completion of the initial enlistment)
among newly enlisted personnel has risen significantly.
These early losses can be attributed, at least in part, to
family problems: One of every five new enlistees is
married; the number increases to two in five during the
first enlistment. Frequent family separations occasioned
by training activities and overseas deployment exacerbated
by money problems strain these early marriages severely.
Funded counseling and social welfare activities at major
military bases would not only help these families
but serve to reduce attrition among first-term enlistees.
A reduction in attrition, in turn, lowers the requirements

[76] James M. Gerhardt, The Draft and Public Policy:
Issues in Military Manpower Procurement, 1945-1970 (Colum-
bus: Ohio State University Press, 1971) pp. 233-35, 358-59.

for new accessions.

7. As suggested above, most military recruits are
drawn from a small segment of the 17- to 21-year-old
cohort. Some expansion of the recruiting pool could
probably be achieved by a restoration of veteran's
educational benefits, long considered one of the most
important and attractive benefits of enlisted service.
Beyond increasing the size of the recruiting pool, restoration of educational benefits would tend to broaden and
diversify the social and political characteristics of the
enlisted force.[77]

8. The Department of Defense should continue to seek
more appropriate policies in those areas affecting military
manpower utilization, especially compensation and retirement
policies. While these policies do not bear directly on the
main issues affecting the volunteer force, more appropriate
policies foster more efficient manpower utilization throughout the services.

Military personnel-procurement policies face a
crisis in the 1980s. None of the actions proposed above
will solve this crisis; individually and collectively
they will help reduce the severeity of the problem.
It may be necessary to resort to a military draft or to
institute a program of national service, but all of the
actions above--and perhaps a major crisis as well--seem
to be prerequisites to the political decision to return
to compulsory military service of any kind.

[77]Bachman, Blair, and Segal, The All-Volunteer Force,
pp. 143-48.

THE ENLISTED RANKS IN THE ALL-VOLUNTEER ARMY

Charles C. Moskos, Jr.

Since January 1973 the United States has sought to accomplish what it has never attempted before--to maintain over
two million persons on active military duty on a voluntary
basis. Five years after the end of conscription, the all-
volunteer force has been analyzed, attacked, and defended
in a seemingly endless series of books, reports, articles,
and Congressional hearings. The commentators tend to
divide into two groups. On the one side, there are those
who convey their belief that the all-volunteer force is a
success which at most requires only certain changes in
personnel-management policies. On the other, there are
those who see little prospect of a viable defense force
short of returning to a form of compulsory military service. I place myself in neither camp.

    This study focuses on that component of the all-volun-
teer force that relied most directly on the draft--the enlisted ranks of the Army; and it is this part of the military system where the outcomes of all-volunteer recruitment
are most quickly evident. It is important to stress, however, that all services were beneficiaries of the selective
service system. It is estimated that about 40% of all voluntary accessions into the military in the peacetime years
between the wars in Korea and Vietnam were draft motivated.
The draft was also the major impetus for recruitment into
the ROTC and our reserve forces. Nevertheless, it is the
enlisted ranks of the Army, the largest of the services,
which most clearly focus the conditions bearing upon the
viability of the all-volunteer force.

    Let me state at the outset that it is unfair and a
gross exaggeration to characterize the all-volunteer
Army as being in a state of crisis. Certainly, Army
recruiters have accomplished a task of immense proportions
in the all-volunteer era. The Army of the late 1970s,
moreover, by many indicators, whether unit effectiveness,

disciplinary rates, or race relations, is noticeably
improved over the Army of the early 1970s. To place the
all-volunteer experience in a more balanced light, however,
it would be better to use the immediate pre-Vietnam period
as a benchmark rather than 1970-73, the worst times in
modern Army history. Furthermore, as the information to
be presented will show, enlistment of an Army primarily
based on marketplace competition most likely cannot insure
a sufficient number of qualified entrants and may well
have a corrosive effect on service integrity. To raise
questions as to the future viability of the all-volunteer
force, however, is not to advocate restoration of conscription. The choices in front of us are not limited to
either tinkering with the all-volunteer status quo, on
the one hand, or bringing back the draft, on the other.
An informed discussion of such choices must be supported
by careful sociological analysis, organizational insight,
and honest presentation of empirical data. This is the
task now before us.

      The plan of this study is straightforward. First,
data from the end of the draft through 1977 are given on
the social background of the Army enlisted ranks. When-
ever possible, comparable data are presented from the
early 1960s in order to assess demographic trends over
two peacetime periods. Second, there is a conceptual
overview of organizational trends within the Army before
and after the end of conscription. Though organizational
developments vary somewhat between the services, they do
share basic commonalities. Third, an account of contemporary enlisted culture is offered. This goes beyond
statistical and conceptual formulations by looking at
actual enlisted life in the all-volunteer Army. Fourth,
there is a discussion of the controversial issues of
"representativeness" and how this relates to soldierly
performance. Finally, in an effort to counterbalance
prevailing econometric analyses of the all-volunteer
force, military service in the ranks is linked to broader
questions of citizen participation and national service.

                        Demographic Trends

Each year since the end of the draft the armed forces
have been seeking to recruit between 400,000 and 430,000
enlisted persons, virtually all between the ages of 17 to
21 years. Of the males in that age bracket, only about a
quarter are considered "qualified and eligible," that is,
physically, mentally, and morally fit and likely to be
available for military service (i.e., excluding full-time
students, those already in the military, veterans, or those

institutionalized).[1] Thus it is calculated that about
three in ten qualified and eligible males must be recruited
from each annual cohort to maintain an active-duty force
slightly over two million persons.

The Army has been recruiting between 180,000 and
200,000 enlisted persons annually since 1973. In FY 1977
the Army recruited 181,000 persons, of whom 85% were non-
prior-service males, 7% prior-service males, and 8% non-
prior-service females. On the whole, the number of entrants
into the all-volunteer Army has matched recruitment objectives. It is true that a major shortfall of 23,000
was experienced in FY 1974, the first year of the all-
volunteer Army, but recruitment achievements in subsequent
years have met or been close to enlistment goals. (In FY
1977, the Army fell 4,000 short of its recruitment target.)
The overall size of the Army, however, has been reduced
from an active-duty strength averaging 920,000 in the
1960-64 period to 782,000 at the end of FY 1977.

While recruitment objectives in the all-volunteer
Army have generally been achieved up to the present,
inescapable demographic constraints appear on the immediate
horizon. In 1977 some 2.14 million males reached 18, in
1980 the figure will decline slightly to 2.13 million, and
then drop precipitously to 1.8 million by 1985, and 1.7
million by 1990. Inasmuch as the recruitment pool consists overwhelmingly of non-prior-service (NPS) males, this
is the group with which most of the ensuing discussion
will deal. The increasing role of women in the all-
volunteer Army will also draw our attention.

Educational Levels

The educational levels of male enlistees in the all-volunteer Army are markedly lower than either the equivalent
civilian population or the Army entrants of 1964, the last
peacetime year before the war in Vietnam. (Because of
higher draft calls, educational levels of Army accessions
increased during the war years of Vietnam.) As reported
in Table 1, 43.9% of NPS males in FY 1977 did not possess
a high school diploma. This compares with 25.4% of nine-
teen-year-old males in the general population, and 28.7%
of draftees and 39.9% of enlistees in 1964. The contrast
between the educational levels of the all-volunteer Army

[1]The concept of "qualified and eligible" was first
introduced in Martin Binkin and John D. Johnston, All-Vol-
unteer Armed Forces: Progress, Problems and Prospects.
Report prepared for the Committee on Armed Services, U.S.
Senate, 93d Cong., 1st sess. (Washington, D.C.: Government
Printing Office, 1973).

and the peacetime draft Army is more glaring when placed in
the context of the overall increase for male high school
graduates, aged 18 to 21 years, in the recent past; from 64%
in 1967 to 72% in 1975.[2] This is to say that while the national trend has been toward improving high school graduation
rates, Army accessions are going the other way.

Table 1. Educational levels of army male entrants (nonprior service)
          and 19-year-old American males

Educational level	1964 draftees	1964 enlistees	FY 1977 enlistees	19-year-old males (1976)
Some college	17.2	13.9	4.9	23.0
High school graduate	54.1	46.2	51.2	51.6
Non-high-school graduate	28.7	39.9	43.9	25.4
Total	100.0	100.0	100.0	100.0

Sources: Accession data from Department of Army statistics; Civilian
data from U.S., Bureau of the Census, Current Population Reports,
P-20, no. 295, p. 59.

     The data given in Table 1 also reveal an even sharper
decline in the proportion of Army entrants with some
college between the pre- and post-Vietnam periods. Where
17.2% of the draftees and 13.9% of the enlistees in 1964
had some college, the corresponding figure is 4.9% of the
FY 1977 enlistees. Not only did the draft directly bring
a sizeable college element into the ranks, but it also
served as an impetus for draft-motivated volunteers who
were educated beyond high school. The 1964 accession data,
if anything, understate the infusion of college enlisted
men into the ranks of the pre-Vietnam Army. During the
small cohort years of the mid-1950s to the early 1960s--the
time when depression babies had reached military age--
college graduates were more likely to be drafted than in
any period since World War II. (Survey data based on
1962 Army entrants show 24.7% of draftees had some college.)

     [2]Richard V. L. Cooper, Military Manpower and
the All-Volunteer Force (Santa Monica, Calif.: 1977),
p. 189.

Racial Composition

The rising proportion of black entrants has generated more
controversy than any other topic in the debate on the all-
volunteer force.[3] This topic has been particularly sensitive with regard to the Army enlisted ranks. In the
early 1960s blacks accounted for about 12% of Army enlisted entrants, a figure corresponding with the black
share of the 18-24 year age group in the total population.
During most of the war years in Vietnam, blacks made up
about 15% of Army accessions. Since the advent of the all-
volunteer Army, the proportion of blacks has more than
doubled over pre-Vietnam levels. As shown in Table 2,
black accessions reached 31.9% of NPS males in 1977.
Although the number of other minorities is not as reliably
tabulated, a figure of at least 5%, principally Hispanic,
would be a cautious estimate. In other words, over a
third of the men now entering the Army's enlisted ranks
are from minority groups.

Table 2. Black proportion of army male enlistees (nonprior service)

Year	Percentage black
1973	26.8
1974	26.5
1975	22.0
1976	27.6
1977 (thru Nov.)	31.9

Source: Department of Army statistics.

Within the enlisted ranks racial content varies by
branch and career-management field. The following figures

[3]Morris Janowitz and Charles C. Moskos, Jr., "Racial
Composition in the All-Volunteer Force," Armed Forces and
Society, 1 (1974), 109-24; Alvin J. Schexnider and John Sib-
ley Butler, "Race and the All-Volunteer System: A reply to
Janowitz and Moskos," Armed Forces and Society, 2 (1976),
421-32; Defense Manpower Commission, Defense Manpower: The
Keystone of National Security (Washington, D.C.: Government
Printing Office, 1976), pp. 160-64; Cooper, pp. 209-21.

pertain to early 1977.[4] Black membership in the combat
arms is about 24%. Thus, even though blacks comprise more
than 30% of the strength in four divisions and are in the
majority in some battalions, it cannot be categorically
stated that blacks are overrepresented in the combat
arms in terms of total enlisted blacks. Of course, blacks
are overly proportionate in the combat arms in relation
to their numbers in American society, but this is because
whites are underrepresented in the all-volunteer Army.
Within the Army, however, it is in support units where
racial inbalance is most clearly evident. Blacks tend
to be concentrated in low-skill fields: 48.5% in petroleum
handling, 41.7% in supply, and 40.2% in wire maintenance.
Whites, on the other hand, are disproportionately found in
such high-skill fields as intercept equipment, signal
intelligence, aviation, and electronics.

The changing racial composition of the Army from
before the Vietnam War to the present is shown in Table 3.
Blacks made up 11.8% of enlisted personnel in 1964, 17.5%
in 1972, and 25.8% in mid-1977. Even at senior noncom
levels (E7-E9) blacks are considerably better represented
in 1977 than at any earlier time. The proportion of black
noncoms can be expected to increase further, owing to the
higher than average reenlistment rate of black soldiers.
In FY 1977, reenlistments at the end of the first term,
were 48.5% for blacks and 30.6% for whites.[5] Blacks
continue to be underrepresented in the officer corps at all
levels although the direction of change is toward greater
black participation. Army projections are for black officer
entrants to exceed 20% by the end of 1979.[6] Whether this
goal will be achieved remains to be seen, but there certainly has been a sharp rise in newly commissioned black
officers since the start of the all-volunteer Army.

It is important to stress that the trend toward increasing black content in the Army predates the all-volunteer force. The rising percentage of blacks operates
somewhat independently of the end of conscription and
can be attributed in part to the dramatic increase in the
proportion of blacks eligible for military service,
specifically, the increasing number of black high school
graduates and the larger percentage of blacks placing in the
upper levels of the mental aptitude tests required for service entry.[7] There is also the combined push of the as-

[4]Army Times, June 27, 1977, p. 40.
[5]Ibid., Sept. 5, 1977, p. 11.
[6]Ibid., June 13, 1977, p. 32.
[7]Cooper, pp. 209-16.

Table 3.   Black participation in the army by grade

	1964	1972	1977
Officers:			
O-7 and above	----	1.8	2.7
O-6	.2	1.5	3.8
O-5	1.1	5.3	5.0
O-4	3.5	5.0	5.0
O-3	5.1	3.9	5.3
O-2	3.6	3.4	8.1
O-1	2.6	2.2	9.8
Warrant	2.8	4.5	5.9
Total Officers	3.3	3.9	6.1
Enlisted:			
E-9	3.3	8.6	16.3
E-8	5.8	14.4	20.1
E-7	7.9	19.9	24.3
E-6	12.2	23.9	20.7
E-5	14.8	16.9	22.4
E-4	12.5	14.1	25.7
E-3	11.9	16.7	28.8
E-2	11.6	18.5	30.5
E-1	6.4	18.4	29.5
Total Enlisted	11.8	17.5	25.8

Source: Department of Army statistics.

Note: 1964 and 1972 figures as of December 31; 1977 figures as of
       31 July.

toundingly high unemployment rate among black youth and the
pull of an institution which has gone further than any
other to attack racism.

Race and Education

It is a well-recognized fact that the educational levels of
blacks in America have trailed far behind those of whites.
The trend, however, has been toward a narrowing of the gap.
Looking at males age 19 in 1970, for example, 44.1% of

blacks compared to 12.9% of whites had not completed
high school. By 1974 the high school dropout rate for
blacks had declined to 30.6% while the white race increased to 18.4%.[8] Still, even for the more recent
figures black educational attainment contrasts markedly
with that of whites.

Contrary to national patterns, however, the inter-
sect of race and education is quite different among male
entrants in the all-volunteer Army. Since the end of the
draft, the proportion of black high school graduates
entering the Army has exceeded that of whites, and this is
a trend that is becoming more pronounced. In FY 1977,
as shown in Table 4, high school graduates accounted for
60.5% of entering blacks compared to 40% of entering
whites.[9] In point of fact, today's Army enlisted ranks
are the only major arena in American society where black
educational levels surpass those of whites, and by quite
a significant margin!

Table 4. Percentage of high school graduates of army male enlistees
          by race (nonprior service)

Fiscal year	Black	White
1974	47.6	46.2
1975	59.4	46.9
1976*	63.6	47.1
1977	60.5	40.0

Source: U.S. Army Recruitment Command.

*Includes transition quarter July–September 1976.

What may be happening in the all-volunteer Army, I
suggest, is something like the following. Whereas the
black soldier is fairly representative of the black community in terms of education and social background, white
entrants of recent years are coming from the least-educa-
ted sectors of the white community. My stays with Army
line units also leave the distinct impression that many

[8]Information Please Almanac (New York: Golenpaul, 1976),
p. 739.
[9]The U.S. Army Recruiting Command obtains the distribution of high school graduates by race from a separate data
source; therefore these distributions may not exactly corres-
pond to other NPS male data.

of our young enlisted white soldiers are coming from non-
metropolitan areas. I am even more impressed by what I do
not often find in line units--urban and suburban white
soldiers of middle class origins. In other words, the
all-volunteer Army is attracting not only a disproportionate number of minorities, but also an unrepresentative
segment of white youth, who, if anything, are even more
uncharacteristic of the broader social mix than are our
minority soldiers. Though put far too crassly, there is
an insight in the assessment given me by a longtime German
employee of the U.S. Army in Europe: "In the volunteer
Army you are recruiting the best of the blacks and the
worst of the whites."

Mental Aptitude Levels

All recruits are classified into mental aptitude levels
according to their score on entrance tests, formerly
known as the Armed Forces Qualification Test (AFQT) and
more recently as the Armed Service Vocational Aptitude
Battery (ASVAB). The tested population is categorized into
percentile groups: I, 100-93; II, 92-65; IIIA, 65-50;
IIIB, 49-31; IV, 30-10; and V, 9-0. The Army in competition
with the other services seeks to recruit from the average-
and-above portions of the mental aptitude spectrum. (Category V individuals are not eligible to join the services.)
By and large, the Army has achieved its goals since the
end of the draft. Table 5 shows that close to nine in
ten NPS male entrants since FY 1975 have been in category
IIIB or above; and, excepting FY 1977, about half of the
entrants were in categories I through IIIA, which constitute the top 50 percentile. Supplementary data show,
moreover, that in comparison with the draft Army of the
pre-Vietnam period, there has been a decided shift toward
the middle mental levels in the all-volunteer Army. Category I made up about 8% of entrants in the early 1960s
compared to 2% in the late 1970s; over the same period,
category IV entrants decreased from about 17 to 10%.

    The usefulness of mental aptitude scores to evaluate
soldierly potential has been intertwined with the controversy over the inappropriate characteristization of racial
groups by their differential performance on intelligence
tests.[10] The replacement of the AFQT by the ASVAB was an
effort toward elimination of cultural bias in earlier tests.
As a result, "the observed effect was clearly substantial:
the nonblack Category I-III percentage hardly changed, but
the black Category I-III percentage increased by nearly 50

[10]See, for example, Allan Chase, The Legacy of Malthus
(New York: Knopf, 1977), pp. 432-47.

percent."[11] The appropriateness of using mental aptitude
scores to assess the all-volunteer Army presents other
difficulties as well. A sophisticated and comprehensive
study of racial differences in promotion progress found
that black enlisted men had slower promotion rates than
their white counterparts even when mental group level was
held constant.[12] Also, as will be discussed in detail
later, formal educational levels are a much more powerful
predictor on almost all measures of enlisted performance
than mental group level.

Table 5. Mental aptitude levels of army male enlistees (nonprior
          service)

Fiscal Year	I-IIIA	IIIB	IV
1974	47.3	33.2	19.5
1975	48.3	40.8	10.9
1976*	51.2	40.3	8.5
1977	40.4	49.6	10.0

Source: Department of Army statistics.

*Includes transition quarter July-Sept., 1976

Marital Status

Though usually uncommented upon by students of all-volunteer trends, a most dramatic change has been in the
marital composition of the Army. From 1965 to 1976,
the proportion of married enlisted men increased from
36.4% to 56.9%. Over the same period, the average number
of dependents per enlisted man increased from 1.02 to 2.47.
These significant changes have occurred only since the end
of the draft in 1973. The figures are all the more re-
markable in that they reflect almost entirely a change in
the marital composition of the junior enlisted ranks. In
1977, 43.7% of E-4s, the modal lower enlisted pay grade,
were married. Though comparable data by pay grade are
not available for the pre-Vietnam period, the number of
married junior EM was certainly a much smaller fraction
than current levels.

[11]Cooper, p. 213.
[12]John Sibley Butler, "Inequality in the Military,"
American Sociological Review, 41 (1976), 807-18.

The changes in the marital composition of the enlisted ranks runs directly counter of national trends.
Table 6 summarizes some of the relevant data. From 1960
to 1976, the median age of males at first marriage increased by one year, and the number of never married men
at age 22 rose from 51.6 to 61.1 percent. An anomaly
is evident, however. The number of never married men at
age 19--typical recruitment age--actually decreases
slightly in recent years.

Table 6. Marital status of American males

Year	Median age at first marriage	Percent never married, age 19	Percent never married, age 22
1960	22.8	87.1	51.6
1970	23.2	89.9	52.3
1976	23.8	87.9	61.6

Source: U.S. Bureau of the Census, Current Population Reports,
         P-20, No. 306, pp. 1-3.

     The anomaly revealed by the census data on marriage
rates--generally later marriages coexisting with an increase
in 19-year-old marriages--is striking because it parallels
the previously described educational data--generally
rising educational levels accompanied by an increase
in the high school dropout rate for 19-year-old white males.
These anomalies in the census data suggest, in effect,
that we now have two quite different youth groups within
the white population. One group, the numerical majority
with middle class origins or aspirations, is characterized
by increasing educational attainment and later marriage.
The other group, with declining educational levels and
propensity to enter young marriages, seems headed toward
a marginal position both in class and culture terms. It
is from this latter white group, along with racial minorities, that the all-volunteer Army has been overrecruiting.

Women

Perhaps no change in the makeup of the all-volunteer force
has received as much media attention as the growing numbers
and the role of women soldiers. A strong argument could be
made that it has been the sharp rise in the number of
female entrants, nearly all of whom possess high school
diplomas, which has been the margin of success in the all-

volunteer Army. As given in Table 7, the proportion of
women in the enlisted ranks has climbed from 0.9% in
1964 to 6.7% in 1977. The racial composition of enlisted
women--24.2% black in 1977--is equivalent with that of
enlisted men. Table 8 shows that females account for about
8% to 9% of all enlisted accessions in recent years.
This is slightly below the 10% female of its active
strength which the Army envisions in the next five years.
A Brookings Institution study, however, has estimated that
close to a quarter of all enlisted personnel could be
female without major changes in current assignment policies.[13]

Table 7. Female participation in the Army for selected years

Year	Percent female	
	Officers	Enlisted
1964	3.4	0.9
1973	3.7	2.4
1975	4.9	6.1
1977	5.7	6.7

Source: Department of Defense statistics.

Table 8. Female proportion of Army enlistees

Fiscal year	Percent female
1973	4.5
1974	7.7
1975	9.1
1976*	8.0
1977	8.2

Source: U.S. Army Recruitment Command
* Includes transition quarter July-Sept., 1976.

[13]Martin Binkin and Shirley J. Bach, Women and the
Military (Washington, D.C.: Brookings Institution, 1977),
p. 105.

The increasing utilization of women in the all-
volunteer Army is an indisputable fact. Starting in the
early 1970s virtually every occupational specialty has
been opened up to women except those in the combat arms.
There has also been an elimination of discriminatory prac-
tices: in 1971 the Army lifted its ban on the enlistment
of married women; in 1973 a Supreme Court decision required
that married women in the military get the same family
allowances that married men have long received; in 1975
the Army dropped its policy of discharging women soldiers
who became mothers; and in 1976 the minimum 18-year-old
enlistment age for women was lowered to 17--the same as
that for men.

The crux of the issue remains the prohibition of
women in the combat arms. Congressional statute presently
bans women from duty on combat aircraft and ships, a
principle which has been codified into Army regulations
pertaining to exclusion of females from the ground combat
arms. Leaving aside the considerable normative and organizational difficulties in the employment of women in the
combat arms, a removal of the ban cannot be viewed as a
solution to all-volunteer recruitment. There are already
indications that the available pool of highly qualified
women is being tapped close to its maximum. More important, it is highly unlikely, to say the least, that women
will show any greater eagerness than men to join the combat
arms.

Service Differences

The Army, of course, is not the only service competing
for qualified people in the all-volunteer era. It
suffers, moreover, by being identified as the least
attractive service by those high school males who are most
qualified for military service. Youth surveys consistently
show the most positive evaluations are given to the Air
Force, followed in order, by the Navy, Marine Corps, and
Army.[14] The Army, thus, starts out as the most handicapped
service in the recruitment effort. This state of affairs
is reflected in a comparison of the average proportion of
high school graduates among NPS male entrants since 1973:
about 90% for the Air Force, 75% for the Navy, 60% of
the Marines, and 55% for the Army.

All the services, with the partial exception of the
Air Force, have encountered recruitment difficulties since

[14]Market Facts, Youth Attitude Tracking Study (Chicago: Market Facts, 1977), p. 142.

the end of the draft. A 1977 market research study
concluded: "It is apparent that it is becoming increasingly more difficult to attract people to enlist in the
armed services."[15] More telling, each of the services had
been plagued by shockingly high attrition rates. Close
to 40% of servicemen, in each of the services, do not
complete their initial enlistments and, instead, are
discharged for disciplinary problems, personality dis-
orders, or job inaptitude. The majority of these losses
occur six months after service entry. In some ways it may
be the all-volunteer Navy which is confronting the most
severe problems. Recruiters publicly bemoan that many
high school graduates seeking to join the Navy simply
cannot read at acceptable levels.[16] Moreover, the Navy's
desertion rate in 1976 was higher than in any previous
time in its history, including the Vietnam War. Even the
well-situated Air Force saw its high school enlistment
rate drop to 80% in 1977, a post-Vietnam low.

Whatever the all-volunteer parallels between the Army
and the other services may be, it is the Army's social
composition which most contrasts with its pre-Vietnam
form. The lower ranks of the peacetime Army between the
wars in Korea and Vietnam were never a mirror image of
America's class system. It is undeniable, however, that
the all-volunteer Army is much less representative of the
American middle class than was the pre-Vietnam Army.
Whether or not this speaks to the success or failure
of the all-volunteer Army is a separate issue. But there
can be no question that since 1973 the Army has undergone
a metamorphosis in its enlisted membership. The real
question is how high-powered commissions and well-financed
studies come up with the opposite conclusion.[17]

The demographic transition of the Army is only part
of the story of the all-volunteer force. The Army and
the other armed services are also undergoing changes in
their public definition and institutional workings.
These organizational trends in the all-volunteer military
are the subject to which we now turn.

[15]Ibid., p. 12
[16]New York Times, Dec. 8, 1977, p. 18.
[17]Prominent examples of this myopia follow. "There
is no evidence to suggest that the armed forces are now
or are in danger of becoming a 'poor man's Army'" (Defense Manpower Commission, p. 167); "The evidence presented here thus shows that the American military has not
been nor is it becoming an army of the poor or the black"
(Cooper, p. 231).

The All-Volunteer Force: An Institution or an Occupation?

The military can be understood as an organization which
maintains levels of autonomy while refracting broader
societal trends. It is from this standpoint that two
models--institution versus occupation--will be presented
to describe alternative conceptions of the all-volunteer
force. These models are evaluated as to which best fits
current indicators. The basic hypothesis is that the
American military is moving from an institutional format
to one more and more resembling that of an occupation.
This tendency pervades all grades but is most apparent
in the enlisted ranks of the all-volunteer force. This
is not to hold that such a trend is either desirable or
inevitable. But only recognition of the trend can focus
attention on measures which can reverse it.

The contrast between institution and occupation can,
of course, be overdrawn. For reality is complicated in
that the armed forces have had and will continue to have
elements of both the institutional and occupational
types. The typology, nevertheless, is deemed a valid way
of understanding the emergent structure of the all-volunteer force. It allows for a conceptual grasp of the basic
hypothesis that the overarching trend is the erosion of the
institutional format and the ascendancy of the occupational
model. Even though terms like <u>institution</u> or <u>occupation</u>
have descriptive limitations, they do contain core conno-
tations which serve to distinguish each from the other.
For present purposes these distinctions can be set forth
as follows.

An <u>institution</u> is legitimated in terms of values
and norms, i.e., a purpose transcending individual self-
interest in favor of a presumed higher good. Members of an
institution are often seen as following a calling. They
are commonly viewed and regard themselves as being different or apart from the broader society. To the degree
one's institutional membership is congruent with notions
of self-sacrifice and primary identification with one's
role, it will usually enjoy esteem from the larger community. Although remuneration may not be comparable to
what one might expect in the economy of the marketplace,
this is often compensated for by an array of social
benefits associated with an institutional format as well
as psychic income. When grievances are felt, members of
an institution do not organize themselves into interest
groups. Rather, if redress is sought, it takes the form
of "one-on-one" recourse to superiors, with its implications of trust in the paternalism of the institution to
take care of its own.

Military service has traditionally had many institutional features. One thinks of the extended tours abroad,
the fixed terms of enlistment, liability for 24-hour
service availability, frequent movements of self and
family, subjection to military discipline and law, and
inability to resign, strike, or negotiate working conditions. All this is above and beyond the dangers inherent
in military maneuvers and actual combat operations. It
is also significant that a paternalistic remuneration
system has evolved in the military corresponding to the
institutional model: compensation received in noncash
form (e.g., food, housing, uniforms), subsidized consumer
facilities on the base, payments to service members partly
determined by family status, and a large proportion of
compensation received as deferred pay in the form of
retirement benefits. Moreover, unlike most civilians
for whom compensation is heavily determined by individual
expertise, the compensation received by military members
is a function of rank, seniority, and need.

An occupation is legitimated in terms of the marketplace, i.e., prevailing monetary rewards for equivalent
competencies. Supply and demand rather than normative
considerations are paramount. In a modern industrial
society employees usually enjoy some voice in the determination of appropriate salary and work conditions. Such
rights are counterbalanced by responsibilities to meet
contractual obligations. The cash-work nexus emphasizes
a negotiation between individual and organizational needs.
The occupational model implies priority of self-interest
rather than that of the employing organization. A common
form of interest articulation in industrial--and increasingly public employee--occupations is the trade union.

Traditionally, the military has sought to avoid the
organization outcomes of the occupational model. This
in the face of repeated recommendations of governmental
commissions that the armed services adopt a salary system
which would incorporate all basic pay, allowances, and tax
benefits into one cash payment and which would eliminate
compensation differences between married and single personnel, thus conforming to the equal-pay-for-equal-work principle of civilian occupations. Such a salary system would
set up an employer-employee relationship quite at variance
with military norms. Nevertheless, even in the conventional military system there has been some accommodation to
occupational imperatives. Special supplements and proficiency pay have long been found necessary to recruit
and retain highly skilled enlisted personnel.

For the single-term draftee before Vietnam, the Army
was also very much an institution. The selective service
system was premised on the notion of citizen obligation--a

"calling" in the almost literal sense of being summoned
by a local draft board--with concomitant low salaries for
junior enlisted men. It is worth remembering that from
1952 to 1964 military pay for the first two years of
service--the term of a drafted soldier--did not rise at
all! Selective service was also defended on the desira-
bility of a broadly representative enlisted force (though
this ideal was not always realized in practice). To be
sure draftees by definition were serving under a form of
compulsion. Yet the peacetime draftee--underpaid, acquiring no civilian skills, not even eligible for the GI
Bill--was by all accounts the equal if not superior of
his volunteer counterpart.

    Although antecedents predate the appearance of the
all-volunteer force, the end of the draft served as a
major thrust to move the military toward the occupational
model. This philosophy of military service clearly
underpinned the rationale of the 1970 report of the President's Commission on an All-Volunteer Force ("Gates
Commission Report").[18] Instead of a military system
achored in the normative values of an institution, captured
in words like "duty," "honor," "country," the Gates
Commission explicitly argued that primary reliance in
recruiting an armed force should be on monetary inducements guided by marketplace standards. Subsequent reports
have seconded this tendency. The turn away from a socially
representative enlisted force was implicitly endorsed by
the 1976 report of the Defense Manpower Commission.[19]
Perhaps the best example of viewing the all-volunteer
force as an occupation is to be found in the 1977 Rand
Corporation volume on manpower in the all-volunteer force.[20]
The Rand study advocates recruitment and retention policies
by which military compensation is calibrated to supply and
demand conditions in the civilian economy. Yet it is
questionable to the extreme whether the market system is
the way to motivate an Army or cost-benefit analyses the
way to strengthen a service institution.

    The system of military compensation reflects not
only the so-called X factor--the unusual demands of service
life--but the corporate whole of military life. The
military institution is organized "vertically," whereas an
occupation is organized "horizontally." To put it in as
unpretentious manner as possible, people in an occupation
tend to feel a sense of identity with others who do the
same sort of work, and who get about the same pay. In an inst-
tution, on the other hand, it is the organization where

[18]The Report of the President's Commission on an All-
Volunteer Force (Washington, D.C.: Government Printing Office, 1970).
    [19]Defense Manpower Commission, pp. 167-72.
    [20]Cooper, pp. 356-80.

people live and work which create the sense of identity
that binds them together. In the armed forces, the very
fact of being part of the services has traditionally
been more important than the fact that military members
do different jobs. The organization one belongs to
creates the feeling of shared interest, not the other way
around. From this perspective, the sense of community
in the military thus runs up and down, not sideways across
--religiously, racially, as well as occupationally--as in
civilian society.

Actually, the move toward making military remuneration comparable with the civilian sector preceded the
advent of the all-volunteer force. Since 1967 military
pay has been formally linked to the civil service and
thus, indirectly, to the civilian labor market. From
1964 to 1974, average earnings in the private economy
rose 52% while regular military compensation--basic pay,
allowance, tax advantages--rose 76% for representative
grade levels, such as lieutenant colonels and master
sergeants.[21] Even more dramatic, recruit pay from 1964
to 1976 increased 193% in constant dollars compared to
10% for the average unskilled laborer.[22] Indeed, the
Rand report mentioned above concludes that career military
personnel are now better paid than their civilian
counterparts.[23]

Termination of the draft and the rise in military pay
have been two of the most visible changes in the contemporary military system, but other indicators of the trend
toward the occupational model can also be noted.

Service Entitlements

Nothing has caused more alarm within the military community than actions and proposals to eliminate a host of
military benefits, such as subsidies for commissaries,
health care for dependents, government quarters for
families, and major restructuring of the retirement system.
The concern with "erosion of benefits" is understandable
because nonpay elements make up about half of all career
military compensation compared to less than a quarter in

[21]Steven L. Canby and Robert A. Butler, "The Military
Manpower Question," in William Schneider, Jr., and Francis
P. Hoeber, eds., Arms, Men, and Military Budgets (New York:
Crane, Russak, 1976), pp. 186-87.
[22]Tulay Demirles, "Adjusted Consumer Price Index for
Military Personnel and a Comparison of Real Civilian and Mi-
litary Earnings, 1964-1973," Technical Memorandum, TM-1200
(Washington, D.C.: George Washington University, 1974), p. 9.
[23]Cooper, pp. 376-80.

most civilian compensation packages.[24] Not so well
understood is that the institutional features of the
military system may have been unwittingly traded off for
the relatively good salaries enjoyed by military personnel
in the all-volunteer force. Current dissatisfaction is
great precisely because, while the military organization
has moved in the direction of the occupational model, much
of its membership harkens to the social supports of the
older institutional format. A kind of "devil's bargain"
may have been struck when military pay was geared to
comparable civilian levels. There is no way that service
entitlements can be maintained at past levels if military
salaries are to be competitive with civilian scales.

Military Unions

The possibility that trade unionism might appear within the
armed forces of the United States was barely more than a
remote thought just a few years ago. Today, there are
signs that such an eventuality could come to pass.[25]
Reliance on supply-and-demand econometric analyses and
monetary incentives to recruit and retain military members
is quite consistent with the notion of trade unionism.
Several unions, notably the American Federation of
Government Employees (AFGE) affiliated with the AFL-CIO,
have indicated an interest in organizing the military.
In the fall of 1977, however, the AFGE decided, at least
for the time being, not to organize the military. Also
in 1977 the Department of Defense issued a new directive
which, while not banning unions outright, forbade any
union from engaging in collective bargaining or job actions
on a military installation. Additionally, bills have been
introduced in congressional sessions to prohibit any
organizing activities whatsoever of the armed forces.
To make military unions illegal, however, may inadvertently
push organizing activities away from mainstream unions
toward more politicized groups which see themselves as
a continuation of the radical troop dissent movement of the
Vietnam War years. In any event, whatever the legal restrictions placed on organizing the armed forces, the
underlying dynamics of the occupational ascendancy are still

[24]Ibid., p. 379.
[25]The literature on military unions, nonexistent a few
years ago, is rapidly growing. See, for example, Ezra S.
Krendel and Bernard L. Samoff, eds., Unionizing the Armed
Forces (Philadelphia: University of Pennsylvania Press,
1977); Alan Ned Sabrosky, ed., Blue-Collar Soldiers (Philadelphia: Foreign Policy Research Institute, 1977); William
J. Taylor, Jr., Roger J. Arango, and Robert S. Lockwood,
eds., Military Unions (Beverly Hills: Sage, 1977).

operative. It would seem a fair judgment to hold that
developments of 1977 have only temporarily capped
rather than undercut the trend toward military unioniza-
tion.

Enlisted Attrition

In the pre-Vietnam Army it was considered aberrant for an
enlisted man not to complete his assigned tour. During
the late 1970s, however, four in ten soldiers were failing
to finish their initial enlistments. The attrition
phenomenon is probably as much an outcome of changing
policies and procedures of military separation as it is
a reflection of objective changes in the quality of the
entering enlisted force. Put in another way, the all-
volunteer military, like the industrial organizations, is
witnessing the common occurrence of its members "quitting"
or being "fired." In time, it is possible that a general
certificate of separation will replace the present discharge classification system. Unlike an older era, there
would no longer be a stigma for unsuccessful service.
Such a development would make the Army that much more consistent with the civilian work model. In all but name,
the all-volunteer force has already gone a long way down
the road toward indeterminate enlistments.

Work and Residence Separation

A hallmark of the conventional garrison Army has been the
adjacency of work place and living quarters. As late as
the mid-1960s, it was practically unheard of for a
bachelor enlisted man to live off-post. Not only was it
against regulations, but no one could afford a private
rental on a draftee's pay. Today, although precise data
are not available, a reasonable estimate would be that
as many as 30% of single enlisted people in stateside
posts have apartments away from the military installation.
To the increasing proportion of single EM living off-post,
one must add the growing number of married junior enlisted
people, all of whom also live on the civilian economy.
Like civilian employees, many junior enlisted personnel
are now part of the early morning and late afternoon exodus
to and from work. One of the outcomes of the salary
raises needed for an all-volunteer Army has been the ebbing
of barracks life.

The Law and the Military

From the 1950s through the 1960s, the Court of Military Appeals and the Supreme Court brought into military law almost

all of the procedural safeguards available to a civilian
defendant while narrowing the purview of military jurisdiction.[26] The highwater point in this trend was
O'Callahan vs. Parker (1969), in which the Supreme Court
struck down court-martial jurisdiction for non-service-
connected offenses. The significance of O'Callahan
was that the off-duty or off-post soldier was to be regarded like any other citizen. Since the early 1970s, however,
the Supreme Court and lower courts have emphasized the
uniqueness of the armed forces and the appropriateness
of its special system of courts-martial. The trend
toward an occupational model, nevertheless, has continued
under a different framework. In U.S. vs. Russo (1975)
and U.S. vs. Larionoff (1977), the Supreme Court applied
basic contract law to the legal status of enlistments.
This dovetails with the rising tendency of active-duty
personnel to bring enlistment grievances into litigation.
The net effect of recent court decisions is to move toward
a legal redefinition of the military from one based on
traditional status toward one consistent with generally
accepted contract principles.

Military Wives

In a manner of speaking, the role of institutional membership in the military community extended to the wife of the
service husband. (It was only in 1960 that court-martial
jurisdiction over civilian dependents of servicemen was
completely ended.) Wives of career personnel were expected
to initiate and take part in a panoply of social functions,
such as formal visits, receptions, luncheons, teas, cock-
tail gatherings, and dinner parties. Military wives clubs
contributed funds and time to such activities as support
of orphanages, hospitals, area welfare work, youth
activities, and other volunteer projects. In recent years,
however, there has been a perceptible heightening in the
reluctance of wives at both junior officer and noncom levels to participate in such customary functions. With the
rising proportion of service wives working outside the
home, moreover, there are bound to be less women who have
either the time or inclination to engage in the volunteer
work which has structured much of the social life of military installations. It is not so much that female libera-
tion has arrived among Army wives, though this is not absent,
as it is the growing tendency for wives to define their

[26]This capsule summary of the law and the military is
taken from James B. Jacobs, "The Impact of Legal Change on
the United States Armed Forces since World War II," paper
presented at the meetings of the Inter-University Seminar
on Armed Forces and Society, Chicago, Illinois, Oct. 20-22,
1977.

roles as distinct from the military community.

Contract Civilians

One manifestation of recent organizational change departs
entirely from formal military organization. This is the
use of civilians, especially those hired on contract,
to perform jobs previously in the domain of active-duty
servicemen. These tasks range from routine housekeeping
and kitchen duties to quasi-combat jobs such as "tech
repś" aboard warships, manning missile warning systems in
Greenland, and ordnance repair and assembly in war zones
as occurred in Vietnam. From 1964 to 1978, contract-
hire civilians rose from 5.4% to 14.5% as a proportion
of total defense manpower.[27] Almost all of this large
increase corresponded to a proportionate decline in enlisted strength from 57.3% to 48.0% over the same period.
Presumably considerations of task efficiencies and costs
bear upon decisions to substitute contract civilians for
uniformed personnel.[28] Nevertheless, the increasing reliance on civilian employees, whose institutional affilia-
tion with the military is attenuated, is yet another indication of the direction of organizational change in the
defense establishment.

     The sum of the above and related developments is to
confirm the ascendancy of the occupational model in the
all-volunteer military. This approach can be faulted for
presenting too monolithic a picture of trends. There are,
of course, always countervailing forces in effect. But
our concern is to grasp the whole, to place the salient
fact. Was it more than happenstance that the recruiting
slogan used in the first years of the all-volunteer force
was "Today's Army Wants to Join You'."? This carried the
impression of a military organization seeking to conform
to individual needs rather than the institutional ethic
where individuals conform to organizational imperatives.
This is not to argue that all such trends are unwelcome.
It is to say that a major transformation is occurring
within the all-volunteer Army--in terms of social organization as well as social composition--which has not generally been appreciated by policymakers or the citizenry
at large.

[27]Cooper, p. 11.
[28]A comprehensive discussion of the expansion of the
civilian component in the defense system is Martin Binkin
with Herschel Kanter and Rolf Clark, Shaping the Defense
Civilian Work Force. Study prepared for the Committee on
Armed Services, U.S. Senate, 95th Cong., 1st sess. (Washington, D.C.: Government Printing Office, 1977.)

The Enlisted Culture

To generalize about the enlisted culture of the Army may
seem to be an act of sinning bravely. It goes without
saying that the Army encompasses a wide range of locales
and people. Even within like units, soldiers may find
themselves in companies ranging from "route-step" outfits
(a term which has generalized from noncadence marching to
describing anything slipshod or sloppy), to units--"strak"
seems to be the new term--where the organizational climate
is conducive to both mission effectiveness and high morale.
This account is a reflection of having spent most of my
professional life studying soldiers, a group of men--and
lately women as well--whose company I have always treasured.
Ever since my own enlisted days twenty years ago, I have
lived with soldiers on more occasions and in more places
than I can remember. The reaction soldiers have accorded
a sometimes too persistent guest has nearly always been
one of openness, and, most often, good fellowship as well.

     In the summer of 1977, I was again privileged to have
an extended visit with American soldiers, this time in
Germany with the U.S. Army in Europe (USAREUR). Besides
talking to literally hundreds of soldiers throughout Germany, I conducted an attitudinal survey of junior enlisted
men in three line battalions. More important, I was able
to lead the life of a soldier--as much as any middle-aged
outsider could--and to interact informally with the men
on many levels: in the barracks, in the field, in their
work capacities, and off duty. What follows is a sociological interpretation of enlisted life in line units of the
all-volunteer Army. Nearly all appraisals of the all-
volunteer Army have failed to deal with the social context
of the ordinary soldier who serves in it. This account
is an attempt to correct that imbalance.

     One overriding impression of Army life in 1977 is the
decided change for the better since 1973. The recovery of
USAREUR especially over that period is an achievement of no
small measure. But it would be misguided to use--as is the
custom of most observers--the years just before and after
the end of the war in Vietnam as the sole reference point.
If the more appropriate peacetime period of the early 1960s
is used as a benchmark, comparisons of soldierly behavior
and performance are less favorable.

     On the job, most importantly in the field, things get
done. The impact of the newly instituted Skill Qualification Test (SQT), which combines hands-on and written examinations, has had a positive impact on training and promotion procedures. There is, however, a growing feeling--and
only some of it can be put down to normal grousing--that
too much is being asked for (and still being given) in too

little time. It is not so much that "shamming" (today's
GI term for avoiding work) is hard to carry off as it may
be that the all-volunteer Army is causing an excessive
workload in cutting back its administrative and support
services. For conscientious soldiers at all ranks,
hours are appallingly long.

In the barracks, the edge of violence which characterized many line units in the early 1970s has largely reced-
ed. Barracks crime is a problem, however, though some of
this is because there is more to steal from today's better-
paid soldier than there was from the peacetime draftee.
A level of raucousness, if not rowdiness, does exist
which exceeds the decibel count and temper of the pre-
Vietnam Army. Not that the drafted peacetime Army was a
sanctuary of decorum, but the tone of barracks life is
no longer modulated by conventional middle class standards
as it was a decade or so ago. The youth with a stable
job in his future or bound for college is much less likely
to be found in today's enlisted force than in times past.
In particular, the college-educated enlisted man, often
from leading universities, has all but vanished from the
ranks. The days when many enlisted men might be better
educated than their sergeants has gone, to the dismay,
surprisingly, of many senior sergeants. A visitor is
struck by the fond reminiscences the older sergeants have
for the university graduates who worked under them.

One source of discontent which exists in the all-
volunteer Army has no real parallel in the peacetime draft
Army. This is the postentry disillusionment resulting
from expectations as to what the military would offer.
The peacetime draftee never held high expectations as to
what he would encounter and therefore was not unpleasantly
surprised; indeed, he might often--at least in hindsight--
find the Army favorable on its own terms. In all-volunteer
recruitment, however, a consistent theme has been the stress
--out of necessity, to be sure--on the instrumental aspects
of military service, that is, what can the Army do for
the recruit in the way of skill-training transferable to
civilian jobs. Because the new volunteer often sees the
military as a last alternative to limited chances in
civilian life, he is understandably irate when his expectations are not met. The visitor is bombarded by
stories--surely with a strong dose of selective memory--
of recruitment promises not kept.

Postentry disillusionment in the all-volunteer Army
underlies many morale and disciplinary problems; it
speaks directly to the excessive attrition rate. For
once a soldier has decided he wants out, he will not be
particular as to the kind of discharge that will accomplish
the purpose (though he will regret this once again on the

outside). Almost every Army unit at any time will have
an individual or two loitering around waiting to be
processed for premature separation. The effect of this on
borderline soldiers is incalculable, but it most certainly
pushes some across the line toward an early out. Although
the all-volunteer concept shies away from it, the irrecon-
cilable dilemma is that many Army assignments--mostly, but
not exclusively in the combat arms--do not and cannot have
transferability to civilian jobs.

   Postentry disillusionment in German assignments is
often aggravated. Many soldiers, rightly or wrongly,
believe they were misled as to the length of their USAREUR
tour. A three- or four-year volunteer will typically
serve 30 to 36 months in Germany when assigned to USAREUR.
My own observations as well as survey data collected by
the Army Research Field Unit in USAREUR show convincingly
that there is a severe decline in soldier morale around
the end of the second year in Germany. It should be
remembered that the somewhat idealized draftee, recollected
by USAREUR senior sergeants, served only 18 months in
Germany. Also, it is hard to deny that the new volunteer
soldier is less likely to take advantage of travel opportunities in Europe than his drafted counterpart. Where a
quasi-touristic ambience characterized the draftee peer
culture, the all-volunteer soldier is more likely
to berate the "rads" (Germans) and harken to teenage life
back in the United States. As a kind of loose measure of
the growing isolation of soldiers in Germany, I have
noticed over the years a decreasing amount of German
phrases in everyday GI language.

   The soldier's reluctance to get out of the Kaserne
is often laid to the fact that, unlike the draftee of an
earlier period, today's volunteer soldier is no longer relatively affluent compared to German civilians. In the past
few years, especially, the declining value of the dollar
relative to the mark has made German duty even more costly.
Yet, when all is said and done, the actual buying power of
today's GI in Germany (in light of pay raises since 1968)
is comparable to that of the draftee of a decade or two ago.
Directly to the point, even the excellent and inexpensive
"Rec Center" tours are often canceled because of undersub-
scription. The typical soldier will save money, not to
travel in Europe but to buy an inordinately expensive stereo
system--the big souvenir he will take back to America--and
fly commercially to the United States to take his 30-day
leave back home.

   Soldiers' complaints about Army haircut regulations are
endemic. Few soldiers, however, argue for complete removal
of haircut restrictions. The consensus is that haircuts
ought to conform to moderate civilian styles, that is, down

to the collar and over the ears. Some of the haircut
griping is pro forma, but there is also the reality that
present Army haircuts can put the GI at a disadvantage in
meeting women. Also, as one soldier put it, "If we are
supposed to be representatives of our country, why can't
our hair look like our Congressmen's?" (Even though
my own pate has been likened to that of Telly Savalas,
I have no satisfactory answer to that question.)

        Like civilian youth, marijuana (hashish in Germany)
usage is widespread among young enlisted men. Accurate
figures are difficult to come up with, but when queried
as to how many of their fellow enlisted men regularly
smoked marijuana (defined as at least once a week), the
estimates ranged between 50% and 80%. Even if one discounts
these figures somewhat, marijuana use is much less covert
than it used to be. Men would smoke it (off duty) in
my presence even after I declined to join them. Though
unit policies vary greatly, the unofficial trend is for
senior sergeants and company grade officers to be officially concerned with marijuana only when it interferes
with duty performance or is the cause of barracks troubles.
This may in fact be the most pragmatic way to deal with
what is almost a cultural trait among young people. Marijuana stories of both a humorous and empathetic nature are
becoming part of service lore, much like that already
found in the retelling of alcoholic incidents. (One example of latrine graffiti bears repeating: "Getting promoted in the Army is like sucking a joint . . . the
harder you suck, the higher you get!"

        The situation regarding hard drugs is quite different.
One can still sadly read, several times a month it seems,
the brief reports in the Stars and Stripes of a private or
corporal found dead in his bunk, the reading between the
lines being that of an overdose fatality. Yet, almost
surely, heroin usage has declined markedly over the past
few years, although it still presents a problem in certain
units. (Personal contacts in the ranks claim the less
addictive cocaine is on the rise, however.) Significantly,
in a group of surveyed soldiers, over 90% favored the legal-
ization of marijuana while only a very few wanted to
legalize heroin. The social acceptance of amphetamines
and barbituates is less clearcut, though they appear to
fall somewhere between heroin and marijuana.

        Although the military, as in civilian society, will
continue to confront an illegal drug problem into the foreseeable future, excessive alcohol use is of greater command concern, and properly so. One does have the strong
impression that the consumption of alcoholic beverages is
higher than in years past, no mean statement; and that one
runs across more twenty-year-old reformed alcoholics than

there used to be. The USAREUR response to alcohol and
drug abuse has been particularly well conceived in its
Community Drug and Alcohol Assistance programs, the new
Alcohol Treatment Center set up in 1977, and the broadly
gauged moral reinvigoration activities of the Community
Life Program. Just to name such programs is to indicate
some of the features--not entirely attributable to the
all-volunteer force, of course--in enlisted life and command
concerns in today's Army.

A welcome improvement in the Army since the Vietnam
era is the noticeable reduction--though by no means
absence--of interracial tension among the troops. Informal groupings by race are still the rule off duty, but not
nearly as rigid as several years ago. One good unobtru-
sive measure of the relaxation in race relations is the
much greater frequency of mixed groups to eat together in
dining facilities than before. Although far from perfect,
the armed forces have gone further in attacking racism
than any other institution in American society. These
endeavors must be pursued with the fullest vigor and there
must be a continuing monitor of all sources of institutional
racism such as bias in promotions, assignment, and punish-
ment. Equal Opportunity and Race Relations instruction
is to be commended for both its practical and symbolic
importance. (Though one unexpected consequence of such
instruction may be to heighten the soldier's sense of
inequity in other areas, for example, female soldier per-
ogatives, Navy facial hair regulations, officer and
sergeant perquisites, civilian amenities.)

My conversations, however, quickly revealed that
many black soldiers still perceive certain "racist"
features in military life, and many white soldiers perceive "reverse prejudice" in the military. Occupying
somewhat of a midposition are Hispanic soldiers who see
themselves as the most dutiful and least complaining, and
thereby most likely to be selected for menial details.
Thought we should be alert to these sentiments, they should
be placed in the context that an overwhelming majority of
surveyed soldiers--six of seven blacks, and three of our
whites and Hispanics--favor serving in racially integrated
units.

The recent improvement in the racial climate of the
Army, however, must be qualified by a potentially calamitous
omen. I detected a degree of latent klanism among some
white enlisted men. A few would show me klan cards in
their wallets (in USAREUR acquired from Americans in German
railroad stations, in the United States from klansmen at
bus terminals). It would be erroneous to view latent klanism as a form of white backlash. The potential emergence

of klan activity in the Army--it has already come into the
open in the Marine Corps--would derive more from social
composition than reactions to equal opportunity policies
within the military. We remember from the earlier presentation of demographic data that all-volunteer recruitment--
in addition to a large number of blacks--was drawing disproportionately from white high school dropouts. Could
it be that the all-volunteer Army is attracting a segment
of white youth more than normally susceptible to klan-
like appeals? (On the same score, what is to be made
of the small number of white satanic cultists one comes
across in some Army units?)

   To fill its ranks, the all-volunteer Army has recruited an increasing number of young men who have wives or
will marry soon after joining. Under long-standing policies, the military does not pay transportation for wives
of most men under the rank of sergeant, nor does it
provide them with low-cost housing on military bases.
All service dependents are eligible for post privileges,
however. Just about every Army post in the United States
today is ringed by trailer camps or shoddy apartment com-
plexes where most of the young marrieds live an existence
close to the poverty line. In USAREUR, problems are
compounded when young marrieds live on the Germany economy
where they face cultural isolation as well as financial
distress. It is a sign of the times that in 1976 alone
the Deutsche Bundespost reported that American soldiers
living on the economy with their families left behind
$11,000,000 in telephone debts![29] The convenience and
abuse of direct dialing to the United States by lonesome
spouses undoubtedly explain these gigantic arrears.

   It is somewhat beside the point whether or not many
of these young soldiers should have ever been married in
the first place. It is to the point, however, that the
Army is going to encounter more and more young marrieds
whose considerable marital problems affect soldierly performance. Proposals to authorize command sponsorship for
lower-ranking enlisted families must be well thought out
lest they be counterproductive. A recurrent topic among
single soldiers, only half in jest, is to get married in
order to move out of the barracks. The paradox is that
while young married soldiers confront special problems
precisely because they are married, single soldiers often
see marriage as a way of avoiding night details, being less
liable for personal inspections, and a way of obtaining
more privacy. Improvement of the situation of young marrieds deserves utmost attention, but in the long run it
would be best to consider ways to reduce the proportion of
married soldiers in the lower enlisted ranks.

[29] International Herald Tribune, Aug. 3, 1977, p. 3.

Relations among Enlisted Men, Sergeants, and Officers

It is a truism that the link between the individual soldier
and the Army system is the noncommissioned officer.
Enlisted/sergeant relations, however, have undergone important shifts in modern Army history. During World War
II, the overriding organizational cleavage was that
between enlisted men (including sergeants) and officers.
This has been attested to by sources as varied as James
Jones's brilliant novel From Here to Eternity, the war
cartoons of Bill Mauldin, the monumental surveys reported
in the volumes of The American Soldier, as well as the
personal experiences of countless soldiers.

     During the peacetime years between Korea and Vietnam
another cleavage appeared, this one within the lower
enlisted ranks. The "US" versus "RA" distinction arose;
US was the prefix of the service number of the drafted
soldier while RA signified a regular Army volunteer.
The US versus RA distinction also overlay differences
between higher educated draftees and lower educated
volunteers. The term RA was used by draftees as a negative adjective to describe compliance with Army rituals
or to denigrate those seen as not being able to get a
decent job in civilian life.

     During the Vietnam War, the sergeant became the prime
object of enlisted animus. In the Vietnam era, moreover,
EM/sergeant strain could typically override that between
enlisted men and officers. Whereas the pejorative term
in World War II was "the brass" connotating an officer,
the equivalent expression in the Vietnam period was "lifer,"
almost always a senior sergeant. Another organizational
difference between World War II and the war in Vietnam
was that in the earlier conflict men served for duration
regardless of how they entered the service; thus sergeants
were often draftees themselves. In the more recent war,
on the other hand, virtually all sergeants were reenlistees.

     In the all-volunteer Army, yet another pattern has
emerged. There has been a reinvigoration of the sergeant
role. Much of this change can be attributed to the payoff
of Army policies, which have explicitly sought to emphasize
the responsibilities, recognition, and professionalization
of the noncommissioned officer. The prevailing antagonism
of lower ranking soldiers toward NCOs, moreover, is noticeably lower than five or ten years ago. At the same time,
EM/officer friction has become more pronounced with occa-
sional insolence toward company grade officers. This is in
the context that the educational gap between officers and
enlisted men is at its widest in modern times.

Sergeants also have some general complaints in the
all-volunteer Army: a sense that the Army is too hyper
and seeking to operate in an error-free environment, a
belief that there is too much diversion from regular
training to civilian education and personnel problems, a
feeling that there is overdirection by officers in the
work setting and not enough in the barracks, a view that
the military justice system can work to the disadvantage
of the enforcer of discipline rather than of the offender,
and a concern that the quality of clerks is deteriorating
(with resultant snafus in the processing of promotion
lists, notifications of transfers, school assignments, and
equipment requisitions).   Most important, there is the
real concern with erosion of service entitlements.   Discussion of military unions with career sergeants reveals
a curious ambivalence.   When thinking of the military
mission and the chain of command, the NCO finds the notion
of unions abhorrent.   But when looking at diminishing entitlements and a perceived lack of societal appreciation,
trade unionism becomes a more congenial option.   The public
definition of the military is one which will have profound
consequences on the career soldier's self-definition.

Women Soldiers

While standing at a USAREUR bus stop by the Heidelberg
PX, I struck up a conversation with a woman Specialist
Four.   She remarks, in passing, that she is proud, unlike
many of the men in her company, when the Star-Spangled
Banner is played at USAREUR movie theaters.   Obviously
bright, she has just been given an early promotion and
is thinking to make the Army a career.   A young soldier
in the company of his wife and preschool daughter also
arrive to wait for the bus.   The little girl eyes the
woman soldier and says to her parents that she wants to
join the Army when she grows up.   The father retorts in
earshot of all, "Only funny women join the Army."   My
acquaintance is furious but pretends not to hear.   Such a
vignette captures some of the perplexities of the role
of women in the all-volunteer Army.

The increasing participation of women, despite some
resistance, has been one of the most important developments
in the all-volunteer force.   Had it not been for the low
quality of many male volunteers, however, it is unlikely
that the acceptance of women would have gone as far as it
has.   Women get the same pay for the same rank.   They are
trained just as rigorously as the men are.   They are, however, excluded from the Army's purpose for being: combat.
This means they cannot advance to the highest ranks and
that they are sparsely represented even at comparatively

low levels of command, in most of the decision-making
processes. Nevertheless, for enlisted women, as for
enlisted men, failure to enter command positions is not
a salient issue. Still the clear trend is toward opening
up more and more positions for women soldiers. In December
1977, yet another barrier fell when women were allowed
into combat brigade headquarters and firing jobs in air
defense units.[30] It is tacitly acknowledged, moreover,
that in the event "the balloon goes up" in Western Europe,
women soldiers are already in positions where they would
definitely suffer casualties.

Three reasons are usually given to explain why women
are barred from combat units. The first is that our
cultural norms will not accept women dying in battle.
Leaving aside whether or not a dead body retains any gen-
der significance, the fact is that we have already crossed
that line in our present deployment of women soldiers.
Second, it is argued that women do not possess the physical strength required for the heavy labor of ground combat. Yet women have performed gruelling labor on many
occasions; and have even taken part in ground combat in
other times and places, albeit not as a common occurrence.
That many soldiers feel women skirt their full responsibilities and that the men end up with added labor, more doub-
ling of their workloads, and late night shifts may speak
more to policy and desire than to innate capabilities.
Third, there is the issue of eroticism in having mixed
sexes living together in close circumstances. That, in
view of the integration that has taken place elsewhere in
the Army, should not be an insurmountable problem. We
also have evidence that women receive good marks in field
maneuvers.[31] (There are, however, the underground rumors
of rapes and special guard details for women in the field.)

The real reason why women are excluded from the mainstream of the Army is simply there is little pressure to
let them into it from either men or women. Certainly
enlisted women are not clamoring for a major expansion of
their numbers into the combat arms. "They also serve,"
seems to be their motto. It is likely, moreover, that the
recruiting successes in attracting high-quality women
into the all-volunteer Army would be reversed if combat
assignments were given females.

[30]Army Times, Jan. 2, 1978, p. 1.
[31]Ibid., Jan. 16, 1978, p. 4.

Is a Representative Enlisted Force Desirable?

It is no longer a question that the enlisted ranks of
the all-volunteer Army are much less representative of
middle class youth than the peacetime draft Army. It
is, however, another kind of question whether this is
good, bad, or irrelevant.

The clearest and strongest evidence bearing upon the
effects of social background on soldierly performance deals
with enlisted attrition.[32] One of the main presumptions of
the all-volunteer force was that, with longer-term enlistments and professionally committed soldiers, there would be
less personnel turnover than in a military system which was
heavily dependent upon on draftees and draft-motivated volunteers. This has turned out not to be the case. Personnel turnover has increased at such a pace that the all-volunteer force is becoming something of a revolving door for
many of its entrants. Five years after the end of conscription, the Army, along with the other armed services,
is confronting an unacceptable high rate of enlistees--four
out of ten--who do not complete their first term of service.

The data given in Table 9 present attrition rates by
educational and mental aptitude levels. The striking
finding is that high school graduates are almost twice as
likely than high school dropouts to complete their enlistments. Most revealing, this finding is virtually
unchanged when mental aptitude is held constant. High
school graduates from the lower aptitude levels are actually much more likely to finish their tours than high school
dropouts in the higher aptitude levels. Supplementary data
from 1972-74 which make black-white breakdowns indicate
that overall attrition rates between the races are comparable, with the exception that blacks in the lower aptitude
levels do better than their white counterparts.[33]

Other measures of soldierly performance, such as enlisted productivity and low disciplinary actions, show precisely the same correlates as found for attrition rates.[34]
High school graduates significantly outperform high school
dropouts, higher mental levels do better than lower mental

[32]An overview of the attrition phenomenon is found in
H. Wallace Sinaiko, ed., First Term Enlisted Attrition, Pro-
ceedings of a Conference held at Leesburg, Virginia, April
4-7, 1977.
[33]A. J. Martin, "Trends in DOD First-Term Attrition,"
in Sinaiko, ed., pp. 20-21.
[34]On the correlates of formal educational and mental
aptitude levels on enlisted productivity and disciplinary
actions, see Cooper, p. 131.

levels, but education is a much more powerful predictor
than mental aptitude. Possession of a high school diploma,
it seems, reflects the acquisition of social traits (work
habits, punctuality, self-discipline) which make for a
more successful Army experience. The conclusion is
inescapable. The all-volunteer Army will be better served
by attracting more high school graduates or, even better,
college bound youth, that is, a more representative cross-
section of American young men.

Table 9. Army attrition rates by educational and mental levels
(FY 1974 enlistees as of July, 1977)

	Attrition percent by months after service entry		
	3 months	12 months	36 months
Total	10.7	21.7	39.8
All high school graduates	7.3	13.7	26.7
Mental level:			
I-IIIA	5.9	11.6	24.1
IIIB	8.6	15.5	29.4
IV	9.7	17.2	29.8
All non-high-school graduates	13.8	28.6	51.4
Mental level:			
I-IIIA	12.1	26.2	49.4
IIIB	14.2	29.4	52.6
IV	15.9	31.3	52.5

Source: Department of Army statistics.

Despite the overwhelming evidence that the higher the
quality, the better the soldierly performance, one too
often hears the statement that there are many manual tasks
for which bright soldiers are less suited than the not so
bright. Or as it has been put more formally: "Higher-
mental-aptitude individuals may become very dissatisfied in
(minimal ability) jobs because of lack of challenge."[35]
This assertion has a surface plausibility and it also has

[35]Ibid., p. 132.

the added attraction of making a virtue out of a necessity
in the all-volunteer force. But it is patently contradict-
ed by the facts. The evidence is unambiguous that on measures of enlisted productivity, higher educated and higher
aptitude soldiers do better in low skill jobs as well as
in high skill jobs.[36] This confirms what every NCO has
always known.

Most of the heated discussion about representativeness
has centered around the racial content of the all-volunteer
force. Though some researchers studiously avoid the
obvious, it is incontrovertible that there has been a
sharp rise in black participation--well over double the
proportion in the general population--in the Army's enlisted ranks. As noted earlier, the rise in black content
reflects both the large increase in the proportion of
blacks eligible for military service (through higher
educational levels and better aptitude scores), and the
unprecedently high unemployment rates among black youth
in the 1970s. Nevertheless, to look at the racial composition of the Army solely in terms of social forces
impinging upon and internal to the black community ought
not foreclose attention on the participation--or lack of
it--of the larger white middle-class population. To what
degree the changing racial composition of the Army also
reflects white reluctance to join a truly integrated system
is unknown. We do know, however, that changing racial
patterns in urban areas result almost entirely from the
preference of whites to live in segregated neighborhoods.[37]

The military has always recruited some youth, white
and black, who had no real alternative job prospects.
The recently advanced view that the armed forces ought to
be an outlet for otherwise unemployed youth, while seemingly
persuasive in the short term, is deceptive on several
grounds. It fails to take into account the preponderance
of minority and other disadvantaged youth in low-skill
enlisted jobs which have marginal, if any, transferability
to civilian employment. We are also confronted with the
understandable, but still disconcerting, fact that blacks
are virtually identical to whites to the extent they
downgrade the prestige of an occupation on the basis of the
percentage of blacks in that occupation.[38] Moreover, with
such a large proportion of volunteers--black or white--fail-
ing to complete their enlistments, the all-volunteer force
is producing large numbers of what are, in effect, two-time

[36]Ibid., p. 139.
[37]Reynolds Farley et. al., "Chocolate City, Vanilla
Suburbs," Social Science Research, 1978, in press.
[38]Paul M. Siegel, "Occupational Prestige in the Negro
Subculture," Sociological Inquiry, 40 (1970), 156-71.

losers. Rather than regarding the military as part of
the marketplace economy; it would be better to redistrib-
ute less advantaged soldiers into positions requiring
extended skill training with attendant longer-term commitments, and, at the same time, to draw middle class
youth into low-skill occupations where short enlistments
are most practical. The military, however, will continue
to draw disproportionately from young blacks as long as
they are victims of certain structural problems in the
national economy--specifically, the steady flow of manu-
facturing jobs away from cities where so many poor blacks
are trapped.

The rising minority content in the Army actually
masks a more pervasive shift in the social class bases of
the lower enlisted ranks, a shift that became apparent in
the combat arms over the course of the Vietnam War, and
one that has become even more pronounced in the all-
volunteer Army. From the 1940s through the mid-1960s,
the military served as a bridging environment between
entering low-status youth and eventual middle class employment.[39] Whatever success the military had as a
remedial organization for deprived youth were largely due
to the armed forces being legitimated on other than welfare grounds, such as national defense, citizenship obligation, even manly honor.[40] In other words, those very
conditions peculiar to the armed forces which can serve
to resocialize poverty youth away from a deadend existence
depend directly upon the military not being defined as a
welfare agency, a definition that is hard to escape unless
enlisted membership is representative of a cross-section
of American youth. Present trends toward labeling the
Army as a last recourse for disadvantaged youth are self-
defeating for the youth involved precisely because they
directly counter the premise that military participation
is one of broadly based national service.

The distinctive quality of the enlisted ranks in
modern times has been a mixing of the social classes. It

[39]Harley L. S. Browning, Sally C. Lopreato, and Dudley
L. Poston, Jr., "Income and Veteran Status," American Sociological Review, 38 (1973), 74-85; Sally C. Lopreato and
Dudley L. Poston, Jr., "Differences in Earnings and Earnings Ability between Black Veterans and Nonveterans in the
United States," Social Science Quarterly, 57 (1977), 750-66;
Wayne J. Villemez and John D. Kasarda, "Veteran Status and
Socioeconomic Attainment," Armed Forces and Society, 4
(1976), 407-20.
    [40]Bernard Beck, "The Military as a Welfare Institu-
tion," in Charles C. Moskos, Jr., ed., Public Opinion and
the Military Establishment (Beverly Hills: Sage, 1971),
pp. 137-48.

was the conjunction of both authoritarian and egalitarian
standards that produced the singular character of the
enlisted experience. It was an experience derived from a
social organization which underutilized--or, if one prefer,
penalized--middle class individuals, while simultaneously
allowing persons from lower-class background to participate with minimal acknowledgement of preexisting social
and educational handicaps. Such an enforced leveling of
the classes had no parallel in any other existing institution in American society. This was the elemental
social fact underlying enlisted service. This is the
state of affairs which has disappeared in the all-volunteer
Army.

An organizational comparison may be instructive at
this point. The Civilian Conservation Corps (CCC) was
set up in 1934 during the depression to recruit unemployed
young men for public works.[41] Throughout most of the
1930s, when the CCC had a membership somewhat representative of a cross-section of men, it received enthusiastic
public support from liberals and conservatives alike, and
was acknowledged to have contributed greatly to the public
benefit and to the individual good of the men who labored
in its civilian battalions. Toward the end of the decade,
however, as outside employment opportunities improved, the
new enrollees were "younger, less self-reliant, and more
prone to homesickness or discouragement."[42] Dishonorable
dismissals, never a problem before, became endemic; crime
and violence in the camps increased; and local communi-
ties, formerly supportive, pressed for the removal of CCC
camps. The CCC precedent, while not a direct precedent
for the all-volunteer Army, does seem to have some transferable lessons: membership representativeness of an organization (if mass based) contributes to internal efficiency,
individual growth, and public esteem.

Another consequence of the all-volunteer force speaks
to ideological representativeness. A major study of active-
duty servicemen in 1973-75 concluded that while there is no
single "military mind," there is a consistent attitudinal
break between those intending to make the military a career
and those who are not.[43] Noncareer military personnel are
very much like their civilian counterparts in attitudes
toward civil-military relations and the military organization. Career military people, on the other hand, are ideo-

[41]Leslie Alexander Lacy, The Soil Soldiers (Radnor,
Pa.: Chilton, 1976).
[42]Ibid., pp. 201-2.
[43]Jerald G. Bachman, John D. Blair, and David R. Segal, The All-Volunteer Force (Ann Arbor: University of
Michigan Press, 1977).

logically different from both their civilian counterparts
and from noncareer military men. The career military "were
telling us--louder and clearer than we are accustomed to
hearing--that they were dissatisfied with present levels of
military influence and preferred a good deal more."[44] The
study concluded that in order to maintain a desirable political balance within the all-volunteer force, extreme caution was in order on proposals to increase the career share
of the active-duty population. Quite the contrary, recruitment ought to be directed at "in-and-outers," single term
servicemen who would represent a broad ideological spectrum.

One of the unquantifiable aspects of combat performance
is the effect of social composition on combat groups. From
a historical standpoint, the evidence is clear that military participation and combat risks in World War II were more
equally shared by American men than in either the wars of
Korea or Vietnam.[45] (The draft per se is thus no guarantee
that military participation will insure class equity.) In
point of fact, soldiers in World War II reflected a higher
socioeconomic background than that of the general population. On the other hand, a careful study of Vietnam War
casualties has documented that low social class (not race!)
was the factor most responsible for the higher casualties
suffered by segments of American society in that war.[46] It
is informative that both supporters and critics of the
American military concur that at least some of the deterior-
ation of American troop behavior in the Vietnam War was due
to the accurate perceptions of lower-ranking enlisted men
that the sacrifices of war were not being equally shared.[47]

In the post-Vietnam context, if U.S. forces are to
fulfill their function of military deterrence, representational concerns are still germane. This is not to argue

[44]Ibid., p. 135.
[45]John Willis, "Variations in State Casualty Rates in
World War II and the Vietnam War," Social Problems, 22
(1975), 558-68; Neil D. Fligstein, "Who Served in the Military, 1940-1973?" CDE Working Paper 76-8 (Madison: Center
for Demography and Ecology, University of Wisconsin, 1976).
[46]Gilbert Badillo and G. David Curry, "The Social Incidence of Vietnam Casualties: Social Class or Race," Armed
Forces and Society, 2 (1976), 397-406.
[47]Charles C. Moskos, Jr., The American Enlisted Man
(New York: Russell Sage, 1970), pp. 135-56; Moskos, "The American Combat Soldier in Vietnam," Journal of Social Issues,
31 (1975), 25-37; John Helmer, Bringing the War Home (New
York: Free Press, 1974), pp. 1-42; David Cortright, Soldiers
in Revolt (Garden City, N.Y.: Doubleday, 1975), pp. 28-49;
Richard A. Gabriel and Paul L. Savage, Crisis in Command
(New York: Hill and Wang, 1978).

that the makeup of the enlisted ranks be perfectly calibrated to the social composition of the larger society,
but it is to ask what kind of society excuses its privileged from serving in the ranks of its Army. If participation of persons coming from minority or blue-collar
background in military leadership positions is used as a
measure of democratic character, it is even more important
that participation of more advantaged groups in the
Army's rank and file also be a measure of representational
democracy.

Serving in the Ranks of the All-Volunteer Army

The time is ready to reassess our stock of knowledge regarding the all-volunteer Army. Such a reassessment must be
based on clear analysis of five years of experience and future probabilities. It ought not to be constrained by policy alternatives--the status quo versus bringing back con-
scription--which dominate debate on the all-volunteer force.
What considerations must be raised in determining who should
serve and what kind of an enlisted force is desirable?
What are the relations between citizen participation and
national security? Econometrically based analyses tend not
to ask these kind of questions, but we must.

Let us summarize the discussion of this study up to
this point. The all-volunteer Army has its difficulties,
but it is working. The Recruiting Command has managed an
accomplishment of immense proportions. In comparison with
the peacetime draft, however, today's Army is much less
representative--and becoming increasingly so--of American
youth. In addition to major demographic changes, there has
also been a shift away from organizational factors conducive to an institutional framework toward one more resembling that of an occupation. A more representative enlisted force will have beneficial consequences for the Army
in terms of military efficiency, enlisted life in the ranks,
and civic definition. Most troubling, even at present
levels of quality and numbers, recruitment will become
progressively more difficult as the cohort of eligible enlistees drops rapidly over the next decade.

Present and anticipated difficulties to recruit an
all-volunteer Army have led to renewed talk of restoring
conscription. This possibility is viewed as remote. The
passions and injustices of the Vietnam years lie too close
to the surface. It is indisputable that public opinion
polls show an overwhelming support for the all-volunteer
concept.[48] A return to the draft would also pose anew the

[48]Chicago Sun Times, March 6, 1977, p. 34.

question of who serves when not all serve. Coercive
induction might well result in troop discipline problems
exceeding what the Army could accommodate. If compulsion
is used, moreover, many will attempt to avoid military
service, which will bring on its own problems. Practical
as well as political considerations foreclose the draft
as a real alternative in the foreseeable future.

If conscription is not feasible, what about management steps that could be taken to improve manpower utilization within the all-volunteer framework? Here we run
into the difficulty that most proposals in this vein--a
kind of suboptimal approach--do not address the core
issue: getting young men into the ground combat arms.
Neither lowering physical standards for men nor increasing
the number of women suits the imperatives of the combat
arms. Similarly, greater reliance on civilian personnel
does not speak as to who serves in the infantry. That
increasing the proportion of women, civilians, or less
physically qualified men in technical support units will
result in releasing more soldiers for assignment into the
combat arms is questionable in the long term. What would
probably happen is that the all-volunteer Army will
experience even greater recruitment and attrition problems
among its male soldiers than presently.

Large raises in military pay were the principal
rationale of the Gates Commission to induce persons to
join the all-volunteer force. This has turned out to be
a double-edged sword, however. Youth surveys show that
high pay motivates less qualified youth (e.g., high
school dropouts, those with poor grades) to join, while
having a negligible effect on more qualified youth.[49]
Better-qualified youth, in fact, have a higher estimate of
military compensation than do lesser qualified youth.[50] To
use salary incentives as the primary motivating force to
join and remain in the military can also lead inadvertently
to grave morale problems. If future military pay raises
were to lag behind civilian scales, as seems likely, the
present grumbling throughout the ranks now limited to
perceived erosion of benefits would then become a rumbling
chorus of complaint.

The central issue remains: is there a way without
direct compulsion or excessive salaries by which a large and
representative cross-section of young men can be attracted
into the combat arms? Or, to put it another way, can we
obtain the analog of the peacetime draftee in the all-volunteer framework? I believe there is. Two proposals are presented for consideration: one moderate, the other more far

[49]Market Facts, pp. 123-27.
[50]Ibid., p. 126

reaching.

The first proposal is a two-year enlistment option (the term of the draftee) to be restricted to the combat arms (and perhaps labor-intensive fields) and be oriented toward an overseas tour. The quid pro quo for such assignment would be postservice educational benefits along the lines of the G.I. Bill of World War II. A college-education-in-exchange-for-two-years-in-the-combat-arms formula would be the means to attract highly qualified soldiers who can learn quickly, serve effectively for a full tour, and then be replaced by similarly qualified recruits.[51] The added costs of generous postservice educational benefits would be partly balanced by budgetary savings in reduced recruiting outlays, less attrition, less time diverted from military training, and, most likely, fewer dependents of lower-ranking soldiers. Such educational benefits would be limited solely to those serving in the combat arms, about a quarter of all enlisted personnel in the Army. (Corresponding formulas could be worked out for the other services.)

Arguments that enlisted occupations in the modern Army demand long terms because of time invested in skill training do not stand up to scrutiny. Close to half of all lower-ranking enlisted jobs do not require more than a couple of months of advanced training beyond basic training.[52] Moreover, because there would be no presumption of acquiring civilian skills in the military, the terms of such short-term service would be unambiguous, thus alleviating a major source of enlisted discontent in the all-volunteer Army.

To go a step farther, the military could set up a two-track personnel system recognizing a distinction between a citizen soldier and a career soldier ("soldier" is used here inclusively for airmen, sailors, and marines, as well). The career soldier would be assigned and compensated in the manner of the prevailing system. The citizen soldier, however, would serve a two-year term in the combat arms or labor-intensive occupations with low active-duty salary, few if any entitlements, but with deferred compensation in the form of postservice educational benefits. Such educational benefits could be tied to military obligations following active duty and thus bolster our sagging reserve forces. There is some evidence that many highly qualified youth would choose a short term in the military under such conditions.[53]

[51]An insightful discussion on the value of postservice educational benefits in lieu of active-duty pay is found in Bachman, Blair, and Segal, pp. 145-48.
[52]Cooper, p. 140.
[53]Bachman, Blair, and Segal, pp. 145-48.

The second and broader proposal assumes that the
definition of military service needs overhauling as badly
as the machinery of selection.[54] Now is the time to
consider a voluntary national service program--in which
military duty is one of several options--which would be a
prerequisite for future federal employment. For purposes
of discussion, a two-year national service program aimed
at youth--male and female--is proposed. Such service
would be expected to take place between school and job, or
between school and college, or between college and professional training. National service would be compensated
for at levels comparable to that given draftees in the pre-
Vietnam era. That is, subsistence plus a little spending
money. It would be directed toward tasks which intrin-
sically are unamenable to sheer monetary incentives, as
diverse as caring for the aged, infirm, and mentally
feeble, performing conservation work, as well as serving
in the combat arms of the armed forces. It would certainly be to the advantage of society to have such tasks performed by low-paid but motivated youth. But at the same
time such tasks need not be considered a lifetime vocation.
In fact, for many in their late teens and early twenties
a diversion from the world of school or work would be
tolerable and perhaps even welcome.

Certainly a national service plan would cause a
readjustment of national priorities. Much discussion is
needed on the manner in which the implementation and
details of such a program could be worked out. But the
core of the proposal is that there ought to be some linkage
between, on the one hand, national service, and, on the
other, future eligibility for government employment.
There will be a reliance on neither compulsion nor altruism.
Such a program has many positive implications. It would
avoid the "stick" of coercion, but still appeal to a
large constituence because of the "carrot" of possible
employment in the government sector. It would meet
pressing national needs in both the civilian and military
spheres. It would be philosophically defensible by connect-
ing future employment by the taxpayer to prior commitment
to national service. It would make public service an essential part of growing up in America. Most important, it
would clarify the military's role by emphasizing the larger
calling of national service.

[54]An excellent study, containing both original thinking and factual information on the relationship between
military needs and national service is William R. King,
Achieving America's Goals: The All-Volunteer Force or
National Service? Report prepared for the Committee on
Armed Services, U.S. Senate, 95th Cong., 1st sess. (Washington, D.C.: Government Printing Office, 1977).

In a democratic society quality of life as well as
life-or-death decisions are topics for the broadest public
discussion and debate evolved through opposing views.
Opinion polls, although fraught with interpretive ambigui-
ties, do offer some reading on public attitudes. Clearly
a large majority of Americans support a massive defense
establishment while opposing a return to military conscription. Yet these same polls show two out of three
Americans favor a year of compulsory national service for
males; 40 percent favor such a program for women. Even
among young men aged 18 to 24, almost half support the
idea and 43 percent would choose military rather than
civilian service.[55] It may be that we are coming to a
realization that many of the things we need as a nation
we can never afford to buy. If we are to have them, we
must give them to ourselves.

The debate about the all-volunteer Army is a continuation of the discussion that surrounded the end of the
draft. The primacy of democratic politics means more than
the tasks of the armed forces as defined by elected
leaders; it also demands an ongoing public discussion which
positions the military in its social, and moral context.
The all-volunteer Army has been presented as either a
failure or a success. Events unfolding today indicate
plainly that it is neither.

[55]New York Times, Jan. 26, 1976, p. 22.

THE BRITISH EXPERIENCE WITH THE

ALL-VOLUNTEER FORCE

Gwyn Harries-Jenkins

Introduction

In 1957 as part of a comprehensive review of national defence
policy, the British Government announced the phasing-out of
conscription. Although the more radical strategic proposals
of the 1957 Defence White Paper were not subsequently implemented, a diminishing number of conscripts were called-up
after this date as the United Kingdom returned to its
traditional policy of relying upon all-volunteer recruitment
to its armed forces. In 1957 National Servicemen numbered
252,600 in a total force structure of 719,100; by 1961 there
were 78,300 conscripts in a smaller force of 525,600. Three
years later, the all-volunteer force totalled 423,100, that
is, less than half the size of the military in the peak
years of conscription in 1952 and 1953.

    For the twenty years after 1957 a consistent issue of
fundamental concern in the United Kingdom has been the consequence of this change in the force structure. This has
raised wide-ranging and far-reaching questions. It has
involved the consideration not only of the strategic and
tactical implications of the 1957 proposals, but also of
the political, social, and economic implications of the
decisions which were taken. In general terms, a review
of the British experience during this period suggests that
the fundamental transformation of military organization
associated with the move to an all-volunteer force has
inexorably led to a number of unexpected and largely
dysfunctional consequences. This has been a period characterized by a constant readjustment of recruiting targets

and force ceilings, a readjustment which coincided with a
consistent reappraisal of the role of British armed forces
in a phase of imperial withdrawal. The hard choice of
allocation within the limits of constrained resources was
initially facilitated by a decline in power status and the
loss of global responsibilities, but this choice has been
subsequently made more difficult by an increasing commitment
to the civil power in Ulster and by a worsening economic
situation. In this context, therefore, the consequences of
the 1957 decision have a particular poignancy, and although
cross-cultural comparisons have to be made with care, the
British experience can be used as the basis for the further
examination of the consequences for other democratic industrialized societies of the decline of the mass armed force.

In examining more critically the dimensions of this
experience, three specific areas have to be considered in
greater detail. Firstly we are concerned with the structural
implications for the armed forces of the return to all-
volunteer recruitment. Secondly, it is necessary to
examine the economic effects of the decisions which were
made. This includes an evaluation of the thesis that a
scheme of economic reward linked to that obtainable in
civilian employment produces the desired number and quality
of military personnel. Finally, an important question is
that of the social consequences of changes in military
organization. This, in turn, draws attention to possible
changes in traditional patterns of civil-military relationships in the United Kingdom and emphasizes the consequences
of all-volunteer armed forces for British society in general.

The central theme of this analysis is that these political, economic, and social consequences are interrelated,
although each element for the purpose of analysis can be
considered as a separate factor. It is argued that the
combined effect of these consequences is such as to suggest
that in an advanced industrialized society, a nation which
is committed to the redistributive goals of the modern
welfare state cannot afford the financial burdens generated
by the creation of an all-volunteer military system. In
this context the notion of "cannot afford" invites an
emotive reaction. For supporters of a comprehensive British
defence policy, economic and, indeed, social costs have to
be subordinated in their importance as determinants of
resource allocation to the criteria of defence needs. The
latter, in turn, are defined in terms of the military capability of a potential aggressor with the result that any
increase in this capability produces a demand for increased
defence expenditure that "has to be afforded." In complete
contrast, at the other end of a continuum of reaction,
opponents of the current level of defence expenditure and
of the size of the military establishment stress that this

inhibits the redistribution of national economic resources
and the development of certain critical minimum standards
in welfare areas. Consequently, it is argued that the
all-volunteer army cannot be tolerated and that there must
be an acceleration of the trend towards establishing clear
national priorities for welfare over defence values.

The Force Structure

Traditionally, Great Britain did not adopt as a means of
military recruiting the levee en masse of continental
Europe. Standing armies of any considerable size in peacetime were unknown before the Second World War. On the
contrary, a historic opposition to the maintenance of any
standing army, irrespective of its size, was a result of
the experience of Cromwell's rule by major-generals. Consistently it was argued that a nonmilitarist nation,
lacking the land frontiers of continental Europe, did
not need to resort to conscription to maintain a mass
army. Despite chronic shortages of military manpower
during the nineteenth and early twentieth centuries, the
force of public opposition to such proposals as those of
the National Service League and to any suggestion of
conscription implied that a hallmark of British citizenship was freedom from compulsory service in the national
armed forces. Consequently the abandonment of the cherished
principle of voluntary recruitment in 1916 and again in
May 1939 were seen only as temporary wartime expedients.

The subsequent decision taken by the Labour Government
in the post-1945 period to maintain conscription in peacetime was, therefore, a notable break with historic British
practice. Surprisingly, it engendered little political
opposition, for the wartime coalition of defence between
Attlee and Churchill was continued.[1] Moreover, the military
need for the maintenance of large-size armed forces could
be readily rationalized in view of contemporary amendments
to traditional British defence policy. The acceptance of
a military responsibility in Europe, in combination with
traditional global and imperial obligations, imposed a
military burden which could only be met through the maintenance in being of a large armed force recruited by
conscription. It was, therefore, the retreat from empire
and the force of internal and external opposition to such
campaigns as the Suez debacle of 1956 which led to the
deliberate political choice to phase-out conscription.

[1]For a further discussion of this point, see, Hugh
Hanning, "Defence and British Public Opinion," Brassey's
Annual (London 1970).

The subsequent contention--that "Defence must be the servant of foreign policy, not its master. Military forces must be designed accordingly"[2]--paved the way for the introduction of new organizational concepts and different orientations within the reformed force. Yet from the very beginning the small all-volunteer force recreated to implement the political decision was beset by a number of persistent problems. Of these, one of the most critical was the difficulty of attaining military manpower targets. Although there was initially considerable criticism of the proposal to reduce the strength of the armed forces, it subsequently became increasingly evident that it would be difficult, if not impossible, to meet recruiting targets and force ceilings.

It can be argued that this difficulty should have been more clearly foreseen since targets and ceilings which were set artificially high did not take into account historical trends in the pattern of military recruitment. An analysis of these trends suggests that three propositions are of particular relevance:

1. In peacetime, the absolute size of the British all-volunteer force consistently declines.

2. Over time, the size of the all-volunteer force declines as a proportion of the adult working population.

3. Over time, the military participation ratio (M.P.R.) associated with the British all-volunteer force declines.

These are explanatory propositions designed to facilitate analysis. They do not purport to indicate either the "absolute" or "normal" size of the British all-volunteer force. What they do suggest is that the historical trends which can be generally observed throughout the twentieth century and which can be more specifically analysed for the post-1963 force structure cast an illuminating light on the problems which have been faced by the United Kingdom. Again it has to be stressed that cross-cultural comparisons have to be made with care. Nevertheless, the British experience may be more generally indicative of the difficulties encountered in other democratic industralized societies which have moved away from the concept of the mass army recruited through some form of conscription.

To look at these propositions in more detail, the first proposition can be initially examined through a simple analysis of the size of British armed forces at yearly intervals during the thirty years from 1946 to 1975.

[2]Ministry of Defence, Defence: Outline of Future Policy /Cmnd. 124_7 (London: HMSO, 1957).

From Table 1 it can be seen that in the early postwar period the size of the military establishment reflected the
wartime mobilization of British manpower, which in 1944
had reached a maximum of 5,022.8 million men and women.
From 1949 to 1952 there was an increase of 12.8% in the
overall size of the peacetime army, the fractional decrease
of 10% in naval manpower being offset by increases of 12%
and 24% in the size of the Army and Air Force, respectively.
During these years of conscription 1952 was the peak year
for the overall size of the military. If this year is
taken as the base year of 100, then in 1957 the relative
size of the armed forces was 81.1; in 1962 this had fallen
to 50.5 and the decline continued through 1967 (47.4),
1972 (42.2) and 1975 (38.6). This trend suggests a marked
decrease in the absolute size of the military, particularly
since in 1947 the size relative to 1953 was 150. The
decrease, moreover, was continuous except for the year 1972
when the strength of the Army increased for that single year
by 3%. This decline is, of course, the result of a failure
to meet recruiting goals, as can be seen from Table 2.
Over the twelve years, 1963 to 1975, the armed forces were
able to recruit on the average only 82% of the requirement
for new enlistees. The impact of such chronic recruiting
shortages on force size is obvious.

    It can also be seen that after the recommendations of
the 1957 White Paper, the decline in the absolute size of
the British military had started even before the last of
the conscripts left the armed forces. Thus in 1962, when
the size of these forces was no more than a half of what
it had been in the peak year of conscription (1952), a
total military manpower of 444,500 included 31,200 (7%)
conscripts. Indeed, the annual rate of decrease was at
its height in the period between the announcement of the
end of conscription and its actual termination. Thus in
the years from 1956 to 1958, the rate of decline varied
between 11% and 12.7% per annum before settling at an
annual rate of approximately 8% for the remaining period
to 1962. Thereafter, the rate dropped to 3% and then,
once conscription had finally finished, fell further to a
fluctuating rate of less than 1% per annum. After a
slight increase of 1% in the total size of the armed
forces in 1972, the decline continued when the annual rate
of decrease accelerated to 4.8% for 1973 before falling
to 2.6% for 1974.

    This pattern of change in the absolute size of British
armed forces seemingly endorses the validity of the first
proposition. Three points, however, must be made. Firstly,
the impact of the final ending of conscription on the military manpower pattern was not as dramatic as the proposition
would seem to imply. The importance of the transitional
period as the time when major reductions in the size of

Table 1. Strengths of the UK armed forces, 1946-75 (in thousands)

Calendar year	Total strength	Calendar year	Total strength	Calendar year	Total strength
1946	2192.6	1956	805.1	1966	419.4
1947	1325.1	1957	713.4	1967	417.4
1948	910.7	1958	622.5	1968	401.8
1949	779.1	1959	574.1	1969	383.0
1950	703.2	1960	524.8	1970	373.0
1951	833.6	1961	479.3	1971	368.0
1952	879.4	1962	444.5	1972	371.5
1953	877.5	1963	427.9	1973	367.0
1954	858.2	1964	425.4	1974	349.3
1955	815.3	1965	424.6	1975	340.1

Sources: 1946-68: British Labour Statistics: Historical Abstract;
1969-75: Statement on the Defence Estimates

Table 2. Tri-Service recruiting results

Fiscal year	Required male entrants	Numbers obtained	Percentage achieved
1963-1964	45,000	35,694[a]	79.3
1964-1965	47,000	42,990[b]	91.4
1965-1966	45,500	37,200	81.7
1966-1967	40,700	39,500	97.0
1967-1968	43,000	31,900	74.1
1968-1969	38,000	28,100	73.9
1969-1970	46,100	34,300	74.4
1970-1971	49,100	38,900	79.2
1971-1972	46,300	46,493	100
1972-1973	43,000[c]	39,120	90.7
1973-1974	43,000[c]	25,800	60.0
1974-1975	43,000[c]	34,960	81.3

Sources: Statement on Defence Estimates for appropriate years; Tri-Service Manpower Statistics, The Regular Forces, Quarterly Recruiting News Release for quarter ended 31 March 1975.

   a. CY 1963.

   b. CY 1964.

   c. Minimum annual requirement, which does not include shortfalls from previous years; Statements on the Defence Estimates 1971, February 1971 (CMND 4952), p. 31.

the military are made, cannot be overlooked. Secondly, this
period may be associated,for reasons which are not entirely
clear, with an unexpectedly high rate of recruitment of
regular and seemingly volunteer servicemen. Thus both of
the years 1959 and 1962 were good years for army recruiting.
As Dietz and Stone comment, "1962 turned out to be a bumper
year for regular recruiting. However, the 36,000 men and
boys who enlisted in the army that year provided an over-
optimistic measure of what could be achieved, and the figure
has never been approached since."[3] By way of comparison there
were 15,863 recruits in 1968 into the Army against an outflow of 24,357 and 26,500 recruits in 1972 against an
outflow of 20,050. In 1973-74 the year of the lowest rate
of recruitment during this decade, only 15,300 personnel,
or 42% of the 1962 figure, joined the army.

     Thirdly,and perhaps most importantly, these changes
which took place in the British armed forces were not the
result of the creation of a new and hitherto unknown force
structure. They marked, on the contrary, the return to the
traditional and long-standing preference for all-volunteer
forces. The transformation of the military, therefore, can
be related to what happened after other major wars even
though the exercise of this preference was before 1945 far
more closely related, in terms of the time-scale, to the
actual cessation of hostilities. Thus, the Second South
African War of 1899-1902, in which some 450,000 troops (of
whom 250,000 were British regulars) were employed to defeat
the Boers, was the last major war to rely exclusively for
its manpower requirements on all-volunteer forces. The
latter then comprised regular, militia, and temporary volunteer servicemen, their total strength amounting in the
peak year of 1901 to 503,300 men. If this year is taken
as the base year (100) for subsequent comparison, then it
can be seen from Table 3 that there was an immediate and
persistent decline in this strength after the war to a
comparative low of 83 in 1907. Thereafter, there were
intermittent fluctuations around the 84 to 85 level until
1914. It was, however, recognized that a force of this
size was insufficient to meet the needs of army mobilization
at the outbreak of a major conflict, and the regular army
was supplemented by a Territorial or Home Force, formed
from the historic militia and volunteer units. By the
beginning of 1910 the Territorials numbered 270,618 officers
and men, that is, 88.5% of their established strength, a
total which exceeded the 244,700 strength of the all-volunteer
regular army.

     [3]Peter J. Dietz and J. F. Stone, "The British All-
Volunteer Army," Armed Forces and Society, 1,2, (February
1975), 164.

Table 3.   Changes in the total size of British armed forces, selected
years 1903-75

Calendar year	Base year 1 1903 = 100	Base year 2 1918 = 100	Base year 3 1943 = 100
1903	100		
1908	85.5		
1913	86.4		
1918	936.5	100	
1923	77.3	8.2	
1928	78.0	8.3	
1933	74.5	7.9	
1938	89.2	9.5	
1943	1092.4	116.6	100
1948	209.9	22.4	19.2
1953	202.0	21.6	18.5
1958	143.4	15.3	13.1
1963	98.6	10.5	9.0
1968	92.6	9.9	8.5
1973	84.6	9.0	7.7
1975	78.4	8.4	7.1

Sources: As Table 1.

This division of the "National Army," which was
instituted under the Haldane reforms of 1907, was to be
the pattern for Britain's peacetime army until the introduction of the Compulsory Training Act of May 1939. The
system,however, was abandoned by Kitchener in the autumn of
1914 when the British set out to create a wartime mass army
by relying first on volunteers for the New Army and then on
conscription. By 1918, the peak year, the armed forces had
expanded to 4,062,900 officers and men, 90% of whom were
serving in the Army and the Royal Flying Corps. If this
year is taken as a second base year, it can be seen that
within twelve months after the Armistice the return to an
all-volunteer force had begun. By 1920 the strength of
the armed forces had been decimated. Thereafter, there was
a progressive decline in numbers until in 1932, at their
minimal level, these all-volunteer forces totalled no more
than 7.4% of the 1918 figure. Although this comparative
size then gradually increased, the 1939 figures in Table 1
indicate that the total strength of the armed forces was
still only 11.7% of the 1918 maximum. Put into practical
terms, this meant that the army, to take the specific
example, could put into the field in Europe thirty-two
divisions, of which six were regular formations, compared
with the German mass army which on mobilization comprised
105 field divisions.

A similar pattern of decreasing military manpower can
be seen to have occurred after 1945. In 1919, the year
after the end of hostilities, armed forces were 40.1% of
their maximum size. Similarly, in 1946, they were 43.6%
of the maximum attained in 1944. In this third post-war
period, however, the retention of conscription prevented
the sudden and dramatic decline in military strength
which had followed the two previous major wars of the
twentieth century. Thus in 1953 Britain's armed forces
still totalled 17.5% of their 1944 size. But it is not
insignificant that ten years after the ending of conscription in 1918, armed forces were 8.3% of the maximum
attained size and that ten years after the decision was
taken to end conscription in 1957, they were again 8.3% of
the 1944 maximum. It would be injudicious to infer too
much from this coincidence, for the time-periods are not
strictly comparable, and indeed in 1973, ten years after
conscription actually ended, the all-volunteer military
was only 7.3% of the maximum size of the 1939-45 mass army.
Nevertheless, it can be inferred from the post-1918 and
the post-1945 pattern of military manpower, that for
Britain, the "normal" size of the all-volunteer armed force
in peacetime apparently lies somewhere between seven to
eight percent of the country's optimum mobilization.

This inference, however, draws attention to a number
of other questions for further investigation. Firstly, it
raises the issue of whether variations in such factors as

recruiting strategies can, in fact, modify to any great
extent the apparent inevitable decline in the size of all-
volunteer armed forces. The critical question is whether
social, political, and economic parameters will, irrespective of changes in their nature, be related to, if not
dependent upon, fundamental limitations on the size of the
peacetime all-volunteer force. Secondly, it can be questioned whether this force is a relatively stable structure
or not, particularly in comparison with the apparent considerable variations in the size of the mass army where
reliance on mass mobilization precluded the establishment
of a military force of a consistent size. Finally, a no
less important question is whether this notion of a
"standard" size all-volunteer force means that specific
branches of the services must compete with each other
to secure a share of the total manpower pool that is
available.

When Table 3 is used as the basis for further analysis,
it can be seen that if 1903, the first year of peace after
the Second South African War, is taken as the base year,
then there is a persistent decrease in the absolute size
of the all-volunteer force not only in the pre-1914 period,
but also during the years of the 1920s and 1930s as well
as in the post-conscription years after 1963. While
specific annual comparisons have to be made with care, it
can be noted that the absolute size of the armed forces at
the lowest point in each of these three phases declined
to between 70% and 85% of the 1903 figure, that is, to
83.7% in 1908, 74.2% in 1933 and 78.4% in 1975. Moreover,
since in this last period of the all-volunteer forces
following 1963 there is ample evidence of a continuing
decline in military manpower, it can be postulated that
the absolute size of Britain's armed forces will inevitably
fall to a total comparable with that of 1933. This would
indicate a force of some 315,000, a total which, although
low, is still in excess of that postulated by David
Greenwood of Aberdeen University, who has suggested that
the combined effect of the 1974 Defence Review and subsequent cuts already requires the shedding over the next
four years of 35,000 service personnel.[4] Irrespective of
the precise nature and size of the "standard" all-volunteer
force in the United Kingdom, what can be concluded is that
both developmental analysis and economic analysis of the
kind utilized by Greenwood separately confirm the proposition

[4]Cited in Tony Geraghty, "How 'Pathetic' are Our Forces?"
The Sunday Times, 24 October 1976. The reference is to two
studies commissioned by the Defence Study Group of the Labour
Party National Executive. The studies prepared by the Centre
for Higher Defence Studies of the University of Aberdeen
examined options for cutting Britain's defence spending.

that the size of the all-volunteer force consistently declines over time.

An alternative way at looking at this long-term trend
and at the postulated conclusion is to consider these
variations in absolute size against changes in the composition of the total adult working population. The underlying
assumption in such an analysis is that in an industrialized
democratic society in peacetime, there is an upper limit
on that percentage of the working population who can be
employed as servicemen. The economic factors which support
this premise will be examined later in this chapter; at
this point, however, it can be argued that historical trends
in the United Kingdom lead to the conclusion that there is
such an upper limit. Initially these trends can be seen
in Table 4.

In Table 4 armed forces are considered as a percentage
of the total UK working population at five year year intervals
between 1903 and 1972. It will be noted that in this Table,
which is based on annual averages of the disposition of the
working population, the strength of the armed forces is not
comparable with that given in Table 1 for these years.
Despite this difference, in the method of calculating the
total size of the armed forces, relative strength figures
are comparable in both tables. From Table 4, therefore, it
can be seen that in the first period of the all-volunteer
army between 1903 and 1913, the initial proportion of military personnel relative to the total working population was
slightly greater than 2%. Subsequently, this proportion
fell to under 2%, with a considerable similarity between
the proportions for 1908 and 1913 despite a marked fluctuation in the numbers of unemployed in these years. An
analysis of each yearly total confirms this pattern, and
the conclusion which can be drawn is that for this period
the size of the all-volunteer force relative to the total
adult working population lay between 1.90% and 2.20% with
a tendency towards the lower percentage for most of this
time.

After the fluctuations of the wartime years, armed
forces declined again to less than 2.0% of the working
population. In this second period, a decrease in the
relative size of the armed forces to the 1933 low of 1.45%
was again unaffected by a marked rise in the number of
those unemployed. Subsequently, in the period of rearmament
prior to the outbreak of the Second World War this relative
size increased, though as late as 1939 this was to no more
than 2% of the working population. Thus for both of the
periods of volunteer service in the years from 1903 to 1939,
the relative size of the armed forces was comparable in
terms of the percentage of the working population serving
in the military.

Table 4. Military personnel as a proportion of the total UK working population, selected years from 1900 to 1972 (employed and unemployed in thousands)

Calendar year	Total in civil employment	Armed forces	Unemployed	Working population	Armed forces as a % of working population	Unemployed as a % of working population
1903	17,720	420	870	19,010	2.21	4.57
1908	17,960	380	1,520	19,860	1.91	7.65
1913	19,910	400	430	20,740	1.92	2.07
1918	17,060	4,430	140	21,630	20.48	0.64
1923	17,758	348	1,567	19,673	1.77	7.96
1928	18,868	336	1,536	20,740	1.62	7.40
1933	18,831	323	3,087	22,223	1.45	13.89
1938	20,986	432	2,164	23,582	1.83	9.17
1943	20,200	4,780	80	25,100	19.04	0.31
1948	22,124	940	300	23,364	4.02	1.28
1953	22,841	868	342	24,051	3.61	1.42
1958	23,609	613	453	24,675	2.48	1.83
1963	24,785	426	540	25,751	1.65	2.09
1968	24,910	398	575	25,883	1.53	2.22
1972	24,088	372	862	25,322	1.46	3.40

     In the third period after 1945, the relative size of
the armed forces in the years of conscription considerably
exceeded this 2% ratio so that in 1953 the military was
3.61% of the total working population. Thereafter, this
proportion began to decline, with the result that in 1963,
when conscription ended, the relative size was 1.65%.
Subsequently, the decrease continued, until in 1972 the
1933 low of 1.45% was almost reached again. Once more,
increases in the level of unemployment did not apparently
affect the decline in the relative size of the armed forces
and this pattern has continued up to the present day.
Indeed, if 1953 and 1973 are compared, then it can be noted
that the comparable sizes of the armed forces and unemployed
relative to the total working population have been reversed.

     From Table 4 and from an analysis of each of the yearly
figures, it can be concluded that the second proposition is
indeed valid for the British all-volunteer armed force. It
suggests that irrespective of changes in factors external
to the military, such as civil employment, government policy,
and so on, the size of the armed force as a modern industrialized nation will decline as a proportion of the adult
working population. This, in a sense, is axiomatic, since
it is most unlikely that Britain today could sustain the
social, political, and economic costs of an all-volunteer
force, the size of which, in 1903, equaled 2.21% of the
adult working population. This 1903 proportion would produce an armed force of 559,616, a figure far in excess of
any in existence during the three periods under consideration. On the contrary, it can be suggested that the
consistent decline in the last decade will ultimately
result in an all-volunteer force which will amount to no more
than a half of the 1903 proportion of the adult working
population, that is some 1.0% to 1.1%.

     This suggested percentage fall, which is derived from
a projection of the noted rate of decline in the other
phases of the all-volunteer force in the twentieth century,
indicates a force structure of between 275,000 and 300,000.
Such a total corresponds closely with the other estimates
which have been previously given. Further confirmation of
this overall decline over time in the maximum size of the
British all-volunteer force is also evidenced by the
analysis of changes since 1900 in the military participation
ratio. The latter can be distinguished from the figures
presented in Table 4 in that this Table is concerned with
both male and female working population while the M.P.R.
is essentially based on changes in the composition of the
male population.

     Table 5 shows the military participation ratio for
British armed forces for selected years from 1900 to 1975.
It is significant that in terms of the M.P.R. the British

Table 5. Military participation ratio in Great Britain, selected
years 1900-75 (male personnel in thousands)

Calendar year	Total male population	Male armed forces	Military par- ticipation ratio
1903	20,491	433.8	2.11
1908	21,410	371.1	1.73
1913	22,150	375.0	1.69
1918	22,322	4,062.9	18.20
1923	21,328	335.6	1.57
1928	21,823	338.4	1.55
1933	22,332	323.3	1.44
1938	22,822	387.1	1.69
1943	23,574	4,285.8	18.18
1948	24,254	871.3	3.59
1953	24,317	853.3	3.50
1958	24,889	608.6	2.44
1963	25,944	410.6	1.58
1968	26,715	386.9	1.44
1973	27,186	352.0	1.29

Sources: As for Table 4.

all-volunteer force has in each of the three periods under
consideration, that is, 1903 to 1913, 1920 to 1939 and 1963
to 1975, shown a consistent decline. What is not most
striking is that in the third of these periods the M.P.R.
has reached a lower figure than in either of the two previous periods. The 1933 low of 1.44 was reached as early
as the end of the 1960s and since then the M.P.R. had
declined still further to less than 1.25. This has occurred despite an increase of some 16% in the size of the
male 15 to 24 years of age group in the decade between 1965
and 1975. What has to be questioned in this context is
whether the rate of decline will continue and whether there
is a base line below which the decline will be arrested.
This also raises the issue of the effect upon such a projected decline of such factors as changes in internal
conditions of service, revised recruiting strategies, and
improved intrinsic or extrinsic rates of reward.

    An alternative question of concern is whether the
decline, if it were to continue, could be offset by more
radical structural changes, such as the employment of an
increased number of women in the all-volunteer forces.
A full analysis of the issues which arise, such as the
cultural constraints affecting such changes, the role of
women in armed forces, the combat capability of women,
and the resultant military self-image, is beyond the scope
of this discussion. What can be noted is that past experience in the United Kingdom after 1947 indicates that the
decline in the male M.P.R. has been paralleled by a corresponding decrease in the female participation ratio. This
can be seen in Table 6.

Table 6. Military participation ratio in Great Britain, selected
years 1948-73 (female personnel in thousands)

Calendar year	Total female population	Female armed forces	Military par- ticipation ratio
1948	25,760	39.4	0.15
1953	26,275	24.2	0.09
1958	26,763	13.9	0.05
1963	27,608	17.3	0.06
1968	28,333	14.9	0.05
1973	28,747	15.0	0.05

Sources: As Table 4.

In looking further at this Table, two points must be
noted. Over the last twenty years the female participation
ratio has remained relatively constant at about 0.05, so
that the marked decline noted in the M.P.R. has not been
duplicated. Even so, the absolute size of the female contribution to the all-volunteer force has varied in the last
decade between a high of 15,900 in 1967 and a low of 14,200
two years later. This absolute size, moreover, includes the
2,500 to 2,800 nurses serving in the all-volunteer force.
At the same time this variation can be attributed more to
changes in the laid-down establishment of these women's
forces--often as a result of economic pressures--rather
than to shortfalls in recruiting. All other things being
equal, the approved strength of these forces, despite a
relatively high rate of attrition, can be readily maintained. It would be very injudicious, therefore, to conclude that higher force levels could not be attained if it
were decided to increase radically the size of the female
contribution to the armed forces. In 1944, for example,
when the absolute size of the women's armed forces was at
its maximum strength of 460,000, this amounted to some 10%
of the size of the male component. A comparable relationship in 1977 would thus indicate a female force of
some 30,000 rather than the 12,000 on establishment. The
addition of the nursing component to the former total would
then produce a force of approximately 33,000, an increase
of more than 100% upon present force strengths.

From Tables 5 and 6 it can be concluded that irrespective of the potential contribution which can be made
by women recruits to the solution of a chronic military
manpower shortage, the male military participation ratio
has declined over time. It can be further argued that
this fall in the M.P.R. will continue in accordance with
historical trends to an ultimate low of approximately 1.00.
This is not to deny the potential advantages of increasing
the absolute size of the female component in all-volunteer
forces in an industrialized democracy. Even so, for as
long as a greater reliance is placed on male recruitment
to these forces, then we are left with a number of continuing and apparently insoluble problems of which the
most acute is the basic difficulty of recruiting and
retaining a sufficient number of qualified personnel.

A subsidiary problem of some importance, however, is
the effect of intermittent fluctuations of force size
within the overall pattern of decline. It is clear that
while there is an overall trend towards a decrease in three
areas--the absolute size of the all-volunteer force, the
strength of such a force in proportion to the total adult
working population, and in the military participation
ratio--there are also significant fluctuations of force
size within this pattern as a whole. Thus in 1972, to

take a recent British example, there was an increase in
the total strength of the armed forces even though both
the Royal Navy and the Royal Air Force continued to decline in absolute size. In view of such variations, the
critical question which arises is whether fluctuations of
this type are indicative of a lack of stability in the
force structure.

The issue of the stability of the force structure in
an all-volunteer force raises a number of important questions about the potential effect of a stable or unstable
structure upon the relationship of armed forces and society. The extreme example which can be taken is that of the
totally stable military organization in which there is neither an inflow nor outflow of personnel. One question which
then arises is whether such a military organization would be
completely isolated from the parent society. At what
point, for instance, does the military in this situation
see itself as a state within a state? Conversely, to
what extent does the parent society see such a military
organization as a caste, membership of which is denied to
the population at large? At the other extreme, the
example of the totally unstable force structure in which
there is a continuous inflow and outflow of personnel
raises questions of equal importance. What, for instance,
is the state of its professionalism? How adequate in this
situation of instability will be those programs of socialization and assimilation which are designed to inculcate a
specific ethos and a sense of unity? To what degree does
an unstable force structure affect the ability of the all-
volunteer force to attain designated organizational goals?

While these are the polar examples, all military
organizations can be located somewhere on a continuum between these two extremes. The issue of the instability of
the military is therefore important in view of the link
between this and wider aspects of civil-military relationships. This is particularly so where the form of the
military structure is that of the all-volunteer force.
Here, the military already exhibits evidence of its partial
divorce from the parent society, notably in the sense that
only a limited number of the adult working population are
serving in the armed forces. As has been noted this
number in the United Kingdom today is in the region of 1.5%.
Similarly, an ever-decreasing proportion of the adult
working population in the absence of conscription has had
any experience of military life whatsoever. Thus in
Britain in the last decade, no more than 830,000 men and
women, or some 3% to 4% of the working population, have
had any direct experience of military life in the all-
volunteer army. A larger number can look back with varying degrees of affection to the conscript armed forces,
but few males under thirty-five years of age have in fact
served in the military organization. A distance between

the armed forces and the parent society is thus already
most marked in the United Kingdom and the critical issue
is whether the effect of this upon civil-military relationships is further affected by the degree of internal
stability within that force.

An initial aspect of this issue of stability which
can be examined is the actual extent of variations in the
size of the annual intake into the all-volunteer force.
In the ten years from 1965 to 1974, the British military,
although its maximum size never exceeded 425,400, received
a total civilian intake of 438,900 men and women of whom
259,000 were recruited into the army. Although the total
intake was less than twice the yearly intake of between
200,000 and 250,000 in the peak years of conscription, the
recurring annual intake to the all-volunteer force shows
considerable variation between the minimum level of 8.3%
of the force strength in 1968 to a maximum of 15% in 1971
to 1972. In some years, the total intake to a particular
part of the armed forces has been notably high, as in 1971
to 1972 when the inflow into the Army amounted to 19.8% of
its total strength.

In examining more closely the size of the annual intake from civilian life into the armed forces, it can be
seen that since 1965 recruitment into the all-volunteer
force has varied from a high of 55,000 in 1971 to 1972 to
a low of 32,400 during the years from 1973 to 1974. For
the greater part of this period, however, the annual intake
has tended to be closer to 45,000, a figure which can be
broadly compared with intakes of 44,400 in 1935 and 48,400
in 1936. Indeed, only in the three years of 1937, 1938
and, 1971-72 did this intake into the all-volunteer force
exceed 50,000 and only in the two years of 1968 and 1973-
74 was it less than 40,000. This suggests a degree of
limited structural stability which contrasts very markedly
with the early years of mobilization into the wartime mass
army when the intake increased dramatically from 426,000
in 1939 to a peak of 1,565,600 in 1940, before falling
away to less than 400,000 in 1944. Even so, the pattern of
recruitment to the all-volunteer army is one of limited
stability only, for the figures from 1970 to 1974 alone
show that if the earlier year is taken as the base year,
then the five-year pattern of recruitment is 100; 118; 99;
69; and 97. If the decade from 1965 onwards is examined
with that year as the base, then the pattern is very
similar: 100; 98; 91; 72; 91; 101; 120; 100; 70; and 98.

It is interesting to compare this pattern with the
five-year period before and after the announcement of the
ending of conscription in 1957. If 1952 is taken as the
base year, then the prior period shows a steady decline in
the number of those recruited: 100; 90; 83; 81; and 85.

In the later period, the comparable figures show a marked
decrease in the intake from civil life: 57; 54; 43; 38;
and 21. Variations here are clearly more marked overall
than in the decade after 1965, but it would be wrong to
conclude that the all-volunteer army is more stable in
terms of its recruitment than the conscript army, for the
figures for the period 1952-57 indicate that before the
White Paper decision of 1957, there was less variation
than in either the period 1970-74 or the period 1965-74.

These variations raise a number of issues which are
outside the considerations of this study, such as the
success of recruiting strategies or indeed the nature of
the ultimate parameters within which these fluctuations
are constrained. One question which can be considered
further, however, is whether the long-term trend in armed
forces is for these variations to become less acute. A
review of the annual intake into the British armed forces
from 1935 onwards suggests that there have been years of
limited stability interrupted by specific periods of
instability which have followed major changes in defence
policy. Thus, the years of 1935 and 1936 were years of
limited stability with a 10% variation in the size of the
intake, although after the decision to rearm, this was
followed by a period of instability. In the postwar era,
the intake from 1948 onwards showed a maximum variation of
20% from the 1952 base-year figure until the decision
taken in 1957 to end conscription. Since the last conscript left the armed forces in 1963, the intake, however,
has shown signs of a greater instability with variations of
up to 30% from the 1965 base. This implies that these variations are increasing rather than decreasing, the result,
perhaps, of what many commentators have seen as the effect
of economic constraints on manpower planning.

A review of variations in the numbers of newcomers
recruited from civil life can only be a partial comment,
however, on the question of the stability of the force
structure. It does not take into account, for example,
variations in the retention rate, so that, in ignoring the
issue of the outflow from armed forces, it only partly
considers the long-term trends within armed forces toward
a stable or unstable force structure. An alternative way
of examining those long-term trends is to consider again
the absolute size of the armed forces and note variations
at an annual rate. A subsidiary issue to which this draws
attention is whether frequent fluctuations in size impose
a considerable strain on military training programs. This
strain has been particularly noticeable as the all-volunteer
force has been confronted by an increasingly complex military technology which necessitates longer, more sustained,
and more costly training. The need to satisfy a consistent
requirement for technicians and tradesmen is difficult to

achieve in a situation of instability where there is a
marked inflow and outflow of personnel. It is particularly
difficult when there is no guarantee that an adequate
supply of suitably qualified recruits will be forthcoming
or that experienced and trained servicemen will be retained.

    A question which arises, therefore, is whether these
fluctuations have declined over time, a question which has
particular relevance in the growing complexity of military
technology. In this context it is possible to compare
directly intermittent fluctuations in each of the three
periods when the armed forces in the years since 1900 have
been organized on a volunteer basis. A preliminary observation is that there was very little force instability in
the period before the First World War. In contrast, the
all-volunteer military in the last of the three selected
periods, that is from 1963 to 1974, shows a marked degree
of fluctuation after an initial period of relative stability. What this does suggest is that the "standard" size
of the British all-volunteer force, that is, a stable
organization of the kind which in 1908 to 1913 totalled
374,000 with an annual variation of less than 1%, has
not been achieved. It also implies that external variables
in the post-1963 period have had, and are having, a considerable effect on the stability of the force structure.

    A tentative conclusion which can be put forward at
this juncture is that the British government in creating
and maintaining an all-volunteer force structure has
encountered a number of complex and fundamental problems.
The initial difficulty, as has been seen, revolves around
the critical question of the size of this structure. An
examination of historical trends in the United Kingdom
since 1900 suggests that in the three areas of the absolute size of this force, the employment of a significant
proportion of the adult working population, and the military participation ratio, there is ample evidence of a
quantitative decline in each area. This evidence is
indicative of the trend over time toward a fall in the
size of the all-volunteer force structure; it does not,
however, provide a commentary on the economic factors,
which are both a cause and effect of changes in the force
structure. To examine these further, the area of enquiry
has to be expanded and it is such an expansion which is
the focus of interest in the next section of this paper.

    In looking more closely at these factors, it has to
be stressed that the British experience with an all-
volunteer force is heavily dependent on a specific
cultural milieu. Historical traditions, social norms,
economic variables, and national attitudes are only some
of the pressures which have affected the all-volunteer

force structure in the United Kingdom. Nevertheless, the
impact of these economic factors is important in terms of
cross-cultural comparative analysis, for, despite their
specific limitations, they are also more widely indicative
of the pressures which are encountered by the all-volunteer
force in the industrialized societies of Western democracy.

The Economic Costs

An initial starting point for examining more critically
these economic factors is to consider changes in the
proportion of the Gross National Product which is devoted
to defense. In this respect, available data have to be
treated with caution, for there are innumerable problems in
reconciling variations among different data sources.
Equally, national governments have adopted varying methods
of data classification in relating defense spending to the
GNP. Certain trends over time, however, can be noted and
these are illustrated in Table 7, which is based on
standardized NATO data categories.

From this data, it can be seen that following the
phasing out of conscription, the proportion of the Gross
National Product allocated to defence expenditure in the
United Kingdom has, with the exception of 1972, declined
consistently. This reflects the specific political decision to reduce a defence commitment which in the 1950s
generated an expenditure averaging 10% of the Gross
National Product and which involved 7% of the working
population either in the armed services or in supporting
functions.[5] It has to be noted, however, that a similar
move characterizes the defence expenditure of most of the
member countries of NATO, other than Greece, Portugal, and
the United States. This suggests that we are witnessing a
common trend in all Western industrialized societies
toward the reallocation of economic resources that were
formerly assigned to defence expenditure, and that this
trend is most noticeable in those countries where the GNP
has increased during the decade under consideration. In
Great Britain, where this growth rate has been less marked,
it is, however, significant that it was found impossible to
bring the proportion of the GNP spent on defence into line
with the Western European average of 4.4% (1973). This
contrasts very markedly with the allocation of resources to
the maintenance of an all-volunteer force in the United
Kingdom in the preconscription period when before 1914
some 3% of the GNP was defence expenditure in the earlier
year, 3.83% in 1938 and 4.7% in 1939. It is thus note-
worthy that to maintain an all-volunteer force in being
under current conditions, the United Kingdom is obliged to

[5]Defence: Outline of Future Policy.

Table 7. Defence expenditure of NATO countries, 1964-73 as a percentage of GNP at factor cost, based on current prices

	1964	1965	1966	1967	1968	1969	1970	1971	1972	1973
Belgium	3.8	3.5	3.5	3.5	3.5	3.3	3.3	3.2	3.2	3.1
Canada	4.2	3.5	3.3	3.4	3.1	2.8	2.8	2.7	2.5	2.3
Denmark	3.2	3.2	3.1	3.1	3.3	2.9	2.8	2.9	2.8	2.5
France	6.3	6.1	5.9	5.9	5.5	5.0	4.6	4.4	4.2	4.2
Federal Republic of Germany	5.9	5.5	5.3	5.6	4.7	4.7	4.3	4.5	4.8	4.7
Greece	4.1	4.0	4.2	5.1	5.6	5.8	5.8	5.6	5.3	4.8
Italy	3.7	3.7	3.8	3.5	3.3	3.0	3.0	3.3	3.5	3.4
Luxembourg	1.6	1.5	1.5	1.3	1.0	1.0	0.9	0.9	1.0	1.0
Netherlands	4.7	4.3	4.1	4.3	4.0	3.9	3.8	3.8	3.8	3.7
Norway	3.9	4.2	4.0	3.9	4.0	4.0	4.0	3.9	3.7	3.7
Portugal	7.3	6.8	6.9	8.0	8.2	7.6	7.9	8.3	8.4	7.5
Turkey	5.6	5.8	5.4	5.5	5.2	5.2	5.2	5.4	5.0	4.5
United Kingdom	6.8	6.6	6.5	6.5	6.3	5.8	5.7	5.8	6.2	5.6
United States	8.8	8.2	9.1	10.2	10.1	9.5	8.7	7.8	7.3	6.8

Source: NATO document ISM (73) 7, dated July 16, 1973.

spend a disproportionately high percentage of the GNP on
defence, a proportion that is greater than the European
average and is in excess of that spent on the all-
volunteer force in the past.

In examining this trend further, it can be argued
that this is largely attributable to the higher costs of
supporting the all-volunteer force. This suggestion is
echoed in the report of the West German Force Structure
Commission where it was projected that about 6.2% of the
1973 GNP would have had to be spent on a professional
Bundeswehr in comparison with the 4.7% spent on a conscript army with a volunteer content of just under 53%.[6]
Whilst this projection seemingly supports the contention
that "the luxury of a volunteer force may be beyond the
fiscal means of a social welfare state,"[7] a distinction
has to be drawn between the economic and budgetary implications of this initial conclusion. The economic
consequences of utilizing conscription as a means of
raising military manpower have been examined in a number
of studies.[8] The conclusion generally reached is that
conscription is a tax which is exacted and paid in
unremunerated labour.[9] If correct labour prices were
charged and military operations moved to a more capital-
intensive mix, then the same level of military output,
it is argued, could be achieved, with the civil sector
actually increasing output by using the labour released

[6]Report of the Force Structure Commission of 17 Novem-
ber 1972, quoted in Federal Ministry of Defence, White
Paper 1973-74 (Bonn: Government Printing Office, 1974)
p. 81.
    [7]Thomas A. Fabyanic, "Manpower Trends in the British
All-Volunteer Force," Armed Forces and Society, 2, no. 4,
(Summer 1976), 570.
    [8]See for example, Paul Cockle, "Military and Civil
Relations: The Economic Nexus," Paper presented to a
Conference on the French and British Military System,
Institute d'Etudes Politiques de Toulouse, September 1976;
W. Y. Oi, "The Economic Cost of the Draft," American
Economic Review, (May 1967); S. H. Altman and A. E. Fechter,
"The Supply of Military Personnel in the Absence of the
Draft," American Economic Review (May 1967); W. L. Hansen
and B. A. Weisbrod, "Economics of the Military Draft,"
Quarterly Journal of Economics (August 1967); A. C. Fisher,
"The Cost of the Draft and the Cost of Ending the Draft,"
American Economic Review (June 1969); Gavin Kennedy, The
Economics of Defence (London: Faber and Faber, 1975).
    [9]The Military Balance 1975-76 (London: IISS, 1975),
p. 103.

from the military sector.[10] Cockle summarizes the point:
"The cost to society of conscription is this foregone
output. Artificially low wages results in an inefficient
allocation of resources between military and civil com-
munities and far from being cheap is quite expensive."[11]
Implicit in this argument, however, are certain assumptions
about economic rationality which do not appear to have been
an acceptable determinant of British manpower planning
after 1957. In the first place, the shift to a capital-
intensive system--which in the 1957 White Paper was planned
to be a concomitant of the abolition of conscription--has
not been implemented to the extent that was envisaged.
There are many reasons for this. In part the failure was
a reflection of the determination to reduce overall defence
expenditure even though the result was that the budget was
not large enough to permit a high level of capital investment. This was exacerbated by a period of excessive
inflation and also by the disproportionate increase in
that part of the defence budget allocated to personnel
costs. Secondly, many facets of the role of Britain's
armed forces still demand a labour-intensive manpower
system. Correlli Barnett succinctly summarizes some of
the reasons for this in a review of British strategy after
1957. "Britain was left therefore with an imperial army
in a European role. Yet British history and recent history
in particular, made plain that Britain needed for this role
not a small, all-regular force, but a large field army
formed by the mobilizable trained manpower of the nation."[12] To these reasons can be added the effects of having to utilize troops in aid of the civil power, a task
which equally demands the employment of large bodies of
men rather than the use of sophisticated labour-saving
equipment. Thirdly, the rational operation of a price and
wage mechanism has been, and is, constrained by bureaucratic rules which are based on the principles of parity of
income for equivalent rank levels within the military
organization and the provision of a career structure. Consequently, increases in service pay, which were introduced
in 1968 due to evidence of a serious manpower shortage in
the services and failure to meet recruiting targets[13]and
which were again implemented in 1969 to overcome the

[10]Kennedy, The Economics of Defence, pp. 96-102.
[11]Cockle, "Military and Civil Relations: The Economic
Nexus," p. 5.
[12]Correlli Barnett, Britain and Her Army, (London:
Allen Lane, The Penguin Press, 1970), p. 493.
[13]National Board for Prices and Incomes, Report No.
70, Standing Reference on the Pay of the Armed Forces,
First Report, May 1968 /Cmnd. 3651/ (London: HMSO, 1969).

existing serious manpower shortage,[14] had a universal
applicability which increased total personnel costs. The
alternative of simply increasing pay to attract and retain personnel in areas of specific shortage, that is, to
adopt a differential system of reward based on the
rationality of supply and demand, was unacceptable even
though the adopted solution was an inevitable cause of
increased costs. As a result, the move away from conscription to an all-volunteer force has been consistently
associated with the spending of a disproportionate percentage of GNP on defence, for the savings which were envisaged
in theory by the maximization of available resources have
not materialized in practice.

        The overall result of these constraints on the
exercise of economic rationality is that manpower planning
has continued to be determined by budgetary and not economic cost consideration. This is very understandable. The
exercise of economic rationality in manpower planning is
affected by a large number of constraints. An awareness
of the social costs of postulated changes in the force
structure is, for example, one factor which may inhibit
the exercise of a rational preference. To this may be
added the constraining effects of the wish to perpetuate
traditional aspects of the military culture, the reluctance to abandon completely traditional military roles,
the insistence on high standards of performance which may
not be justified in terms of pure economic costs, and so
on. Most importantly, economic rationality has to be
subordinated to the exercise of political preferences.
As Greenwood has pointed out, "Species of budgetary
'constraints' have been _instrumental_ in bringing about
the reshaping of the defence effort in the postwar period.
But they have not been 'decisive'--in a strict, imperative sense. For budgetary constraints are not some _deus
ex machina_. They are produced by 'the machine' itself,
the bureaucratic process, as expressions of central
public choice."[15] Consequently, attempts to limit the proportion of the GNP spent on defence have in this field
resulted in repeated reductions to the proposed size of
the all-volunteer force and to a revision of the envisaged
role of the military in the postconscription period.

        Yet it can still be concluded that within the finite
resources of the modern democratic state, the maintenance

[14] NBPI, _Standing Reference on the Pay of the Armed
Forces, Second Report_, June 1969 /Cmnd. 4079/ (London:
HMSO, 1969).
        [15] David Greenwood, "Constraints and Choices in the
Transformation of Britain's Defence Effort since 1945,"
British Journal of International Studies 2 (1976), 24.

of the all-volunteer force imposes an unacceptable burden
on national resources even after these amendments to the
size and role of the force. For the United Kingdom it
can be argued that the share of the GNP which can be allocated to defence spending cannot exceed the 1976 NATO
average of 3.9%. This would mean a reduction from the
present level of 4.9%. The available options for cutting
expenditure, however, are relatively limited. The initial
constraint has been clearly spelt out by Geraghty: "The
fallacy in deriving defence requirements from GNP calculations is, of course, that while our GNP is less than
most others in NATO, our defence needs are not. Arguably,
they are greater."[16]

A second limiting factor is that even if force levels
can be marginally reduced, a reduction in the share of GNP
allocated to defence is not inevitable. This conclusion
is evidenced by the British experience during the last
decade. Personnel costs within the allocated budget have
consistently continued to rise even though the size of the
force has diminished. Thus total personnel costs have
increased from 39.4% of the defence budget in 1966-67 to
46.2% in 1975-76, although force levels dropped from
417,400 in the earlier year to an estimated 333,900 on
April 1, 1976.[17] The trends which have taken place during
this period are shown in Table 8. Again, the presented
data have to be treated with caution, and it is possible
that the specified percentage of the budget ascribed to
personnel costs is an underestimate of the true position.
Fabyanic discusses this further in reviewing current
British personnel costs, for since official figures do
not include personnel-related costs such as personnel
movements, clothing, and certain food costs, he estimates
that a further 10% to 12% can be added to the government's
figures.[18] It also has to be noted that the personnel
costs given in Table 8 relate to active-duty personnel
only; that is, they exclude the cost of pensions, even
though these are a significant item of expenditure in an
all-volunteer force.

From this table it can be seen that there is a clear
trend towards personnel costs absorbing an increasing
share of the total defence budget. A question for further
discussion, however, is the extent to which this trend is
repeated in those nation-states which continue to rely on

[16]Tony Geraghty, "How 'Pathetic' are Our Forces?'
[17]Statement on the Defence Estimates 1968 /Cmnd. 3540/
(London: HMSO, 1968), and Statement on the Defence Estimates 1975 /Cmnd. 5976/ (London: HMSO, 1975).
[18]Fabyanic, "Manpower Trends," n. 50, p. 572.

Table 8. Expenditure on military personnel in the United Kingdom,
1966-75

Year	Defence[a] expenditure	Personnel[a] costs	%	Total[b] strength
1966	2,172.11	821.75	37.83	419.4
1967	2,205.12	867.33	39.31	417.4
1968	2,271.19	939.59	41.36	401.8
1969	2,265.85	960.33	42.38	383.0
1970	2,279.98	1,041.52	45.68	373.0
1971	2,343.06	1,228.93	52.44	368.0
1972	2,455.72	1,271.20	51.76	371.4
1973	2,838.90	1,413.00	40.60	367.0
1974	3,469.43	1,492.88	43.02	349.3
1975	4,314.60	1,868.70	43.31	340.1

Source: Statements on Defence Estimates, 1966-75, and Supply
Estimates, Ministry of Defence.

[a] In thousands of pounds.
[b] In thousands.

conscription as a means of manpower recruitment. In West
Germany, official figures suggest that the percentage of
the defence budget spent on personnel costs, excluding the
cost of pensions, was 44% in 1975 and 42.5% in 1976. This,
however, is not based on total defence expenditure. Thus
in 1975, when the latter totalled DM 47.6 thousand million,
DM 13.7 thousand million were attributed to expenditure on
personnel, that is, 28.78%. By way of comparison, DM 10.5
thousand million or 22.1% of total defence expenditure
was allocated to the costs of the Parliamentary Commission
for the Armed Forces, NATO civil budget, military aid,
expenditure on behalf of allied forces stationed in Germany, and expenditure on Berlin.[19] In a comparative study
of the situation in France and the United Kingdom, Kelleher
et al. have shown that the percentage of expenditure on
personnel in France has from 1966 to 1975 fluctuated
between a low of 33.72% in 1968 and a high of 38.64% in
1971.[20] The trend here is toward a mean of 36%, which is a

[19] Federal Ministry of Defence White Paper,1975-76,
pp. 210-15.
[20] Catherine M. Kelleher, Richard D. Erchenberg, and
Christopher D. Carr, "The Post War Cost of Defence in
Britain and France: Guns and Butter Revisited," Paper
presented at the Institut d'Etudes Politiques de Toulouse,
September, 1976.

proportion considerably lower than that spent in the United
Kingdom. The suggestion that the higher cost is a reflection of reliance on a volunteer-force is confirmed by the
American situation, where it has been estimated that at
least 52% of the current defence budget is absorbed by these
personnel costs.

A closer look at the data relating to expenditure on
personnel costs within the United Kingdom confirms that the
real level of expenditure for defence has not declined but
has in fact increased.[21] What has declined, as Kelleher
et al. have stressed, is the relative share of the GNP and,
indeed, of central government expenditure devoted to defence.
In Table 9, which is based on original calculations by
Kelleher and her colleagues, expenditure on personnel is
shown in constant (1970) US Dollars, as is the cost per head
of defence manpower. By way of comparison, the constant
cost per head of defence manpower in France is shown as a
percentage of the British figures.

The Table shows clearly the contrast in trends in the
respective cases of an all-volunteer force and a conscript
army. For the former, it is clear that while manpower
strengths have declined, the real level of expenditure for
personnel costs has increased dramatically. Thus while the
overall size of the armed forces has declined from 419,400,
a figure already well below the peak conscription size of
879,400 in 1952, to 340,100, expenditure on personnel,
expressed in constant dollars against a basic year of 1970
(100), has risen from 94.26 to 129.45. The magnitude of
this increase is more clearly seen when the expenditure is
considered in terms of the cost per head, for, as Table 9
shows, this has steadily risen throughout the period from
224.74 to 380.62. In contrast, the French have been able
to maintain in being a force of relatively constant size
for which personnel costs have remained at a more stable
figure. Because these total costs have fluctuated between
93.27 and 114.35 (1970 as the base year of 100) while the
force has remained constant in size, costs per head expressed in constant US dollars have only risen from 166.55
to 197.49 over the decade. As a percentage of the United
Kingdom costs per head, as Table 9 illustrates, the French
costs have declined to a point where they are one half of
the British costs.

The further significance for the all-volunteer force
of these trends in the United Kingdom can be illustrated by
considering the relationship of upward and downward movements in the three areas of expenditure on personnel,
manpower strength, and expenditure per head. If 1970 is

[21]Ibid., p. 2.

Table 9. Expenditure on personnel, manpower strengths, and cost per head of defence manpower, 1966-75

	United Kingdom[a]			France	
Year	Expenditure on personnel	Defence manpower (N in thousands)	Costs per head[b]	Defence manpower (N in thousands)	Cost per head as a % of U.K. costs
1966	94.26	419.4	224.74	560	74.10
1967	96.83	417.4	231.98	560	73.36
1968	100.68	401.8	250.57	565	65.18
1969	97.67	383.0	255.01	563	70.00
1970	100.00	373.0	268.09	566	65.89
1971	113.13	368.0	307.41	566	60.21
1972	113.32	371.4	305.11	559	64.17
1973	118.59	367.0	323.13	574	61.19
1974	112.86	349.3	323.10	573	55.51
1975	129.45	340.1	380.62	579	51.88

Sources: Exchange rate figure and common price under figures for the 1970 base are obtained from IMF International Financial Statistics (December, 1974 and August 1976); U.K. manpower strength is obtained from Statement on the Defence Estimates; manpower strength for France is obtained from The Military Balance, 1966-75 (London IISS). The figures include the strength of the Gendarmerie.

[a] Base year = 100.

[b] Expenditure in constant (1970) U.S. dollars.

taken as a base year for both expenditure and manpower,
the relationship is as given in Table 10.

Table 10. Relationship between manpower strength and personnel
costs, United Kingdom, 1966-75

Year	Expenditure on personnel	Manpower strength	Cost per head[a]
1966	94.26	112.44	83.82
1967	96.83	111.90	86.53
1968	100.68	107.71	93.46
1969	97.67	102.68	95.12
1970	100.00	100.00	100.00
1971	113.13	98.66	114.66
1972	113.32	99.57	113.80
1973	118.59	98.39	120.53
1974	112.86	93.64	120.51
1975	129.45	91.18	141.97

Note: Base year 1970 = 100.

[a]Expenditure in constant US dollars.

Real costs per head have increased very significantly
since the base year of 1970, and although a certain degree
of stability has been achieved from time to time, as for
example in 1973 and 1974, increases in pay had a noticeable
effect on manpower costs. It is significant that while
manpower strength since 1970 has declined by some 9%,
expenditure on personnel has increased by 29% in real
terms. One interesting question which arises is whether
the continuation of this trend produces by 1980 a situation
where, all other things being equal, manpower declines to
a total strength of 300,000, that is, to a level some 20%
below the 1970 figure, while expenditure on personnel
rises to a level that is at least 60% to 70% greater than
in 1970. If this were to happen, costs per head would at
constant prices be more than double those of 1970. Even
if this situation were not to arise, the current trends
affecting the all-volunteer force in the United Kingdom
can be seen to contrast very sharply with French experience. In France, the manpower strength has shown much
less variation, so that if 1970 is taken as the base year
(100), the fluctuation is between 98.93 in 1966-67 and
102.29 in 1975, the actual increase since 1970 contrasting
very markedly with the British experience. Similarly,
when 1970 is taken as the base year (100) for the French

costs per head of expenditure on personnel, the figures
for 1966 in constant dollars equate to 94.27 and to 111.78
in 1975. The increased expenditure in France between 1970
and 1975 in constant figures is thus significantly less
than in the United Kingdom and it has to be inferred that
much of this increase can be attributed to the additional
pay increases awarded in the all-volunteer force. The
conclusion which has to be drawn from this comparison is
that while the economic costs of conscription may be high,
budgetary data emphasize that an inexorable effect of the
transition to the all-volunteer force is a reduction in
total manpower and a concomitant increase in total personnel costs and real costs per head. This supports the
contention that in an industrialized democracy, with its
finite resources, the luxury of an all-volunteer force
imposes a severe fiscal burden upon the parent society.

From this conclusion, it can be argued that in the
case of the United Kingdom the need to reduce defence
expenditure to the NATO average necessitates further
reductions in the force size. These cuts to achieve this
aim would have to total some 35,000 service personnel,
that is, to the suggested force level of 300,000, and
20,000 civil servants, but a further issue of concern is
whether costs per head even after such force reductions
would still continue to rise and subsequently necessitate
further force reductions. The two critical questions in
this context are why these personnel costs should rise in
the first place and whether the rises are an inevitable
concomitant of the pay policy which has been adopted for
the all-volunteer force.

In answering these questions, rises in costs are
frequently attributed to the need to compete in the open
labour market for service manpower. This is a popular
explanation, particularly amongst servicemen themselves,
for increased personnel costs can be rationalized as the
result of external market factors rather than the effect
of a conscious choice of resource allocation.

It is difficult to assess, however, how far increases
in pay which largely account for increased personnel costs,
can be directly related to attempts to counteract shortfalls in recruitment and retention rates within the
framework of lowered force levels. In 1969 and 1974, percentage increases in pay were specifically requested by
the Ministry of Defence because of existing manpower
shortages and continued recruitment shortfalls. At the
same time, the introduction of a "military salary" in
accordance with the recommendations of the Second Report
of the National Board for Prices and Income (1969) brought
into being the notion of comparability between earnings

in the civilian sector and in the armed forces.[22] Subsequently, pay increases have been governed by the
findings of an independent civilian committee, the Review
Body on Armed Forces Pay, which reexamines both pay and
charges in the light of the principles laid down by the
National Board for Prices and Incomes. Some of the economic effects of this have been summarized by Cockle:
"The review mechanism reinforces the organic linking of
military and civil economic experiences, by stimulating
the direct effects of government economic and social
policies within the military sector--military wages have
a sound economic base inasmuch as wage costs are related
to alternative civil earnings and work preferences."[23]

    In practical terms this has meant that the armed
forces have been awarded pay increases of 7% in August
1971, 10% to 11% in 1972, and 6.5% in 1973. In 1974,
when the services asked for a 20% increase in pay and other
associated benefits, actual raises were less than requested
but in 1975 increases averaged 29.5%. Whether these increases could be justified in terms of movements in the
civilian labour market or because of the effects of inflation upon wage rates are two important questions. The
alternative and more pertinent issue in the context of
this chapter continues to be whether the need to compete
in a labour market or the wish to establish comparability
can be said to impose unacceptable demands upon budget
allocation and thus detract from other defence programs
such as capital expenditure.

    The fundamental problem which has to be faced here
is that a designed pay policy has to meet a number of competing and often conflicting objectives. Firstly, it has
to be a means of competing in an open labour market by
offering a rate of remuneration which is comparable with,
if not superior to, that offered by the civil sector. In
this context the decision taken in the United Kingdom in
1969 to introduce a "military salary" based on the principle of pay comparability with the civil sector has had
far-reaching economic and social consequences. Although
the latter will be discussed as a later part of this
chapter, it has to be noted at this point that the initial
economic consequence of this decision has been the increased cost of paying new entrants into the military

_____
[22]NPBI, Standing Reference on the Pay of the Armed
Forces, Second Report, June 1969. The "military salary"
was actually implemented in 1970 in NPBI Report No. 142
Standing Reference on the Pay of the Armed Force, Third
Report /Cmnd. 4291/ (London: HMSO, 1970).
        [23]Cockle, "Military and Civil Relations: The Economic
Nexus," p. 14.

organization. For the conscript army, in contrast, the basis of reward need not be related to the amount that would entice the individual to choose a military career. "Therefore most conscripts receive less than that which would notionally attract them voluntarily."[24] In the United Kingdom, on the other hand, the pay system was designed scientifically to attract volunteers through a wage structure which would be amenable to comparison with civil earnings.

The question which has to be asked is whether these increases in pay have in fact attracted the desired number of recruits. Fabyanic in reviewing the trends since 1970 points out that structural improvements to military pay coincided with a period of higher unemployment and stable military force level projections by the government. Pay improvements were made therefore amidst the most favorable circumstances.[25] Even so, recruitment and retention rates have not been satisfactory. Table 11 illustrates the trends in this area since 1970.

Table 11. Force strength, recruitment, and unemployment

Fiscal year	Force[a] strength	Required male recruits	Numbers obtained	Percentage achieved	Percentage unemployment
1970-71	373.0	49,100	38,900	79.2	3.3
1971-72	368.0	46,300	46,493	100.0	3.7
1972-73	371.4	43,000	39,120	90.7	2.6
1973-74	367.0	43,000	25,800	60.0	2.5
1974-75	349.3	43,000	34,960	81.3	3.3

Sources: Fabyanic, Table 4; Statement on Defence Estimates 1971-75.

[a]In thousands.

What emerges from this table is that while improvements in pay have produced immediate increases in recruits, the correlation between unemployment and recruitment may be more indicative of long-term trends. What is also clear is that since 1970 the long-term requirement of recruiting some 43,000 male entrants annually has been met on one occasion only. This suggests that despite adjustments to the pay structure of the armed forces, the all volunteer force finds it difficult to compete in the open labour market simply by raising pay, although this is not to suggest that the Grigg Committee was correct in

[24]Cockle, p. 5.
[25]Fabyanic, "Manpower Trends," p. 567.

assuming that a given pay level did not constitute a deterrent to recruitment or that increases would not attract
recruits of the right quality.[26]

While increased personnel costs can be associated
with a recruitment policy, these increases are also derived from the other objectives of an adopted structure.
A pay policy has to be related to the problems associated
with the need to retain within the volunteer armed force
an adequate number of trained personnel. Here, an established optimum rate of turnover can further determine the
level of reward offered to recruits through giving one
rate of pay to the short-term recruit and another to those
prepared to serve for longer periods. In the British Army
this has produced three scales of pay for newly recruited
enlisted men: Scale A with a per diem rate for a private
of 4.68 pounds (1975); Scale B for those committed to
serve for more than six years but less than nine years of
4.98 pounds; and Scale C for those committed to serve for
nine years or more of 5.43 pounds. For officers, a newly
appointed second lieutenant receives 4.92 pounds per diem
on commissioning or 6.25 pounds if the officer is attending a Regular Career Course immediately after attending
the Standard Military Course at the Royal Military Academy
Sandhurst. For enlisted men, these differentials are retained throughout the pay structure and are further
expanded by relating pay to the various demands placed
upon the individual by the job specification. An evaluation of this when formulating the military salary
produced the conclusion that service employment could be
banded in groups so that for a corporal, for example, nine
different rates of pay are linked to a per diem rate varying from 7.48 pounds to 9.39 pounds (1975). For a staff
sergeant, twelve different rates give a spread of 8.56
pounds to 11.29 pounds per diem. The issue of the extent
to which this difference has produced earnings rates which
can be compared favorably with pay in the civil sector
invites subjective evaluations. A major difficulty which
remains unsolved is that although a highly sophisticated
system has been established to create and maintain the
principles of pay comparability, the system itself cannot
eradicate individual perceptions of imagined exploitation
or relative deprivation. The social issues which occur in
this area will be discussed in a later part of this chapter.
What is clear is that if pay scales are affected by the
principle that increased pay is necessary to implement a
retention policy, then inevitably this will increase total
personnel costs, if only because this produces "overlapping"
rates of reward in the sense that an individual on a long-
term engagement has to be paid more than those who are less
committed to the military career.

[26]The Grigg Report /Cmnd. 545/ (London: HMSO, 1958).

An alternative objective of an adopted scale which is
in many ways similar to the retention goals is that of
creating and rewarding a career structure. The genesis of
such a structure owes much to the Weberian notion that in
the rational-legal bureaucracy, staff should be promoted
on the basis of seniority or ability or on a combination
of these two factors. In the all-volunteer forces in the
United Kingdom, this concept of a career has particularly
governed the establishment of a pay structure for officers.
Whereas the review of enlisted men's pay focused on trade
skills as well as on rank and thereby produced overlapping
scales, it was decided that in the case of officers, rank
and skill were on the whole closely correlated.

Consequently, the adopted structure reflected two
assumptions. Firstly, that pay should rise on promotion
from one rank to another and, secondly, that experience in
a rank justified income growth within that rank over a
period of time, which varied according to the rank. Both
assumptions may seem to be self-evident, but there are
innumerable examples drawn from the system applied in
other armed forces and in the civilian sector to suggest
that the validity of these assumptions is not beyond question. When these assumptions, however, are implemented,
then it is axiomatic that costs will increase. In the
first place, the sum of total personnel costs will vary,
in direct relationship to the number of people who are
retained over time in a given rank level and who receive
successive increments. Whilst this may be offset by the
number of people leaving whose replacements are paid at a
lower point on the scale for the rank, the tendency for
costs to increase is accentuated by the goal of providing
a career structure for individuals. In providing this
career structure, it is inevitable that when individuals
receive virtually automatic promotion to a career grade,
the shape of the notional pyramid of the ideal-type
bureaucracy changes into a rhomboid as a larger number of
officers are retained at a middle rank level. In turn,
this "rank inflation" increases overall personnel costs.
The broad-based structure of the conscript army, in which
a large proportion of personnel receive minimum rates of
pay, is replaced in the all-volunteer army by a structure
in which a high proportion of servicemen have to be paid
at an enhanced level to satisfy their expectation of
achievement within a promised career.

A comparison of the trend toward career provision in
the all-volunteer force of today with provision in the
past emphasizes the complexity of the changes that have
taken place. Traditionally, in a less technological system,
officership was identified with a short-term commitment to
the military environment. The need for a large number of
officers in junior appointments was thus satisfied through

such devices as the short-service commission with its
very limited transfer to a permanent career. The notion
of a military career was at a discount. Conversely, enlisted men were engaged for long-term periods with a very
limited prospect of promotion that was comparable with the
system that was, and still is, a feature of civilian
employment. Now, the trend toward providing a career
structure for officers is balanced by the provision of
short-term enlistment for enlisted men. In both instances,
personnel costs inevitably increase. For officers, as has
been noted, the expectation of promotion produces on its
realization higher total expenditure. For enlisted men,
the official wish to move away from short-term engagements,
where the training overhead is not justified by subsequent
productivity, has resulted in the provision of additional
incentives to encourage a commitment to a longer-term
career. Both factors inevitably necessitate allocating
an increasing share of a limited budget to manpower costs.

Underlying this wish to provide a career structure
for servicemen is the explicit awareness of a further
objective of the adopted pay structure. In determining
the remuneration of both officers and enlisted men, a
common feature of the pay policy in the all-volunteer
force is the recognition of the goal of establishing a
socially just reward. Traditionally, this was achieved,
if indeed it was acknowledged, through the medium of paying allowances and through the provision within a custodial
management framework of ancillary benefits. Since these
were not necessarily paid at a fixed rate of universal
applicability, these allowances and benefits could be
readily amended in response to such factors as a shortfall
in recruiting, a wish to retain selected personnel, the
removal of grievances, and so on. In the United Kingdom,
however, the overriding principle that in order to facilitate comparison with the civil sector the wage structure
should be as simple as possible led to the consolidation
of a mass of allowances within the military salary. Once
the wage structure was established on the basis of comparability, then to meet the demand for social justice it was
necessary to weigh the relative advantages and disadvantages of the military way of life. In Britain the net
balance was considered to be adverse and a compensatory
payment defined as the "X-factor" was added to the basic
rate of pay. This was and is a straight percentage
increase on salaries--originally fixed at 5% for all
servicemen irrespective of rank but increased to 10% in
April 1974. This has thus produced a straightforward
increase in total personnel costs, partly mitigated by
reducing the percentage paid to senior officers on the
grounds that they are less affected by the postulated
disadvantages of military life.

When the notion of social justice is looked at more
critically, however, it can be argued that the adopted pay
structure created economic pressures which were an inevitable result of an unresolved and fundamental problem.
Comparability, on the one hand, presumes such a degree of
convergence between civilian and military skills that the
latter can be evaluated in terms of criteria applicable
to the former. The introduction of the "X-factor," on the
other hand, recognizes the degree of divergence between
the two sectors.

The interaction of these two presumptions created
and continues to create a number of problem areas in which
solutions aimed at producing a socially just reward for
military personnel cannot be strictly based on rational
economic criteria. This is not to suggest that the desir-
ability of achieving social justice is unwarranted. On
the contrary, it can be argued that the uniqueness of the
military task is such as to justify a rate of reward which
can reflect fully the particular needs of different members of an all-volunteer force. What is less satisfactory
in terms of its economic effects is the attempt made to
equate two systems of remuneration with widely divergent
base criteria and then add an element of reward which
recognizes the uniqueness of the military way of life.

One specific difficulty in this context is that, in
seeking to establish comparability, evaluation could not
fully recognize the extent to which a given rate of reward
in the civilian sector was not simply based on the relative
effect of the seven factors chosen as the basis for evaluating comparability[27] but was also a recognition of the

[27] The seven factors which were used to assess both
military and civil job sizes were: previous training and
experience; consequences of error; physical or mental
skill; responsibility for materials, equipment, and confi-
dential information; responsibility for supervision; mental
demand; and working environment. Each factor had a "maximum point range" within which points were awarded
according to the various demands placed upon the individual
by the job. Five factors had a maximum score of 100 points
or less; "responsibility for supervision" attracted a maximum of 160 points, while "previous training and experience"
merited 340 points as a maximum. To provide a coarse measure of comparison, each factor was broken down into a
number of levels of sub-ranges, four levels being the common categorization except for "previous training and
experience" which was given five levels and "working environment" which had three levels for "conditions" and a
further three for "incidental hazard." Upon analysis, it
was found that all military job sizes for enlisted men
could be grouped under three distinct headings, each with
a modest range of points.

presence of an "X-factor" within civilian employment.
Thus the comparison of civilian and service wage rates
for enlisted men was based on earnings, rather than on
basic pay excluding overtime, in 728 jobs in 321 civilian
organizations. What is uncertain is the extent to which
these civilian wage rates reflected not only the operations
of a prices-and-wages mechanism but also the recognition
with the civilian sector of such variables as lack of job
security, the monotony of work, unsocial hours, productivity, the provision of motivation, and so on. Some of
these had doubtful relevance in the military system or, if
they were relevant, were in the adopted structure doubly
recognized in the sense that the civilian "X-factor" was
supplemented by the military "X-factor." While it may be
socially just to recognize that the particular features of
military life justify a rate of pay that is at least comparable with that obtained by the civilian, it has to be
questioned whether this justifies the recognition of the
disadvantages of the employment situation in the two
sectors of society.

    The search for social justice in the field of remun-
eration in the all-volunteer army has thus had the effect
of increasing total personnel costs. This is perhaps
inevitable, for the notion of social justice is founded
on specific normative considerations which may or may not
reflect economic rationality. It is particularly significant in this context that pay and reward has been determined
not by a global figure representing the total amount that
can be "afforded," but by shifts in a civilian labour
market over which the military have no control. The consequent fiscal pressures are not unique to the all-
volunteer force. Other public service bureaucracies in
which the principle of pay comparability governs rates of
remuneration are equally affected by external movements
in civilian pay. In all these cases the wish to promote
social justice implies that if public service employees
are to be paid at pay levels commensurate with those
obtainable in civilian employment, then the total personnel cost has to be met. This also suggests that the
reference to what can be "afforded" in budgetary terms is
a denial of this justice and the exploitation of these
employees. The harsh reality of the situation, however,
is that there is a perpetual dilemma of rising demands
and insufficient resources which forces some amendment to
existing dispositions.[28] The declared preference for the
all-volunteer force in the United Kingdom was for the
furtherance of social justice even though this produced an
inevitable rise in total personnel costs.

    In the United Kingdom, therefore, a situation has
arisen in which there is clear evidence that personnel

[28]Greenwood, pp. 24-25.

costs absorb an increasing percentage of the defence
budget. This is taking place in a financial climate within which there is strong pressure for a reduction of
defence spending to a level at which the share of GNP allocated to this sector of public expenditure does not
exceed the NATO average. The British experience suggests,
however, that the pay policy which has been adopted for
this all-volunteer force inevitably increases personnel
costs as it strives to meet the needs of competing in a
civilian labour market for recruits, of retaining trained
personnel, of implementing a career structure and of providing a socially just reward for service personnel.
Consequently, if allocation constraints arise as the
government alters priorities in public spending and thereby reduces the share of GNP assigned to defence expenditure,
very little discretionary choice remains available. On the
one hand, capital expenditure can be cut back further,
although there must be a limit below which this expenditure
cannot fall without some damage to military effectiveness.
On the other, the size of the force can be further reduced
in an attempt to control the growth of total personnel
costs. But, as has been appointed out, per capita costs,
even after force reductions, have continued to rise, and
this does suggest that in exercising a discretionary choice,
options open to the British government are further limited
by the trend toward more expensive manpower costs.

The Social Implications

In evaluating the consequences of basing a force structure
on a system of all-volunteer recruitment rather than on
conscription, economic costs can be seen to be only one of
the major factors which shape policy choice. The social
implications of alterations in patterns of recruitment and
structure may be equally important determinants of resource
allocation. Indeed, from numerous examples, it can be
argued that an awareness of the social implications of
policy decisions is a greater constraint on the exercise of
political choice than strictly economic or budgetary considerations. In this context, the fundamental problem
faced by the decision-maker is that the transition from the
mass army to the all-volunteer force creates a number of
problems. Some of these are linked with the economic
issues which have been outlined previously; others, however,
are associated with more general social issues and it is
often the latter which create particular difficulties for
the military organization.

One of the most significant of these social issues
for contemporary British all-volunteer force is the professional dilemma which is faced by military personnel.
We are currently witnessing changes in the organizational
format of the military, alterations to the demographic

structure of the all-volunteer force, and major shifts in
the attitudes of personnel to the concept of military service. These, in combination, create strains in the military organization, and it is the social implications of
these strains which emphasize the complexity of the problems which affect the British all-volunteer force.

     In looking further at these strains and their effects,
it is evident that different aspects of military professionalism have been stressed at various times as the most
significant indicators of the military ethos. Given that
these various characteristics are all part of the total
concept of professionalism, the application of developmental analysis to a study of the British experience with
all-volunteer forces suggests that there are three separate phases in which each phase can be broadly associated
with the emphasis placed on specific aspects of professionalism. Thus in the first phase, a phase which can be
initially identified with the all-volunteer force before
1914, considerable emphasis was placed on the importance
of service to society. In this situation, the activities
which were undertaken were primarily legitimated in terms
of institutional and societal values; that is, individual
self-interest was seen to be less important than the
belief in public service for the public good was not only
to be found in the military organization. It was equally
a characteristic of other aspects of national and local
government. Consequently, even if individual members of
the military organization were looked upon with disfavor,
armed forces as a whole enjoyed high status and prestige
within the community.[29] To society at large, notions of
self-sacrifice and complete dedication to the concept of
service were fundamental components of the military ethos.
Paradoxically, however, the identification of military
service with the principle of service for the common good
rationalized the low rate of remuneration which was paid
to members of the armed forces. Consistently during the
nineteenth century the political and military elite
stressed that military service was an honour and that remuneration could not be expected to be comparable to what
might be expected in the economy of the country. This
low rate of reward, however, was partially offset by the
fringe benefits received by individuals. Officers, in
particular, enjoyed the privileges of what was to them a
way of life different and apart from the broader society,
and by and large, these privileges were accepted by the
civilian world as concomitants of the military calling.

     In the second phase of development, far greater
emphasis was laid on the identification of the military as

[29]See Gwyn Harries-Jenkins, The Army in Victorian
Society (London: Routlege & Kegan Paul, 1976).

a highly technical and specialist profession. The claims
of individuals to prestige, reward, and status were now
legitimated not only in terms of military service as a
calling but also in terms of expertise, commitment, and
responsibility of individuals. The characteristics of
professionalism in this context are succinctly summed up
in Morris Janowitz's classic study The Professional
Soldier.[30] Initially used as a characterization to describe
the ethos of career officers, the concept of professionalism with its emphasis on specialist skills was soon extended in its use to refer to servicemen of all ranks and
specialties.   Thus in its recruiting strategies the
British Army invited civilians to "Join the Professionals";
the Royal Air Force, not to be outdone, coined the term
"Aerocrats" to describe its professionals. All three
services stressed the extent to which there was job comparability with civilian professionals, particularly in the
field of management, and emphasized the degree to which
their education and training programs closely resembled
those of other civilian professional associations.

This interpretation of "profession" as it was applied
to and interpreted by the military did, however, have a
number of serious methodological and conceptual limitations
derived from the total fusion of profession and organization
in the military. It is beyond the scope of this discussion
to analyse these in depth, but it can be noted at this
point that the analysis of the dysfunctional consequences
of military professionalism was a constant theme of organizational analysis in the late 1960s and early 1970s.[31]
It was, however, ironic that much of this analysis, when
it was applied to the British all-volunteer force, took
place in a situation in which the third aspect of professionalism was receiving increasing emphasis. This is
not to suggest that such organizational analysis lacked
purpose or direction. It was simply that much of the
evaluation which took place did not take into account the
realities of a situation in which there was a marked shift
toward a third phase of organizational development.

Before this third phase of development is looked at
more closely, however, it has to be pointed out that the
three phases to which reference has been made are not
totally divorced one from the other. Contemporary

[30]Morris Janowitz, The Professional Soldier: A Social
and Political Portrait (Glencoe, Ill: Free Press, 1960).
    [31]For a further discussion of this point, see Gwyn
Harries-Jenkins, "The Dysfunctional Consequences of Mili-
tary Professionalization," in Morris Janowitz and Jacques
Van Doorn (eds), On Military Ideology (Rotterdam:
Rotterdam University Press, 1971).

professionalism in the all-volunteer force is an amalgam
of the characteristics which have been outlined; all that
has changed is that there has been a variation in the degree of stress laid on a particular aspect or aspects of
the total concept. Thus, the legacy of the identification
of the military with the notion of public service dies hard.
As in other professions, noticeably the caring professions,
considerable emphasis continues to be placed on the idea
of service to society. Moskos, in describing the military
as a "calling," draws attention to some of those features
of life in the armed forces which can be associated with
the notion of service: "One thinks of the extended tours
abroad; the fixed terms of enlistment; liability for 24-
hour service availability; frequent movements of self and
family; subjection to military discipline and law; and
inability to resign, strike or negotiate over working conditions."[32] In sum, the legacy of the concept of "public
service" remains an important component of the military
ethos and a significant determinant of military culture.

Equally, the stress which was placed on the importance of such features of the concept of military professionalism as expertise, commitment, and responsibility
continues to be most marked. The emphasis placed on
academic qualifications as initial determinants of military
suitability, the postulated code of conduct, a sophisticated
system of extended training and educational programs, sub-
ordination of the armed forces to civilian control and a
system of reward and promotion geared to peer evaluation--
are all indicative of the perpetuation of the stress placed
on these aspects of professionalism. In short, we are
witnessing the development and maintenance of the bureaucratic profession in a manner which is also to be found in
other occupational groups.

Yet in recent years there is marked evidence in the
British all-volunteer force of a move toward a third phase,
in which increasing emphasis is placed on the need for
public recognition of the uniqueness of the occupational
task. At one level this is reflected in the demand for a
rate of reward which is commensurate with the demands
placed upon service personnel. At another level, this move
towards a third phase of development is associated with the
dissatisfaction shown toward long-standing features of
military life. Two significant indicators of this third
phase have already been noted. Firstly, it has been seen
that significant pay increases have been given to the armed
forces in an attempt to make the rate of reward for the
military professional competitive with that of civilian

[32]Charles C. Moskos, Jr., "The All-Volunteer Military:
Calling, Profession or Occupation?" Parameters, Journal
of the US Army War College, Vol. VII, no. 1, 1977, p. 2-9.

appointments. Secondly, the British government introduced
the radical innovation of the military salary, thus making
civilian-military remuneration directly comparable. These
steps totally changed the traditional characteristics of
the military system of reward and considerably modified
the established perception of conditions of service for
the military professional. Their effect was to suggest
that the military as a profession merited a rate of reward commensurate with that of other professionals in
civilian employment.

These innovations, however, have had a number of dysfunctional consequences. The emphasis placed upon the
importance of extrinsic reward within the military organization is interpreted by many traditionalists within the
organization as a shift to a situation in which the military is legitimated in terms of the marketplace. The
demand for public recognition of the uniqueness of the
military task is then interpreted as a demand for more
money. This implies to many traditionalists that individuals are primarily motivated by self-interest rather than
by the notion of professional obligations.

For other servicemen the emphasis placed upon the need
for public recognition of the uniqueness of the occupational
task has had a second dysfunctional consequence. This can
be summarized as the change in primary motivation amongst
officers and other ranks (enlisted men). Here, the emphasis consistently placed on pay comparability and on the
high degree of convergence between military and civilian
specialities, has encouraged the emergence of a sense of
relative deprivation. Individuals, rather than looking
upon the military task as a unique exercise of specialist
skills in which job satisfaction is derived from task
performance, have tended to evaluate their function against
the conditions of employment enjoyed by their perceived
civilian counterparts. Other servicemen experience a
sense of frustration and dissatisfaction when they conclude that society is not prepared to give them the degree
of public recognition which is afforded to other professional groups. These perceptions, in turn, generate
interest in the potential advantages to be gained from the
establishment of some form of group representation among
servicemen. In its extreme form, this group representation
is identified with the creation of a trade union as a common means of interest articulation. Such an organization,
it is argued, could ensure that the armed forces received
a rate of reward commensurate with that paid to civilians
and could exert pressure for increased public recognition
of the uniqueness of the military task.

An alternative and important indicator of the trends
within this third phase of professional development is

the dissatisfaction shown with traditional aspects of
military life. This is essentially the conflict between
the expectations and the realities of life within the contemporary all-volunteer force. Part of the dissatisfaction
stems from the belief that conditions of service are not
those which a professional can legitimately expect to
receive. There has thus been criticism of the traditional
system of regimental care and responsibility in which the
commanding officer of a unit plays a paternalistic role in
exercising his overall responsibility for the welfare of
his men and their families. Similarly, there has been an
expressed dissatisfaction with a whole range of aspects of
military life from the standard of accommodation to the
effects of excessive turbulence. There is also evidence
of a resistance on the part of military wives to participate
in their customary social obligations, their argument reflecting their perception of the role of the professional
in an organization. All of this dissatisfaction is evidence of a general reaction to a situation in which the
professional in the all-volunteer force is seen to have
the status of a "second-class" citizen in comparison with
workers in civilian occupations.

One of the most significant characteristics of this
phase of organizational development is the change in
primary motivation among many servicemen. Initially, it
can be noted that there are a number of basic differences
between motivation in the traditional mass army and motivation in the all-volunteer force. In the former, conscription as a means of recruitment was closely identified
with the rights and obligations of citizenship,[33] and
although opposition to this system and to the associated
perception of individual motivation was, and is, not
unknown, the legacy of the relationship between conscription and citizenship continues to be most marked. Thus
in West Germany, the 1973-74 White Paper on Defence
stresses that through military service, conscripts develop
a sense of allegiance to "our democratic state." Former
conscripts, it is argued, display more mature democratic
awareness and possess a more positive disposition toward
"our political and social system."[34] This theme is also
followed in the 1974-75 White Paper in which reference is
made to the link between the obligations of citizenship and
military service: "The Federal Government adheres to the

[33]For an expansion of this point, see Morris Janowitz,
"Military Institutions and Citizenship in Western Soci-
eties," in G. Harries-Jenkins and J. Van Doorn (eds.),
The Military and the Problem of Legitimacy (Beverly Hills:
Sage Publications, 1976) pp. 77 ff.
    [34]Federal Ministry of Defence White Paper, 1973-74,
pp. 56-57.

principle of universal conscription. Compulsory military
service will continue to be a keystone of our defence
effort. It is an essential civic duty."[35] In neither the
United States nor the United Kingdom, however has the
identification of military service with the rights of
citizenship been accepted as a justification for the retention of the mass army. Moreover, it has never been
agreed that conscription can be seen as a hallmark of
citizenship because it is the means of implementing a
universal obligation to defend the democratic State.
Consequently, the hypothesis which Janowitz has advanced
in respect of the mass army seems to have little applicability to the all-volunteer force of the kind found in
the United Kingdom: "To the extent that mass armies defined
their recruits in terms of political and normative notions
of citizenship, military service functioned as an essential
and necessary contribution towards political institutions."[36]

     The normative-based ideology which underlies this
hypothesis, however, was a consistent feature of the culture of the traditional British all-volunteer force,
although it has to be noted that there have been considerable differences between the attitudes of officers and
enlisted men. For the former, their traditional commitment
to military service was closely linked with a wider social
obligation to carry out a wide range of public duties.[37]
These obligations in turn were a general reflection of an
upper-class sense of guardianship with its emphasis on
traditional shared values and a sense of personal obligation.   In short, this was characteristic of the model of
the military as a profession which demanded service to the
community at large.

     For enlisted men, however, the initial commitment to
military service was much more utilitarian in its origins.
The tendency to recruit individuals who were in some way
deprived and who were thus attracted to military service
by the rewards which it brought was balanced by the consistent recruitment of personnel who were motivated by an
awareness of the eventual rewards to be gained from a
military career. But for both these latter groups a

[35]Federal Ministry of Defence White Paper, 1974-75,
p. 161.
     [36]Janowitz, "Military Institutions and Citizenship,"
p. 79.
     [37]One of the characteristic features of the British
All-Volunteer Force in the period before 1914 was the way
in which officers readily transferred to senior appointments in both national and local government. The tradition of "service" in both political and administrative
posts has persisted although bureaucratization and professionalization have diminished the available opportunities.

structured, normative-based ideology was developed through
secondary socialization within the ship, regiment or
squadron. Hence the importance of the traditional regimental system of care and responsibility for the basic
utilitarian philosophy of the enlisted men was consistently
counteracted by the paternalistic ethos of the group leaders.

The dimensions of this concept of care and responsibility are admirably summed up in the Report of the Army
Welfare Inquiry Committee (The Spencer Report), which was
published in 1976: "This is a concept that it is rooted in
history; its origins lie in the days when soldiers were
recruited from the ranks of the poor and unemployed and
were then fed, clothed and nurtured by their regiment. This
inspired great affection for the regiment and led to the
idea of the regiment as a family."[38] The Spencer Report is
here referring to the Army, but the philosophy which is
implicit in the notion of care and responsibility is equally applicable to the other two services. It is normative-
based ethos very much associated with the person of the
commanding officer, for it presumes that he will relate
the operational needs of his unit to all the factors that
affect the persons serving in it, take the decisions that
are necessary to preserve the right balance between them,
and be accountable for the decisions which he has taken.[39]

In the contemporary British all-volunteer force
structure, the legacy amongst officers of this normative-
based ideology dies hard. Garnier, for example, in an
analysis of the relationship between technology, culture,
and officer recruitment notes that the traditional patterns
and criteria of recruitment still prevail even in a highly
technological army.[40] But the search for ideological conformity based on a normative commitment to the military is
now increasingly affected by the appearance of calculative
orientations amongst both aspiring and serving group members. This is particularly noticeable in contemporary
recruitment propaganda where the tone of advertisements has
changed considerably from the time when considerable emphasis was laid on the importance of "duty," "honour,"
"service," and so on. Thus a recent advertisement designed
to attract into the Army newly qualified entrants to university stressed that "Undergraduates can now get 900

[38]Ministry of Defence, Report of the Army Welfare
Inquiry Committee (The Spencer Report),(London: HMSO, 1976)
p. 22, para. 53.
    [39]Spencer Report, p. 22, para. 54.
    [40]Maurice Garnier, "Technology, Organizational Culture
and Recruitment in the British Military Academy," Journal
of Political and Military Sociology, 3, no. 2, (1975), 141-51.

pounds a year without signing their lives away." In the
text, which emphasized that selected students would receive financial help during their university course,
considerable emphasis was placed on the instrumental advantages which would be forthcoming: "The only difference
between you and other students will be the Army's financial
backing for your degree and the guarantee of an exacting
and rewarding job when you graduate." This selected example is illustrative of the extent to which the seen need
to compete in an open labour market has encouraged a
policy of recruitment deliberately designed to appeal to
the calculative orientations of potential officers. To
a certain extent, the excessive effects of such orientations are checked by the selection processes to which
Garnier draws attention. Nevertheless, these schemes of
recruitment are based on a realistic awareness of a
situation in which it can no longer be presumed that potential officers will be primarily attracted to the armed
forces through a sense of public duty.

Among these aspirants, therefore, there has been a
marked shift from a normative ideology, with its concomitant sense of moral commitment, to a utilitarian-
calculative perception of the advantages of military
service. Such a shift, moreover, may be particularly
pronounced amongst those candidates destined to serve in
units which are concerned with the secondary and tertiary
levels of military functions, that is, with the "nonfight-
ing" units. This point is made clear in Garnier's
analysis of the degree of ideological conformity to be
found amongst cadets at the Royal Military Academy at
Sandhurst. He concludes that the fighting regiments--
aristocratic (cavalry) and nonaristocratic (infantry)--
recruit higher proportions of high conformists oriented to
the maintenance of traditions than do the artillery and
engineers who, in turn, recruit more than do the technical
formations. Similarly, cadets destined for "elite"
regiments were, at the time of Garnier's survey, more
likely to support "conformist" ideas, many of which were
derived from the traditional normative ideology, than were
cadets who had been accepted by technical regiments.[41]

A similar hypothesis can be put forward in respect of
those potential officers who are recruited from amongst
university students. One conclusion which can be drawn,
therefore, is that even if the all-volunteer force can
continue to recruit an adequate number of normative-
orientated candidates for the fighting formations, the
maintenance of the remainder of the force structure may be
very dependent upon the recruitment of aspirants who
possess a more utilitarian-calculative orientation. This
dependency, moreover, tends to be increased if the force
seeks to widen the basis of recruitment in striving to

[41]Garnier, pp. 148-49.

ensure that the social composition of the force is truly
representative of society at large. Such a policy reflects an awareness of the thesis that the military in a
democratic state cannot continue to implement a system of
social selectivity. A disproportionate reliance on parti-
cularistic sources of recruitment may ensure that selected
officers are more likely to be included with the desired
normative orientations, but the dysfunctional consequences
of such a policy may outweigh the postulated advantage. A
highly unrepresentative officer corps, for example, weakens
the legitimacy of the all-volunteer force. Selective factors in recruitment are considered to increase the innate
conservatism of the group and this may produce more rigid
attitudes toward innovation and technological change. Yet
a move toward a wider base of officer recruitment raises
the issue of the extent to which in this force a fundamental problem is that of ensuring that aspirants with
initially different motivations will respond equally to a
socialization process which seeks to create a high degree
of ideological conformity. The search for conformity may
be severely affected if the utilitarian-calculative perceptions of some potential officers are indicative of
internalized attitudes which are highly resistant to change.

To a considerable extent, this change in the orientations of potential officers should not be unexpected. It
is a reflection of more general changes within the parent
society and, as such, is not only to be found within the
military organization. Yet it is also apparent that there
is a comparable shift of ideology among serving officers.
Numerous explanations can be put forward to account for
this. Werner, for example, in discussing the growth amongst
Belgian officers of a preference for group representation
within the armed forces, suggests, inter alia, that this
is attributable to a growing sense of relative deprivation
among officers as they become aware of increased economic
reward and improvement of conditions in the civilian sector.[42] Certainly, this sense of relative deprivation can
be noted amongst British officers in the contemporary all-
volunteer force. This was noted by the Spencer Committee
in 1974. Before noting that such dissatisfaction was less
marked amongst single soldiers, where there was a "greater
preoccupation with matters concerning their families and
girl-friends," the committee drew particular attention to
this sense of deprivation:

> Most of our visits and postal surveys were
> carried out before the announcement of the increased
> rates of pay on 16 May 1975. We therefore met with
> numerous complaints about the inadequacies of Army
> pay in a highly inflationary situation, and how the

[42]Victor Werner, "Syndicalism in the Belgian Armed
Forces," Armed Forces and Society, 2,no.4,(1976), 477-95.

military salary concept had not worked out in practice. We heard from a number of officers and men who expressed concern that because the Army lacked the service of a Trade Union, they had to accept whatever was offered to them.[43]

Since this date the sense of relative deprivation has increased. Many officers, even in 1974-75, believed that the contemporary situation was only temporary and that the political power would "look after" them. Those who forcibly expressed dissatisfaction were seen to be lacking in the "right" attitude, but events in 1977 gave rise to a more general sense of dissatisfaction. Two factors in particular generated an enhanced sense of discontent. Firstly, the government proposed further cuts in the Defence Budget, cuts which prompted a number of writers to conclude that morale in the services was seriously affected by a sense of continuing uncertainty.[44] Secondly, the pay proposals put forward by the Armed Forces Pay Review Body were seen to be ineffectual. This prompted one Defence Correspondent to write, "There is a chronic ill feeling about the 'Irishman's rise' last month which increased the Serviceman's pay with one hand and took it away with the other in extra charges for quarters and the good food the Services now enjoy."[45]

Apart from the sense of uncertainty which is created by the prospect of further cuts in the Defence Budget, the present sense of dissatisfaction derives from the introduction of the Military Salary in 1970. Until that time pay was adjusted biannually to all for increases in the cost of living, but food and accommodation for the single serviceman were free, and the married man was given a special allowance to meet his household charges, and a daily ration allowance. The failings of the system have already been noted, yet the introduction of the concepts of the military salary and pay comparability--concepts which have already been seen to be indicative of the

[43]Spencer Report, p. 132, para. 514.

[44]The projected Defence cuts prompted a number of retired senior officers to write to the newspapers. The general tenor of their arguments is epitomized in a comment from Major-General P. L. R. De C. Martin, colonel of the 22d (Cheshire) Regiment: "Let there be no doubt in anybody's mind that the morale of servicemen today is more brittle than senior officers, past or present, can ever remember. One more straw in the shape of further cuts in defence spending or injustice, real or apparent, in pay could break the camel's back," Daily Telegraph, 5 July 1977.

[45]Clare Hollingworth, "Will the Ranks Enlist in Unions" Daily Telegraph, 8 June 1977.

search for public recognition of the uniqueness of the
military task--have enhanced the sense of relative deprivation.

In this context, it is significant that the pre-1970
pay structure was so complex that individuals were unable
to calculate their emoluments. Thus a 1969 survey indicated that 44% of the officers and 51% of the enlisted ranks
were unable to estimate their pay within 10%.[46] One result
of this was that pay comparability was virtually impossible,
and a sense of relative deprivation--where it existed--was
rarely associated with a perception of income differential.
With the introduction of the military salary, however, the
concept of pay comparability encouraged officers to seek
out a reference group, to identify with group members, and
to compare critically conditions of service. This tendency
was reinforced by the increased importance in the all-
volunteer force that was placed on the growing convergence
of the military and civilian system. As part of a noted
change in the basis of military authority, as the authoritarian style of control was replaced by a managerial
style based on persuasion, officers repeatedly concluded
that their roles and skill were directly comparable with
those of professionals in the civilian sector. The stress
thus placed upon comparability of pay, conditions of service, roles, function and skills--particularly management
skills--inevitably led, and still leads, many officers to
identify with an external reference group.

How far the sense of deprivation which is derived
from this notion of comparability is or is not based on
a true assessment of relative positions is very questionable. The figure frequently quoted by many officers is
that they are at least 20% behind comparable civilian
wages. For reasonable parity with civilian jobs, taking
into account "fringe benefits," others are talking of an
increase of 70%. In contrast, civilian commentators,
whilst acknowledging individual cases of hardship, tend
to stress that officers are a well-paid, privileged group.
In practice, however, it is largely unimportant whether
the sense of relative deprivation is or is not based on a
true assessment of respective positions. What is much
more significant is that there is ample evidence of a
sense of dissatisfaction, a sense which is again indicative
of the trend toward a model of professionalism which ex-
pects the public to reward occupational skills and confirm
claims for specific privileges.

The base of this sense, in the absence of objective
and value-free comparisons based on empirical evidence,
is derived from the utilization of an imperfectly selected

[46]Standing Reference on the Pay of the Armed Forces,
Second Report.

reference group as the basis of comparison. Many officers
whose whole career has been spent in the military organization are largely unaware of what is taking place in the
civilian sector. They select a reference group defined in
terms of a narrow range of subjective and personal criteria.
These are derived from "the looking-glass self" and rarely
include an evaluation of such factors as accountability,
the locus of decision-making, the civilian career structure,
and the requisite experience demanded from reference group
members.

The extent to which this sense of deprivation is indicative of a complex set of perceptions is clearly
reflected in a study of the attitudes of Royal Air Force
officers. James, in looking critically at the reaction of
these officers to the question of their social and financial status, shows how the overall sense of relative
deprivation is closely related to the ongoing occupational
activities of these officers. He draws attention to two
very pertinent observations. Firstly, officers who are
employed in roles which have a direct relationship to the
primary objectives of the organization, that is, pilots
and navigators of aircraft, are less likely to be dissatisfied with their social and financial status than
"marginal" officers employed in support roles. This conclusion is thus a confirmation of the hypotheses postulated
by Garnier in his analysis of the attitudes of cadets at
Sandhurst. Secondly, James concludes that the middle-rank
officers who formed the bulk of his sample are considerably
confused about the precise role definition of members of
the reference group with whom they compare themselves:

> However, discussion showed that many officers were
> unable to distinguish between the Chartered Accoun-
> tant, claiming professional status and operating as
> a self-employed consultant, and the employed book-
> keeper or general clerk. Similarly, in discussion
> some officers appeared to have misconceptions about
> the training and function of the Civil Engineer, con-
> fusing him with the civilian engineer or mechanic.[47]

One tentative conclusion which can be drawn here is
that in the all-volunteer structure, in comparison with
the conscription force, there is, despite the proliferation
of skills in the contemporary military, less awareness of
the precise dimensions of civilian job specifications. In
the conscript force, there is an awareness, possibly an

[47]John James, "Concepts of Social Status among Middle
Ranking Military Officers," Paper presented to the British
Inter-University Seminar on Armed Forces and Society,
Selwyn College, Cambridge, March 1975, p. 4.

enforced awareness, of changes in the civilian occupational structure since conscripts bring with them into the
military organization their professional and technical
skills. Clearly the degree of this awareness will be diminished if the mode of conscription is a form of selective
service which largely excludes from recruitment the
possessors of certain occupational and professional skills.
Nevertheless, interaction between civilian and military
occupational structures is still greater than in the all-
volunteer force where there is a tendency, particularly
amongst longer-serving personnel, for military men to live
in occupational and professional isolation.[48]

      This sense of isolation and the associated inability
to establish a rational reference group with whom individual status can be compared is as marked for enlisted men
as it is for officers. Indeed, the former may suffer from
a greater sense of relative deprivation and status uncertainty, for in selecting a reference group, it is often
not clear whether this should represent and reflect claimed
management skills or a basic technical expertise. In
addition, many primary military skills, particularly at
the lower-rank levels, have no directly comparable civilian
counterpart. The consequent status confusion can be most
marked. Again, whether the conclusions which individuals
reach about their status are valid is a largely immaterial
consideration. What is important is the extent to which
the sense of relative deprivation is, by reflecting attitudes and perceptions, indicative of individual motivation.

      The critical question in this respect is whether
enlisted men in the all-volunteer force feel that they are
deprived when they compare their conditions of service,
particularly the rate of reward, with that of their perceived civilian counterparts. If these feelings are a
common characteristic of contemporary attitudes, then it
can be argued that the volunteer serviceman is prone to
conclude that society does not accord to him the just
rewards which he deserves. Such a conclusion does seem to
be endorsed by contemporary reports in the United Kingdom.
The Spencer Report, as has been pointed out, draws attention to this sense of dissatisfaction: "Other persons did
not understand the purpose of the rent rebate scheme and

      [48]The feeling of isolation is more marked in the con-
temporary all-volunteer force than in the past. The
traditional inter-penetration of the political and military
elite and the ready transfer from military appointments to
civilian posts hitherto minimised this feeling. Today,
however, despite the emphasis placed on the comparability
of military and civilian professionalism, the sense of
occupational and professional isolation is most marked. See
John James.

thought it clear proof that the Army's lower ranks were
underpaid and below the poverty line; whilst some pointed
to rates of pay (usually obtained from newspaper reports)
for civilian jobs which were apparently similar to Army
employment and cited them as evidence that comparability
of pay had not been achieved in practice."[49] Similar comments have also been reported for airmen (enlisted men) in
the Royal Air Force. Here, the bone of contention is that
skilled technicians "would be better off on the dole
(welfare payments) or, alternatively would be earning twice
as much in any similar civilian job."[50] Under the heading
"Angry RAF Wives Demand More Pay for Our Men," one newspaper reporter commented that RAF wives were "tired of
scrimping and saving and living on orange boxes--and for
what." The general sense of dissatisfaction was that the
all-volunteer force had been forgotten in "regulation
poverty" whereas other workers in the public sector were
able to obtain more pay through threatening to take some
form of industrial action. It was stressed that these
servicemen wanted some recognition of their efforts:
"While they are being shot at in Belfast or Belize, they
expect to be paid enough to support their family in something better than a military slum."[51]

    Comments of this nature imply that these enlisted men
are likely to suffer from a feeling of general alienation
in that there is an apparent contradiction between their
awareness of the rewards given by society in terms of
prestige and remuneration, and their assessment of the
worth of the service which they render to the community.
It is also apparent that the notion of "reward" which is
implicit in the identification of military life with a
"calling" or, indeed, a "profession" is no longer adequate.
There is some clear evidence of a more instrumental
attitude in which the primary motivation of these enlisted
men has changed considerably since the introduction of the
twin notions of pay comparability and the military salary.

    It can be argued that this sense of dissatisfaction
in the United Kingdom is essentially associated with a
high rate of inflation which has considerably reduced real
living standards. This would suggest that the more than
passing interest shown in the potential advantages of some
form of group representation within the all-volunteer force
is in reality derived from the effect of this reduction in
living standards. Yet the motivational changes which we
are now witnessing have more complex origins than this.

[49]Spencer Report, pp. 132-33, para. 516.
[50]Alison Beckett, "Angry RAF Wives Demand 'More Pay for
Our Men,'" Daily Telegraph, 21 July 1977.
[51]Ibid.

Indeed, the change of attitudes is also to be found within
other armed forces in contemporary Western industrialized
society. Thus Teitler, in tracing the growth of the demand
for trade unionism among Dutch enlisted men, stresses that
the defence hierarchy in the course of the 1960s abandoned
the idea of constructing a normative organization. He
suggests that the inculcated ideology of the military man,
both officer and enlisted man, has never found many supporters in the West. Consequently, during a period of
détente the military authorities set out deliberately to
give to the military the standing of an attractive organization offering chances of promotion, interesting work,
and a good salary. Teitler sums up very clearly the philosophy underlying the innovations which were introduced:
"So instead of appealing, in accordance with tradition ,
to normative compliance, they correctly realized that in
modern Western society an appeal to utilitarian and social-
normative compliance opened up perspectives with regard to
personnel policy, even for the military force."[52] This
would suggest that the transition which is taking place in
the British all-volunteer force cannot be simply attributed
to contemporary dissatisfaction with a reduced standard of
living. Rather, it is indicative of more widespread trends
within Western armed forces as a whole. What is peculiar
to the British situation is that the potential effects of
this trend have been reinforced by the sense of relative
deprivation consequent upon the adoption of a specific
pattern of military remuneration.

The critical social issue for such a force is that
these changing attitudes largely contradict the traditional view of the component parts of the military way of life.
The notion of the profession as a "calling," with the
emphasis placed upon the significance of service, is no
longer widely acceptable. Equally, although the profession
of arms has hitherto been seen as "one of the fundamental
pursuits,"[53]the concepts of commitment, expertise, autonomy,
and responsibility are redefined within the present situation. This rejection of the traditional military ethos
is the nub of the dilemma. At one extreme, the trend
toward a calculative and utilitarian approach to service
in the all-volunteer force, a trend derived from the
emphasis placed by the political and military elite on
economic incentives and advantages, produced, if carried
to a logical conclusion, the creation of a primarily mer-
cenary force. The problem to which this, in turn, leads
is succinctly summarized by Janowitz: "Military men do not

[52]Ger Teitler, "Conscript Unionism in the Dutch Army,"
in The Military and the Problem of Legitimacy, p. 200.
[53]Sir John Hackett, The Profession of Arms, (London:
The Times Publishing Co , 1962) p. 63.

want to think of themselves as mercenaries and a democratic
society cannot treat its military as if they were mercenaries."[54]

At the other extreme, a reaction within the all-
volunteer force to utilitarianism and calculation can lead
to the deliberate conservation of certain traditional norms
and values which are seen to be representative of the
"real military." The effect of this backlash is to create
further dissension within the force as the traditionalists
seek to stem the tide of change. Concomitantly, the parent
society reacts to those measures, the effect of which is to
isolate further the military.

A major dilemma, therefore, for the all-volunteer
force is the difficulty of striking a balance between these
two extremes. The essential problem is the difficulty of
guaranteeing the "required mixture of numbers and quality
of personnel, especially of the most dedicated and inno-
vative types" in an all-volunteer force that has to compete
with other organizations and occupations for the recruitment and retention of personnel.[55] The social and economic
costs of emphasizing the extrinsic advantages of a military
career escalate to the point where they are no longer
acceptable to the democratic society. Conversely, any
overemphasis which is placed on the need to retain as
criteria of selection a highly selected set of normative
values encourages the recruitment and retention of military
men whose attitudes and ideology are seen to be unrepresentative of the values of the parent society.

At the same time, the complexity of the problem is
exacerbated by the conflict between the expectations and
realities of life in the all-volunteer force. This conflict, as has been noted, is evidenced by an expressed
sense of dissatisfaction with various aspects of military
life. Its origins, however, are to be found in the major
changes which have taken place in the pattern of contemporary service life and in the demographic structure of
the force.

Thus until 1967 a large part of the all-volunteer
force was stationed overseas. Indeed, the greater part
of the Army was located outside the United Kingdom. Con-
tractions through successive defence reviews and the
continuing withdrawal from overseas bases, however, have
considerably modified this. It now means that the major
part of the all-volunteer force is located in the United

[54]Morris Janowitz, The US Forces and the Zero Draft,
Adelphi Papers (London: IISS, 1972), p. 1.
    [55]Ibid.

Kingdom and in Europe. This is in accordance with the
proposals of the Supplementary Statement on Defence
Policy, 1967, in which it was argued that the manpower
and fixed installations in overseas bases would come to
cost more than would be justified by the type of military
operations which were foreseen. Since it would be more
economical to rely mainly on sending forces from Britain in
a crisis, forces were consequently withdrawn from their
stations in the Middle East and Far East.[56]

One effect of this withdrawal from empire has been to
concentrate the all-volunteer force in the United Kingdom
and Europe. Thus, some 60% of the Army, for example, is
retained in the United Kingdom; the balance is to be found
overseas, but the largest overseas station is BAOR where
30% of the Army is located. Within the United Kingdom
most RAF and many army units are stationed in isolated
areas so that a large number of servicemen and their families are situated at often considerable distances from
centres of population. The extent to which this geographical isolation is paralleled by a sense of social
isolation and the effect of these factors upon morale is
an interesting tangential issue. The Spencer Committee
looked specifically at the patterns of contact which army
personnel had with the surrounding civilian environment
and the peculiar difficulties which might arise from the
army way of life. It reported that examples of civilian
hostility toward the Army had been widely experienced.
It also concluded that many servicemen felt that army life
prevented friendship with civilians: "The main reasons
given were turbulence, the isolation of army camps, and
because civilians kept their distance on account of the
image of the Army. The young wife felt the difficulties
that arose from geographical isolation and mobility much
more than her husband who felt more readily the negative
attitudes towards the Army by the civilian community."[57]

The conclusion, that 47% of single and married junior
ranks had experienced this civilian hostility and that 38%
of the respondents at the more senior and mature level had
undergone a similar experience, raises a number of questions
about the pattern of contemporary civil-military relationships in the United Kingdom. It suggests that in a society
where a relatively small percentage of the population has
had any direct experience of service in the all-volunteer
army and where a declining percentage has any experience
whatsoever of life in the armed forces, the social isolation of these forces becomes increasingly noticeable.
But the social and geographical isolation of the Army and

[56]Ministry of Defence, Supplementary Statement on
Defence Policy, 1967 /Cmnd. 3357/ (London: HMSO, 1967)
p. 4.
[57]Spencer Report, p. 37, para. 124.

Air Force is also important because of the effect which it has on the internal pattern of military life.

In this context, three elements of military life, elements which are important characteristics of the professional notion of total commitment, are particularly significant because of the way in which they enhance feelings of isolation. The expected mobility of the serviceman, the long periods of family separation to which he may be subjected, and a high degree of turbulence are, in combination, an important determinant of individual motivation. Here, however, it is significant that each of the three services is differently affected by these elements; this partly explains noted differences of motivation in each of the three services.

The most acute problems are faced by the Army, which is severely affected by the effects of mobility, separation, and excessive turbulence. One of the major effects of the revised policy which was outlined in the 1967 Supplementary Statement on Defence Policy has been to overstretch considerably the resources of a shrinking force structure. Thus of the 18,500 officers and 153,000 enlisted men serving in the Army in 1975, a comparatively large percentage had been sent at short notice for periods of up to six months at a time on unaccompanied postings. In November 1975, for example, three major units were serving on unaccompanied tours of this length in Cyprus and Belize. For the twenty-one-month period up to and including this date, no fewer than a total of 75,000 men had been sent on unaccompanied tours.[58] To this number can be added those undergoing separation during training courses. One of the subsidiary effects of the withdrawal from overseas bases has been the difficulty of arranging realistic training within the United Kingdom. Consequently, soldiers are separated from their families during periods of intensive training which to many servicemen seem to be designed to keep them away from their home base.

An important part of this intensive training is the refamiliarization training given to units which have been serving in Ulster. This service in aid of the civil power is the greatest cause of contemporary separation, for units are rotated to Northern Ireland for an unaccompanied tour of duty of four months' duration. Although there is now a minimum break of twelve months between such tours, rather than the seven to eight months' break which was the norm until early 1975, this rotation has meant that some units stationed in the United Kingdom have now been to Ulster for their sixth tour of unaccompanied duty since 1969. The cumulative effect of this separation and mobility is that some units have been away from their home base for almost

[58] Ibid., p. 19, para. 44.

two-thirds of a two, three, or four year period. Looked at
from another point of view, in one of the major garrison
towns, Colchester, in September 1974 some 45% of the families in quarters were without the head of the household.

The Spencer Committee in looking more critically at
these periods of separation, found that for corporals and
below the mean number of weeks of separation in a twelve-
month period was between eleven and fifteén weeks; for
sergeants and above it was between nine and fourteen weeks;
for junior officers it was between eleven and sixteen
weeks; and for senior officers the period of separation lay
between eight and eleven weeks. In all these instances,
the lower of these periods was experienced by the "other
arms," that is, the corps other than the Infantry, the
Royal Armoured Corps and the Royal Artillery. In the combat
arms, less than 10% had experienced no separation in the
previous two years while a substantial proportion had
experienced more separation than the mean figures suggest.
Thus 20% of all ranks up to and including junior officers
in the combat arms had experienced six months or more
separation in the last year.[59] In general the incidence of
separation, and its length particularly, affected the
junior other ranks, suggesting that the problems of overstretch in the all-volunteer army were most noticeable at
this rank level.

The problem of meeting worldwide commitments with a
reduced force structure whilst concomitantly effecting a
reasonable balance between overseas and home service also
generates a high degree of turbulence. This uncertainty
of army life, stemming from the policy of posting individuals and units at fixed intervals and to meet sudden
emergencies is evidenced by the number of people claiming
disturbance allowance upon posting. During 1973 to 1974,
for example, in a twelve-month period some 40% of the
enlisted men and almost a half of the officers claimed
disturbance allowance for the movement of their families.
The high degree of turbulence which is experienced by
many families is also shown in Table 13, from which it can
be seen that the degree of family mobility exceeds that
which is normally associated with the two to two and a
half years tour of duty at a given location. This turbulence is considerably in excess of that experienced by
the most mobile sector of the civilian community, and it
can be deduced that the feeling of social and physical
isolation to which reference has been made, is in part
derived from the constant mobility of the military family.

Before the effects of this mobility, family separation,
and turbulence are considered in more detail, however, it

[59]Ibid., p. 21, para. 48. Additionally, see Tables
17 to 23: "Separation for Service Reasons."

Table 13. Number of times families moved in the past five years:
Army personnel

Number of times moved	Corporals and below %	Sergeants and above %	Junior officers %	Senior officers %
0	14	7	10	8
1	16	13	11	11
2	20	20	16	19
3	24	28	24	29
4+	26	32	39	33

Source: Calculated from General Household Survey: Introductory
Report, 1971, OPCS, 1973, p. 155.

has to be noted that many of the problems which are encountered are more significant in the Army than in the
other services. This is not to suggest that the problems
and their effects are absent in the Royal Navy and the
Royal Air Force. It is, however, apparent that for a
number of reasons these two services have been able to
adopt alternative planning policies which ameliorate the
encountered difficulties. Thus, in the Royal Navy the
longer periods of enforced separation are balanced by the
concept of the "home port" and by the encouragement given
to naval personnel to buy their own houses by offering
advantageous terms to longer-serving married men for the
advance of a cash sum. In contrast, the Royal Air Force,
although it has not adopted the home base concept, has
been able to soften the worst effects of excessive turbulence and mobility by extending the length of the tour at
a particular station. Both the Royal Navy and the Royal
Air Force are still affected by the problems created by
mobility, family separation, and turbulence, for these
continued to be endemic features of life in the contemporary all-volunteer force. Even so, the magnitude of their
problems is far less than that of the Army. The latter is
essentially a mobile force, for its ability to respond as
a crisis organization, involving personnel of all regiments and corps at a wide range of rank levels, is its
very raison d'etre.

    The fundamental problem shared by all these services
is that the all-volunteer force was established on the
premise that it would be able to act quickly in the satisfaction of defence commitments. The acceptance of this
premise justified force reductions, for it was consistently argued that the United Kingdom needed small but
mobile armed forces. This, in turn, implied that in the
ideal all-volunteer force servicemen would be free from
extraneous obligations and responsibilities that could
interfere with their expected degree of mobility. In short,

the ideal serviceman would be single, living on base, and
totally committed to the notion of service for twenty-four
hours a day.

The reality of contemporary life in the all-volunteer
force, however, is that a majority of personnel are married, that there are strong pressures to live outside the
military cantonment, and that a developed sense of relative
deprivation has encouraged a more limited commitment to
the notion of "total service." The Spencer Committee thus
noted that an army strength of some 171,500 was paralleled
by some 92,000 wives and 156,000 children, so that the
total number of dependents far exceeded the number of uniformed members. Perhaps the most significant change in
this context is that the national trend toward early
marriage has been reflected in the all-volunteer force.
Before the introduction in 1970 of the military salary
which gave equal pay to both single and married personnel,
a number of disincentives to early marriage existed.
Marriage allowance was not given to enlisted men below the
age of 21 or to officers below the age of 25; nor was
married accommodation provided officially below those ages.
These disincentives, however, were removed with the
introduction of the military salary, and, at the same time,
married quarters became more readily available following
an expanded building program which implemented a policy
laid down in the 1966 Statement on the Defence Estimates:
"If we are to attract and retain sufficient recruits, we
must not only offer good pay and a decent career; the
Serviceman must also be well-housed. Although much has
been accomplished in recent years, we still have a lot to
do before the armed forces have sufficient housing. We
therefore attach great importance to providing modern,
well-designed houses for married Servicemen and their families."[60] These changes no doubt encouraged a marked
increase in the number of young married servicemen. Thus,
although the overall army strength fell by 3.8% between
1969 and 1974, the number of families actually rose by
5.4%.[61] A similar trend was also noticeable in the Royal
Air Force and the Royal Navy, thus justifying the conclusion that the all-volunteer force was a "married man's
military."

It is also significant that there has been a marked
fall in the age at marriage both of husbands and wives.
Table 14 shows the average age at marriage of a representative sample of servicemen and their wives:

[60]Ministry of Defence, Statement on the Defence
Estimates, 1966 Part II /Cmnd. 2902/ (London: HMSO, 1966),
p. 74, para. 1.
   [61]Spencer Report, p. 18, para. 41.

Table 14. Average age at marriage of army personnel and their wives

Rank	Servicemen	Wives
Corporals & below	21.7	20.3
Sergeants & above	23.8	21.4
Junior officers	24.8	23.2
Senior officers	26.8	23.9

Source: Calculated from Spencer Committee Report, Tables 8 & 9.

From this table it can be seen that the enlisted men in
the lower ranks and the junior officers are now getting
married at an earlier age than did their seniors. Indeed,
between 1969 and 1974 the proportion of junior enlisted
men married at the ages of 19 and 20 almost doubled.
Moreover, families with small children now predominate in
the contemporary all-volunteer force, for almost two-thirds
of the junior enlisted ranks who are married have a child
below school age. The significant feature of this trend
toward earlier marriage is that we are looking at a force
structure in which there are a large number of young
married officers and soldiers. In the Army, for example,
22% of the junior enlisted men are below the age of 19
and a further 42% are under the age of 25; similarly, 24%
of the junior officers are under the age of 25.[62] Expressed
in terms of absolute size, this means that some 67,000 army
personnel are below the age of 25. Of those who are married, particularly the junior enlisted men, a large number
of wives are under the age of 25. Thus the Spencer Committee found from a representative army sample that more
than half the wives of the junior enlisted men were under
the age of 25; almost 10% were 19 and under. It is, therefore, these young servicemen and their wives who are
especially affected by the demands placed upon them by
the needs of the all-volunteer force, demands which give
rise to the problems engendered by mobility, family separation, and turbulence.

     Until the Spencer Committee looked at these problems
in depth, much of the comment which was made on the difficulties of servicemen and their families was impression-
istic. The Report of the committee, however, provides a
detailed analysis of the social difficulties which are
experienced by all ranks and their families. The general
observation of the Report is that matrimonial and family
problems form the largest matter for concern facing
servicemen today. Above all, the Report stresses, "the
consequences of loneliness stand out as a major problem."[63]

[62]Abstract of Army Manpower Statistics, No. 82
(December, 1974) pp. 7,14.
     [63]Spencer Report, p. 49, paras. 167, 168.

One part of the Report is of particular significance:

> The isolation felt by the wives of junior ranks is
> particularly noticeable. Some of this, no doubt,
> is caused by their having very young children to
> care for; much of it however is compounded by their
> high rates of separation and turbulence, the system
> for allocating married accommodation, an inability
> to drive, a lack of social amenties, and of course
> stress produced by their new relationships without
> having the ready assistance of their mothers to hand
> when difficulties arise.[64]

The traditional method of meeting these difficulties has
been the system of regimental care and responsibility to
which reference has been made. It is now, however, apparent that this system is not able to cope with the
demonstrated problem. This is particularly so where the
source of dissatisfaction is major changes in the perception of realities of service life. There is, for example,
increasing evidence of the importance of paid employment
to the wives of all ranks in the all-volunteer force. Two
of the consequences of this are of particular importance.
Firstly, it is evident that there is a sense of dissatisfaction among those wives who would welcome paid employment
but who find that the opportunities for this are very
limited, particularly outside the United Kingdom. In turn,
the demand for employment, especially amongst officers'
wives, conflicts with the traditional role ascribed to
military wives, since the concept of regimental care and
responsibility has relied very heavily on the participation
of these wives. Now, it is clear that a smaller number of
wives are prepared to accept those commitments which hitherto have been seen as an extension of the husbands' role
within the force structure. Secondly, the nonsatisfaction
of this demand for paid employment has been followed by
a demand for improved welfare services; these, it has been
argued, should include, for example, the provision of
kindergartens and nursery schools. Additionally, improved
welfare services are needed, it is said, to compensate for
that higher degree of loneliness and boredom which is
partly attributable to this inability to obtain paid employment.

These expressed strains and stresses draw attention
to one of the fundamental questions to be answered for the
all-volunteer force. To what extent does such a force have
to divert resources to meet the needs of military families?
Associated with this question is a whole range of subsidiary, but no less important, issues. The operational
tasks of the British all-volunteer force are most readily
satisfied by the recruitment of a small and mobile skilled

[64]Ibid.

military. Does the provision of extensive facilities for
the support of families have dysfunctional consequences?
Do such facilities encourage early marriage, which reduces
the mobility of that force? Does the military organization
in contemporary society still have a responsibility for the
provision of these facilities? Or is it the custodial,
paternalistic style of management, which is implicit in
such provision, at variance with a concept of professionalism that stresses, inter alia, the importance of individual responsibility and commitment.

    Recognizing that the pattern of life in the contempor-
ary British Army had changed, the Spencer Committee
recommended the establishment of a professionally staffed
Army Social Work Service to assume responsibility for
promoting social welfare within the Army and for offering
army members and their families professional social work
support. This proposal, however, was rejected, but
although the Army was criticized by the media for its lack
of action the decision taken can be rationalized in the
light of the questions which have been posed. The critical
issue is the extent to which the Army and, indeed, the
other parts of the all-volunteer force are identified as
a professional fighting force or as an ancillary social
welfare agency. Given that the problems of mobility, family
separation, and turbulence are endemic features of a crisis
organization, at what point does concern within the social
implications of these features of military life outweigh
concern with operational commitments and task attainment?
Put into simple terms the question is whether the military
force, despite its traditional pattern of care and responsibility, can still be expected to respond as a total
organization in some areas, when members of the organization have often rejected personal obligations of total
commitment. How does the all-volunteer force reconcile
individual perceptions of convergence between the military
and civilian organizations in terms of pay comparability
with perceptions of divergence in terms of the social
consequences of military life? How is the demand for public recognition of the uniqueness of the professional task
equated with the demand for an extension of a paternalistic
system of organization?

    To these and similar questions there are no simple
answers. What is certain is that the problems associated
with the harsh realities of mobility, family separation,
and turbulence create very real difficulties for the development of the all-volunteer force. The problems are
symptomatic of the conflict of the expectations and
realities of service life. In turn, the degree of stress
and strain which is associated with the conflict is
exacerbated by changes in the primary motivation of many
officers and enlisted men. No longer can it be presumed
that all servicemen will be motivated by a structured

normative-based ideology. The calculative orientations of
many servicemen thus lead them to look very critically at
the possible conflict between their military and family
responsibilities. All of this can be seen to form part of
a sense of relative deprivation, the importance of which
is that it erodes positive attitudes toward the all-
volunteer force. Thus the social implications of the contemporary force structure in the United Kingdom are very
considerable, for we are witnessing a stage of professionalism in which dissatisfaction with the low level of
public recognition of the uniqueness of the occupational
task is paralleled by dissatisfaction with longstanding and
traditional features of military life.

Conclusions

This survey of the experiences of the British all-volunteer
force structured in the two decades since the announced
phasing-out of conscription has concentrated on three
issues: changes in the force structure, the costs of
volunteerism, and the social implications of the readoption
of the traditional method of recruitment. It is not
claimed that this is an exhaustive analysis of the noted
problems and postulated solutions. There are whole areas
of concern which merit a fuller discussion. Such issues
as the effects of the current retention and retirement
policy, the pattern of promotion, the provision of education and training programs, and the effectiveness of
recruitment and resettlement strategies are examples of
these additional areas which deserve further analysis.
Equally, in looking in more detail at the social problems
encountered by servicemen and their families, more attention could be paid to the problems of children's education,
to the dysfunctional consequences of a housing policy which
through raising to an economic level the charges for
accommodation encourages the purchase of houses outside the
cantonment, and to the wider issue of the single man's
reaction to wnat he sees as positive discrimination in
favor of the married man.

Nevertheless, from a survey of the three designated
issues certain tentative conclusions can be drawn. It
has to be stressed that because these are derived from the
British experience since the ending of conscription, they
may have a limited applicability in cross-cultural comparative analysis. Conversely, it can be argued that the
issues and solutions which are noted in the United Kingdom
have a wider applicability in that they are indicative
of the general problems faced by the all-volunteer force
structure in a Western industrialized society. The
conclusions reached, therefore, may be illustrative of more
universal trends. To look at these more specifically:

The contemporary all-volunteer force structure in the United Kingdom reflects certain well-defined historical trends. An analysis of the force structure during earlier phases of the twentieth century indicates three propositions which have a continuing applicability:

1. In peacetime, the absolute size of the all-volunteer force consistently declines.

2. Over time, the size of the all-volunteer force declines as a proportion of the adult working population.

3. Over time, the military participation ratio in a country with an all-volunteer force structure declines consistently.

These are explanatory propositions designed to facilitate analysis. They do not purport to indicate either the "absolute" or "normal" size of the all-volunteer force. Nevertheless, the historical trends suggest that the structure in size and composition is determined by these trends:

1. The normal size of the all-volunteer force in peacetime is related to a figure which is a given percentage of the country's optimum mobilization. For the United Kingdom, a figure of 7% of the optimum mobilization indicates a force of some 315,000 personnel.

2. The size of the all-volunteer force approximates to a given percentage of the adult working population. The maximum percentage for the United Kingdom is no more than 1.25%; a continuing decline, which reflects previous trends, indicates a fall to somewhere between 1.0% and 1.1%.

3. A consistent decline in the military participation ratio, despite fluctuations in the size of the age group from which recruits are primarily drawn, indicates a "baseline" M.P.R. For the United Kingdom, historical trends indicate an M.P.R. of no more than 1.20 to 1.25.

This analysis of the size and composition of the all-volunteer force structure in peacetime does not take into account the possible effect of external variables. It is derived from developmental analysis which entails historical reconstruction, trend specification, and the establishment of a future model toward which actual events are progressing.[65] Essentially, as Moskos has pointed out, it "emphasizes the 'from here to there' sequence of present and hypothetical events."[66]

[65]Heinz Eulau, "H. D. Lasswell's Developmental Analysis," Western Political Quarterly, 2 (June 1958) 229-42.
[66]Moskos, p. 2.

The utility of such a model of analysis is, however, confirmed when we look more specifically at the external variables which affect the contemporary all-volunteer force structure. In this context, concern with the economic costs and consequences of volunteerism is a marked characteristic of societal reaction to the creation and maintenance of this type of force structure. Here, three factors are of particular importance:

1. The economic costs of the all-volunteer force in an industrialized society inevitably increase to a level which becomes politically unacceptable. Not only are the total costs, in terms of the share of the Gross National Product allocated to defence expenditure, seen to be unacceptable, but the costs of foregone alternatives also becomes an issue of considerable concern.

2. In an attempt to overcome the stress which arises as a consequence of the demand for a reduction in defence expenditure, specific policy decisions are made. These follow an established pattern which is confirmed by both historical and contemporary examples:

a. Those overseas commitments which are seen to be anachronistic and of peripheral importance are reduced in the light of a more rigidly defined national defence policy.

b. As costs continue to escalate, the redefined role is marginally amended. The primary role has to be maintained, but objectives here have to be attained with a substantial reduction in allocated resources.

c. These cuts are progressive until the point is reached at which the military establishment and the political power disagree about the ability of the force structure to sustain the amended and diminished role.

3. Despite the operation of planned cuts, the effect of increasing personnel costs is such that there is a marked shift in the proportions of the defence budget allocated to personnel (including support) costs and to capital expenditure on equipment. Consequently, any savings which were envisaged through the change from a labour-intensive mass army to a capital-intensive all-volunteer force cannot be fully realised.

In looking more critically at the experience of the British all-volunteer force, it is clear, however, that concern with the economic costs of volunteerism is only one of the factors which shape policy choice. One major problem to be faced by the decision-makers is that the force structure, needing to compete in the open labour market for recruits, is faced with the dilemma of reconciling

the expediency of emphasizing the extrinsic advantages of
a military career with a wish to maintain specific normative standards. Any emphasis which is placed on the
former has certain dysfunctional consequences:

1. With the cessation of conscription, the all-
volunteer force over time becomes increasingly unknown to
the public at large. To an everincreasing proportion of
the adult working population, the military is an alien
institution. Evaluation, therefore, concentrates on the
apparently privileged position of the armed forces, largely
ignoring the relationship between the rate of military
reward and the role and function of these forces.

2. Within the force structure, the emphasis placed
on the comparability of the military and other large-
scale complex organizations frequently produces feelings of
relative deprivation as individuals compare themselves
with a selected external reference group.

On the other hand, any tendency to emphasize the need
to maintain an established value system within the force
structure, also creates certain difficulties:

1. The pattern of recruitment is seen by the public
to emphasize the importance as criteria of selection of
a set of values and attitudes which are unrepresentative
of the parent society.

2. These criteria encourage the recruitment from
traditional sources of individuals whose subsequent
promotion through a sophisticated system of social control
seemingly perpetuates the existence of a closed system
which is socially unrepresentative.

The social implications of alterations in patterns of
recruitment and structure are thus very considerable.
Within the contemporary British all-volunteer force structure, alterations in the demographic structure of the
force and major shifts in the attitudes of personnel to
the concept of military service create considerable
strains for the organization. The crux of the problem can
be summarized as the contrast which exists between the
operational imperative, which is the raison d'etre of an
efficient military force, and the social imperative with
its emphasis on the importance of both individual and
family well-being.

So far as the operational imperative is concerned, the
difficulty of meeting defence commitments with a force of
reduced size is accentuated by the need for the enhanced
mobility and readiness of that force. The all-volunteer
force is, however, characterized by a growing dissatisfaction with three elements of military life which are

significant indicators of an expected professionalism:
(a) the enhanced mobility of the serviceman, (b) the long
periods of family separation to which he is subjected and
(c) a high degree of turbulence. This sense of dissatisfaction is thus a reflection of the impact of changes in
the structure of the all-volunteer force, not only in
terms of the substantial growth in the number of military
families, especially younger families, but also in the
values of family life.

The analysis of these three issues of changes in the
force structure, the costs of volunteerism, and the social
implications of the transition to an all-volunteer structure implies that such a structure is characterized by
endemic strain and stress. Yet it would be unrealistic to
suggest that an industrialized democracy can readily accept
the reintroduction of conscription in an attempt to overcome the problems associated with the all-volunteer force
structure. Indeed, there is increasing evidence of an
international shift in the West away from conscription as
a means of recruitment.

Solutions to these problems have, therefore, to be
found within the realities of policy decisions. British
experience suggests that the fundamental problem to be
faced here by decision-makers is that postulated solutions
have traditionally dealt with the symptoms of stress rather
than with the causes. This is very understandable. The
cause of many problems can be attributed to social, demographic, and economic changes within the parent society
rather than to the weakness of traditional facets of
military life. But it is easier for decision-makers to
amend the rules and regulations which govern this life,
than to consider more critically the interrelationship
between armed forces and society. Consequently, the
introduction of such reforms as the creation of the military salary, minor adjustments of the regulations governing
military discipline, and improved conditions of service
may ultimately have disappointing, if not dysfunctional,
consequences. The need is for forms of alternative thinking which focus more directly on the causes of the
difficulties whilst accepting the realities of change
within the parent society.

In summary, British experience suggests that, on
balance, the all-volunteer force has been able to meet
its task commitments, albeit at increasing economic and
social costs. It would be folly to suggest that the
difficulties which have been encountered necessitate or
even justify a return to some form of conscription. Equally, it would be foolish to ignore the consequences of the
strains which arise as the needs of society impose constraints on the share of scarce resources, in terms of

manpower and finance, which can be allocated to the military sector. But the all-volunteer force is not a static
organization. Its created form and structure are not
sacrosanct, and in the final analysis it can be argued
that the military in an advanced society is a reflection
of that society. This suggests that the force is adaptable
and that it can respond to the demands which are placed
upon it. The decisions which have to be taken in this
field, however, are ultimately political ones. Given that
civilian control over the military system is a cardinal
feature of Western democratic society, then the final
decision in areas of resource allocation has to be taken
by the civil power. This may create a degree of civil-
military stress, but in arriving at a decision, the
political power has to accept that both historical trends
and contemporary examples suggest that society ultimately
gets the all-volunteer force which it deserves.[67]

[67]The author wishes to express his grateful acknowledgement of the support received from the US Army
Research Institute for the Behavioral and Social Sciences
during the basic research upon which this analysis is
based.

ROLE OF WOMEN IN TODAY'S MILITARY

Cecile S. Landrum

Coming to the forefront of the recent debate on the success or failure of the military to sustain an all-volunteer force (AVF) is the growing importance of the role
of women. A combination of the predicted dwindling
manpower pool of eligible young men and the fact that the
services are experiencing an all-time high first-time
attrition rate of personnel has turned the thinking to
increase the numbers of women.

Concurrent with this AVF dialogue has been the changing roles of women in society. The 1970s show women
going beyond the traditional jobs, with more and more
entering the legal and medical professions as well as
becoming skilled in engineering and the crafts. Women
are choosing to marry later, delay their families, or not
have children at all. And as the women begin to assert
themselves in the professional world, they are seizing
upon the military as a source for training and education
in diverse fields. The military is more than a source
of challenge and adventure; it has become a source of
job security, which is coupled with such attractive
benefits as health, housing and retirement.

In today's climate, women find themselves doing much
more in the military than just filling gaps in male recruiting, and if this country were to fight another major
war, women would surely play a significant role. Clearly
the issue of the military woman's role is becoming one

Note: The views and opinions expressed or implied in this
paper are those of the author, and not to be construed as
carrying the official sanction of the Department of the
Air Force.

that demands a national policy response.

Recent Pentagon plans call for an increase of the numbers of enlisted women from 104,000 to 199,000 over the next five years. This would be an increase from approximately 6% to 11% of the force.[1] This increase can be appreciated even more when one realizes that five years ago there were only about 43,000 enlisted women in the military.[2] The decade of the seventies will see a sevenfold increase in the numbers of women in uniform. Since the potential manpower pool of teenage youth will be reduced by 15% in the 1980s, women's presence will be of increasing importance.[3]

Even more significant are the kinds of jobs women can now enter. Where just a few years ago women were generally relegated to administrative, clerical, and the healing fields, they are now serving as electrical equipment repairmen, aircraft maintenance personnel, forklift and truck drivers, pilots, communications experts, and telephone linemen--among the many other nontraditional career fields.

Policy decisions concerning the kinds of jobs women can perform, the numbers of women who can serve, the locations in which they can serve, and the personnel policies altering their status sound very encouraging. People cannot, however, be lulled into feeling that all is well because of these numbers of women, or that all of the problems of the AVF will be resolved by the sheer presence of women. Women's capabilities and desires to serve must be supported by policies and by leaders in order to insure their success. Policymakers must examine the impact of these new policy decisions beyond one dimension. The problems of numbers and quality in sustaining the AVF can easily be replaced by problems of managing a military with significant and growing family concerns, or perhaps even by significant attrition problems occurring at different career points than being experienced now. For example, large numbers of dropouts at mid-career will create different problems than large numbers dropping out in the first term.

The Decision to Open the Academy's Doors to Women

Actually, as a matter of public policy, no positive determination has ever been made of the role women would play

[1]Department of Defense, Annual Report, Fiscal Year 1979, p. 328.
[2]Ibid., p. 328.
[3]Ibid., p. 326.

in national defense. Historically, restrictive laws and
policies have denied women the opportunities for education, training, and assignments that are career-
enhancing in the military system. President John F.
Kennedy noted the importance of military education and
training in his address to the West Point graduating
class in 1962 when he said that "you will need to understand the importance of military power and limits of
military power . . . to decide what arms should be used
to prevent fights. Above all, you will have a responsibility to deter war as well as fight it. West Point
was not built to produce technical experts alone. It
was built to produce men and leaders who understand the
great stakes which are involved."[4]

Kennedy's words were still relevant when in the summer
of 1976 women, for the first time in our history, entered
the class of 1980 at the Army, Navy, and Air Force academies. And for the first time women had the opportunity
to participate in the first step of the educational
process that has produced many of the leaders who have
been making such decisions.

Although the issues surrounding the military academies address only officer procurement, from the moment that
Congress passed the legislation allowing women in the
academies, questions emerged concerning combat and the
role of women in the military. Dialogue over women's
capabilities to fulfill the academies' rigorous physical
training requirements and questions of whether the academies planned to lower their physical standards resounded
among concerned parties. To meet the stated missions of
the academies--preparing combat officers on land, sea, and
air--the academies had to maintain their rigorous programs
without compromising their training and without developing
a two-track system.

In 1977, when the women entered the academies for the
second year, they had a better understanding of the
military mission and more realistic expectations. Moreover, they had peer counterparts with whom they could
identify. Whereas dropout rates during the first year
of transition for the women in the class of 1980 were
slightly higher than the men's at West Point and Annapolis,
the rate for the women at the Air Force Academy was 17.1%
compared to 28.6% at the Military Academy and 22.2% at
the Naval Academy. The class of 1981 statistics already
show an overall decline. For example, 9.6% of women

[4]Kennedy, John F., Graduation Address, United States
Military Academy, West Point, New York, June 1962. Text
provided by Public Affairs Office, United States Military
Academy.

dropped out during the summer training at West Point this
year--14.3% dropped out last year. Only 4.4% of the
Naval Academy women dropped out this year, as compared
to 7.4% last year. The Air Force Academy had a negligible
increase from 3.2% to 4.5%--an increase of two cadets.[5]

The Dilemma of Combat

Clearly, combat issues cannot be discussed without gener-
ating emotional arguments--often irrelevant to today's
interpretation of combat and the number of women who would
actually serve. And most of the literature emerging
concerning combat at the time the academy legislation was
passed focused on the very emotional issues. Questions
of whether society was ready for women in combat, intense
examinations of the average physical capabilities (such
as upper arm strength), and debates on women's ability
to complete "beast barracks," and the obstacle course,
etc., were all part of the ongoing dialogue. Of course,
neither all women nor all men are average. There are
both men and women who will never physically qualify for
the rigors of combat and should not go to the academies
or be placed in combat jobs. There are also physically
average women whose will to survive and motivation have
been the keys to their success in the academies and the
military. In fact, the average woman's smaller size
and manual dexterity might be viewed as assets in some
weapon system environments.

The question of whether women are willing to go into
combat is often asked. Some 20% of the military women
with whom the author has spoken have answered that question affirmatively. There is no indication of how
enlisted men would respond if asked the same question.

Women are demonstrating by their high performance
standards that they want to be part of the service;
yet if the combat laws are not changed, what are we
training the women for? One can try to circumvent the
combat laws by changing the interpretation of combat or
by temporarily altering utilization policies until the
balloon goes up. Maj. Gen. Jeanne Holm, USAF (Ret),
in a recent congressional hearing, said: "In this day of
mobile strike forces, tactical and strategic bombing,
guerilla warfare and guided missiles, the rationale of
not assigning women, except nurses, to locations subject
to possible hostile fire escapes me."[6] The question here

[5]Data provided by Department of the Air Force, Deputy
Chief of Staff, Personnel, Academy Group, January 1978.
[6]Statement before Subcommittee on Priorities and Economy in Government of the Joint Economic Committee on the
Role of Women in the Military, 1 Sept. 1977.

really can't be one of whether women can perform in combat. Women have proven themselves under the bombs in World War II in London, in the field hospitals in Korea, and under rocket attack in Vietnam. They have been in combat and in combat zones, but without recognition. It seems that women are being considered to be a manpower pool of last resort. In other words, policymakers redefine the interpretation of combat according to their manpower requirements. As the pool of available men dwindles, policymakers take a more liberal view of what is not combat and permit the use of women as needed.

An alternative recently considered by the Navy is to utilize women temporarily in jobs now defined as combat or combat-related. For example, the Navy would put women aboard ships temporarily, but would replace them with men if a combat situation arises. This means that the experienced women would be replaced by untrained men, because the women would have occupied the combat-related slots, thereby precluding sufficient numbers of men from getting their training. The results, therefore, could well be the diminishing of the mission readiness of the ship and the denial of the right of women to provide the ships with the required readiness.

Everytime a woman is placed in combat-related duties temporarily the services are denying the country and every person in that command the right to a fully-manned unit in a combat environment. An inordinate amount of precious time and energy would have to be spent on removing women from the combat environment, and time, energy, equipment and manhours will be spent on other than the real mission. Any results of tests which indicate that women can do any job they demonstrate themselves to be physically capable of doing is irrelevant if they are not going to be allowed to serve in the mission for which they are trained. Our country cannot afford to gamble with its mission readiness and particularly with those women who have volunteered to serve their country. The concept of sending women into combat assignments on a temporary basis should be totally unacceptable to any American who puts the peace of the United States in the forefront.

Women's Historic Role in the Military

In the history of our country, women's participation in the military dates back to the French and Indian and Revolutionary Wars.[7] Hundreds have even won Purple Hearts

[7]See Martin Binkin and Shirley Bach, Women in the Military (Washington: Brookings Institution, 1977), chapter 2, for an expanded discussion of this topic.

and Bronze Stars; both of these decorations could only be
earned in a combat zone. Yet prior to Vietnam, the laws
and policies stated they could not have been in combat-
related jobs, and subsequently, they were not entitled to
combat pay.

The Army Nurses' Corps came into existence in 1901 to
provide medical care for the U.S. soldiers in the Spanish-
American War. And from that point on, army women began to
be used in those jobs which they could "sufficiently" fill
and free the men for the battlefield. The Navy and
Marines followed suit in 1916 to meet their personnel
shortages. The jobs included traditional female jobs
referred to as "helping occupations." They included
clerks, stenographers, and telephone operators. However,
when the war was over, the women were sent home. This was
also the case during World War II, when once again women
were called to duty as an auxiliary force. This situation
was reflective of their participation in the labor force--
again that of "freeing" the fighting men.

Approximately 350,000 (3%) women served on active duty
in World War II, and their jobs went beyond the traditional
skills. To mention a few, they were pilots, truck drivers,
bombsight maintenance specialists, and link trainer instruc-
tors. Of course, in the civilian sector there was "Rosie
the riveter." At the end of that war, the women did not go
home, but their numbers were severely reduced.[8] Those who
remained were pressured, regardless of their own personal
inclinations, to return to the switchboard, typing pool, or
the other "traditional jobs." Clearly, a return to mother-
hood and the home was desired. Women who were considered
patriots during wartime for accepting jobs in the military
were now looked at suspiciously if they remained after the
conflict. Actually, if the draft had not ended in 1947,
it is doubtful that the women would have been kept on at
all. But it was believed then, as it is today, that women
could be used to fill in where the numbers of male enlistments were inadequate.

In 1948 the Women's Armed Services Integration Act
gave permanent status to the women in all four services;
however the law limited women to 2% of the regular force,
a ceiling that was never reached--even at the height of
the Korean conflict. They also were restricted to a top
permanent rank of 0-5 (Lt Colonel or Commander), with only
one temporary 0-6 (Colonel or Captain) authorized in the
line force in each service. The passage of PL 90-130
(1968) lifted these restrictions; but it was not until the

[8]Delores Battle, "Women in the Defense Establishment,"
Defense Manpower Commission Staff Studies, Vol. 4, May
1976, p. 2.

advent of the AVF in 1972 that recognition of the fact
that women could play a key role in this mission of the
services became apparent. While many of these changes
could not have occurred if women had not begun to be
accepted in the civilian labor market, it was apparent
among the AVF policy planners that women could no longer
be a manpower pool of last resort.

The Enlisted Woman Today

While the numbers of women in the military academies
remain small (a reflection of the previous limited women-
officer procurement program), the major numerical increases
have been in the enlisted grades in the last five years.
The problems generated by this rapid increase have been
accentuated because approximately 87% of these women are
in the lower four grades, a function of the orderly
personnel promotion system which takes years to "grow" its
senior personnel.[9] The services therefore lack significant
numbers of women leaders either in the officer or enlisted
ranks to support these young women in their new endeavors.
Too often, women, in trying to prove themselves in a male-
oriented world, become frustrated when they lack support
or role models for reinforcement.

Additionally, many of the young enlisted women entering the services today find themselves in nontraditional
jobs in which they are uncomfortable, especially in the
male-dominated environment. These enlisted women are
caught in the struggle for full opportunity and equal
responsibility, on the one hand, and their desires to be
properly utilized on the other hand. As women enter the
services with more prior exposure to the nontraditional
fields, as neutral job standards for all jobs are established, as management reflects the standards, and as the
women grow in numbers in the service--this dilemma can be
resolved.

The changes in policies and legislation relating to
marriage, pregnancy, benefits, ceilings, and promotions--
in addition to the expanded job opportunities--have served
as catalysts for the recruiting of greater numbers of
women into the military. Now these policy changes must
be viewed in a context of examining the impact each has on
the others. Without such an examination, women's ability
to perform fully in the AVF can be seriously impaired.

[9]Office of the Assistant Secretary of Defense (Manpower, Reserve Affairs, and Logistics), "Use of Women in
the Military," May 1977, p. 7, Table 3.

Attitudes of Women in the Armed Forces

Very complex attitudinal issues play a subtle but significant role in relationship to all other issues dealing
with the utilization of women[10] The author's contacts with
officer and enlisted women in the field suggest that problems based on attitudes are pervasive. These include
attitudes held by both women and men. These attitudes
clearly impact on the ability of women to perform their
jobs. Women recognize that women leaders will not be
influenced by female wiles the way men are. Yet women
still resist the concept of having other women as
supervisors--a case of fear of the unknown.

Women's Attitudes

As women have moved into this "new" world, it is apparent
that acting out traditional roles has become the modus
operandi for many, often because it is the only known
successful behavior. Their use of the stereotypes to take
advantage of the system thus creates a polarized situation.

A recent GAO report on job opportunities for women
in the military referred to the fact that military women
are partly to blame for their status. With women still
clustering around administrative and medical jobs, the
change is hard to come by.[11]

[10]While much of this section on attitudes is the
author's interpretation of comments made during contacts
with male and female military personnel, many items are
substantiated by surveys. In particular see Joel M.
Sevell and Bary Collins, Soldiers' Attribution of Contemporary vs. Traditional Sex Role Attitudes to Themselves and
to Others, Research Memorandum 75-7 (U.S. Army Research
Institute for the Behavioral and Social Sciences, July
1975); Patricia J. Thomas and Kathleen P. Durning, "The
Military Women and the Navy Wife," Paper presented to the
Eighty-fourth Annual Convention of the American Psycho-
logical Association, Washington, D.C.: "Utilization of
Women in Industrial Career Fields," information sheet pro-
vided by Department of the Air Force, Deputy Chief of Staff,
Personnel staff: Joel M. Sevell, John C. Woelfel, and Barry
Collins, Attitudes Covering Job Appropriateness for Women
in the Army, Research Memorandum 75-3 (U.S. Army Research
Institute for the Behavioral and Social Sciences, July
1975); Kathleen Durning and Sandra Mumford, Differential
Perceptions of Organizational Climate Held by Navy Enlisted Women and Men, NPRDC TR 76 TQ-43, 1973. Also,
Martin and Bach, chapter 5, provides an excellent and extensive treatment of this topic.
[11]Comptroller General of the United States, Job Opportunities for Women in the Military: Progress and Problems,
FPCD-76-26, May 11, 1976.

One of the most difficult tasks for women is that
they must also learn to turn away from dual standards and
accept responsibilities that are not always desirable in
order to achieve real equality.

In general, the author has found that women leaders
would not approve or propose the lowering of standards to
allow women to fill jobs once considered to be male occupations. Equality is perceived as the establishment of
job standards based on specific qualifications other than
sex.

Male Attitudes

Based on the author's discussions with men and women enlisted persons and officers, it would seem that existing
male attitudes may be contributing to the curtailment of
full utilization of women. Some men find the presence of
qualified women in nontraditional jobs to be threatening
to their positions and dominance. Many men want to maintain an image of a tough, active, and hard-fighting man.

Men's attitudes vary from being very paternal toward
women to being resentful of them. Many men feel that
women should be placed on a pedestal and should not be
exposed to distasteful tasks. However, in this protected
role women cannot do their share, and men coworkers feel
imposed upon.

Additionally, men in positions of authority traditionally pick as protégés young individuals as much like
themselves as possible. "Fast burners" (up-and-coming
young officers) need mentors. It is rare for a male senior
officer--who rose to the top in an era when women were
not in evidence except in support functions--to act as
sponsor for a woman officer.

Many men admit that they first view women as sexual
objects--and only later see them as professionals. Some
men can never separate the two. While they want women to
be feminine, many men find themselves very uncomfortable
working with feminine women. Others find that once they
work with women their preconceived ideas change and become
positive.

For many men, women in the services will always create
a negative situation, because it was the absence of female
influences which first attracted them to the military. To
these men, the military fulfills the concept of "male
clubs."

Men who are resentful often reflect the views of those
on the receiving end of paternalistic attitudes. They are

the men who feel that women shirk full responsibilities by
desire or policy and that men end up with added physical
labor, longer rotations away from home, more remote assignments, late-night shifts, and more doubling-up on workloads.

To further complicate these different attitudinal
problems, men also vary in their concepts of equal treatment of women. Some feel that equal treatment means
treating and expecting women to act like men. Some think
that equal treatment is keeping women in traditionally
female jobs.

With such nonstandard treatment, women act frustrated
and react to men's reactions while attempting to maximize
their performance. Women feel that they are performing
their best and are equal to men, although they are not
being fully utilized. Men, on the other hand, often feel
that women are not doing their full share and fail to
recognize that they are the ones not allowing women the
opportunity to do so. Additionally, men fail to communi-
cate any dissatisfaction and would be dissatisfied no
matter what. Similar to the private sector, men have most
often seen women in administrative and clerical roles and
find it difficult to accept them as being successful elsewhere.

It is essential that men and women both be treated
fairly and given equal opportunities for achievement and
advancement and also be held equally responsible for their
contributions and failures.

While attitudes are paramount alone--they have a com-
pounding impact on the other issues to be considered.

Socialization of Women

While much emphasis is being placed on the roles of women,
the real question of their preparation to fill those roles
has not been considered. These new life-styles are still
proving very threatening to many women. According to
Martina S. Horner, president of Radcliffe College, historically women have "converged on the idea that femininity
and individual achievements which reflect intellectual
competence or leadership potential are desirable but
mutually exclusive goals. The aggressive and, by implication, masculine qualities inherent in a capacity for
mastering intellectual problems, attacking difficulties,
and making final decisions are considered fundamentally
antagonistic to or incompatible with femininity."[12] Horner

[12]Martina A. Horner, "Toward an Understanding of
Achievement-Related Conflicts in Women," Journal of Social
Issues, Vol. 28, No. 2 (1972), p. 158.

sees women going as far as purposely avoiding success in
fear of negative social ramifications.

A study of Vassar women implied that the best-
adjusted women were the underachievers, who did not prepare
themselves for an unrealistic future by overemphasizing
academic performance.[13]

From women's early formative years, the sense of
individual competition has been ingrained. Women compete
for affection from their fathers and suitors. Sports
activities for women were traditionally competitive and
not team-oriented or spirited. In moving into professional
roles beyond the traditional nursing, teaching, and clerical
jobs, women have carried over these competitive attitudes.

For many women who moved into the traditional male
domain, a "queen bee" syndrome ensued as the result of
tokenism. Once one or two successful women were in an
organization, the urgency to recruit more competent women
dissipated, and integration was in fact slowed down.
Attitudes will change to some degree if more women enter
into these new career fields in some density. Density is
critical, as problems will continue to arise from existing
isolation of women, while others will prevail because of
the continuing existence of the "queen bee" syndrome.
Yale University, upon opening its doors to women, found out
that until their classes had 20% women, the women did not
adjust or fare well in that environment. (There were the
rare superwomen exceptions.) A recent court case involving a Yale faculty member indicates that despite the
present 1 to 3 density at the university, women are still
subjected to academic problems because of their sex.[14]

                          Resource Pool

Due to the highly structured personnel system, women in the
military have not been able to move readily in or out of
their career field during childbearing years in the way
that other women professionals do (teachers, lawyers,
doctors, accountants). In addition, the up-or-out-system
plays havoc on the potential of a woman choosing to take
time out for childbearing. Needless to say, childbearing
cannot be delayed until later in one's life. Women in the
military, in the past, had to make the choice of career or
family, usually at a time when career opportunities were

[13]Ravena Nelson, "The Changing Image of the Career
Woman," in E. C. Lewis, Developing Women's Potential
(Ames: Iowa State Press, 1968), p. 35.
    [14]Personal interview with Jackie Mintz, Provost, Yale
University, July 1975.

about to develop for them, because pregnancy meant automatic discharge.

Despite the policy changes in 1971 and 1975 relating
to pregnancy and minor dependents, women still must face
the implications of the military mission in making decisions to manage both career and family. This choice
becomes increasingly difficult as the types of jobs change
and levels of responsibility increase.

To intensify the situation, recent work by Matina
Horner and others shows that today's college women are
moving toward a belief that they must choose either a
career or a family.[15] This is a slight turning away from
the concept of balancing both a successful career and
family. This can further impact on the real potential
pool of women and their availability as presently believed
to be substantially beyond a first term.

Married Couples

As more women enter the service, there are bound to be
more service marriages. For example, today 46% of the
Air Force's enlisted women and 31% of the officers are
married. About 80% of these married women are married to
other military members.[16] Already the services are feeling
the impact of these changes. Marriages when only one
spouse is in the service must reflect personal decisions
concerning new assignments. If the numbers of women continue to increase and the percentage of the population of
marrieds grows accordingly, the services will be managing
a significant percentage of joint assignments (keeping
spouses/families together).

Joint spouse moves for schooling and assignments conducive to career advancement that require separation become
another matter. While the economists view these phenomena
as blessings--saving money by moving one family instead of
two to fill two military vacancies; the personnel people
will be faced with an entirely new set of assignment problems. These will include moving two people to a single
base and matching skills, training, and schooling assignments. Training and schooling, while critical to career
enhancement, could place the assignments of the spouse
out of sequence, cause the overmanning of a position, or
move someone to accommodate a spouse, or incur additional
moves to keep them together.

[15]Personal Interview with Martina Horner, April 1977.
[16]Data furnished by the Department of the Air Force,
Military Personnel Center, November 1977.

Military couples can ease the impact of these career planning necessities by developing realistic joint-career game plans which allow for career progression for both spouses, not just the wife tagging after the husband. It takes a mature couple to consider both careers, especially when the woman's is more or at least as competitive as her husband's career. With deployment and training exercises which include joint spouses with dependent families increasing, there already has been evidence of one spouse being left behind to care for the children during these routine exercises. Childcare needs must be considered.

In addition, investments in potential leaders are lost when opportunities are denied because of the desire for joint assignments. This can be both economically costly and in terms of the numbers of quality people.

While the services are presently striving to arrange joint assignments, the increased numbers of marrieds are going to create real and new potential management problems in the future.

Pregnancy Policies

Statistics on pregnancy show that the "fertility" rate with Air Force women is 7 per 100 women per year, half the rate within the U.S. population as a whole. Considering that this rate represents 7% of the female force--or less than one-half of 1% of the total force, it does not constitute a significant manning factor at this time; however, extended absences of pregnant women impact on small units and organizations and, further, with the growing number of women in the service and the consequent increase in military couples, pregnancy will become commonplace.[17] Clearly desk jobs require only a short absence period for childbirth and recuperation for healthy women. For the rare cases with complications, their fitness for service becomes a much longer-term question. However, as women move into the more physically demanding, nontraditional jobs, the woman's ability to perform her job during pregnancy may result in temporary assignment to less demanding work.

Since the childbearing period covers a span of years, assigning women to only desk jobs during that span can hurt their careers, and is logistically impossible. Expecting a woman to get pregnant only during periods of desk assignments is also unrealistic.

While healthy women should be able to do physical

[17]Department of the Air Force, Surgeon General Letter, subject: Non-Effectiveness Rates by AFSC, Sex, Disease Category and Age, 29 July 1976.

activity during pregnancy, problems relating to size,
balance, and environmental hazards, especially for women
who are aircraft mechanics, tank drivers, forklift drivers,
etc., can emerge that have not yet been reckoned with.

Job adaptation during pregnancy will be significantly
different for women in desk jobs as opposed to women in
nontraditional roles. Physical strength may be of no
great concern in a desk job. On the other hand, sheer
size and balance problems could well change a woman's
ability to perform her nontraditional job for as long as
her entire pregnancy.

Pregnancies not only create temporary physical changes,
but often circumstances of the pregnancies put great emotional stress on the women. With the growing numbers of
single-parent households have come more children born out
of wedlock--a situation that is contrary to the family
orientation of this country and which creates serious
questions for the women in the military environment. A
young woman faced with pregnancy under these conditions
must carefully examine her ability to assume the demands
of military life--especially when her job requires full-
time commitments such as with academic life or more than
normal field duty or time away from home. Policies,
created as examples of equality for women, can pose such
strains on a woman that her ability to emerge as a leader
would appear doubtful. This very complex issue tracks to
the more basic requirements such as academy cadets remaining single or women entering more of the nontraditional
career fields.

Single Parents

While the phenomenon of the single parent was brought
into the limelight when the policy relating to single
mothers changed, the issue has had growing importance to
men as well. Thousands of single military fathers, far
greater numbers than single mothers, create concerns of
childcare, especially during deployment, exercises, shift
or night work, and other regular but unusual conditions
relating to the mission. In fact, there are over 3,538
male single heads of household and 1,107 female single
heads of household in the Air Force with dependent children. These include individuals who are widowed, single,
divorced, under interlocutary decree or whose marriages
have been annulled. The children may be that of the parent
or may be adopted.[18]

[18]Data provided by Department of the Air Force,
Military Personnel Center, November 1977.

The Impact on the Family

With these and other changes, such as an emerging role of
the dependent husband, policymakers must begin to examine
these phenomena carefully and plan accordingly, for there
are no historical data that reflect these changes. Hamil-
ton McCubbin, sociologist at the University of Minnesota,
asks the following questions: "How will these changing
situations affect military job assignments, family reloca-
tions, and extended separations? And will members of
military families become less dependent on the system,
more assertive of their personal and family needs, and
less willing to subordinate their lives to the orders of
the military establishment?"[19] McCubbin clearly foresaw
the problems of recruiting, socializing, and retaining
high-quality military personnel in light of the changing
roles of men and women.

Standards

Pay and job security cause women to resist leaving traditional jobs. As women begin to get into new fields, they
have recognized another threat of uncertainty--the
acceptance of additional responsibilities along with
assumptions of rights. Unfortunately, some women are not
ready for these responsibilities and, in resistance,
capitalize on feminine traits. For these women, double
standards have become a way of life. The military career
has become conducive to equal pay for unequal responsibility. Development and dissemination of information on
non-sex-specific job standards--as well as the preformance
of capable women meeting those standards in those jobs--
can rectify this performance shortfall.

As women move into the nontraditional jobs, they are
moving into a male-oriented world. Changes in policies
do not necessarily mean changes in standards. But it is
necessary for people to become aware of and sensitive to
the prevailing male atmosphere in establishing job standards that reflect both mental and physical needs. This
becomes critical to avoid mismatches, unreal expectations,
in an alien atmosphere--all which lead to mismatches,
intensifying of attitudes, and eventually an aura of
failure.

The lines of command must be sharply defined from
the start, especially when a husband and wife are in the

[19]Hamilton I. McCubbin and Martha A. Marsden, "The
Military Family and the Changing Military Profession,"
Paper presented at the Regional Meeting of the Inter Uni-
versity Seminar on Armed Forces and Society, Maxwell Air
Force Base, Alabama, October 1976.

same unit. Many women may face conflicts with their husbands if high performance standards are demanded of them.

It is important that the interlocking issue described
shouls by no means preclude women from fully serving in
the military--especially at a time that their presence is
becoming more important in making the AVF work. What is
essential is that women and men joining the military understand the mission and its priorities--and that the
policymakers consider these issues in defining their requirements.

For whether these women remain in the military and
contribute to our national defense is directly dependent
upon the parameters within which they are allowed to serve--
as equal partners or as an adjunct and disadvantaged
minority.

If this challenge is successfully met, the Defense
Department will have been in the forefront of one of the
major social accomplishments of this century.

UNITED STATES RESERVE FORCES

A HIGH-COST, LOW-RETURN INVESTMENT IN NATIONAL SECURITY

John B. Keeley

The all-volunteer force is comprised of two elements, the active forces and the reserve forces. The success of the all-volunteer force and the viability of current strategic assumptions for the employment of the nation's military forces can only be assessed against the condition of both the active and the reserve forces. In this sense the all-volunteer force must be judged a failure, for the condition of our reserve forces, in their totality, can only be judged as disastrous.

Some might have us believe that the deplorable condition of the reserve forces is not significant; that what counts is the status of the active forces. Let us look at some facts. Assuming that U.S. Army reserve forces were at full strength, they would provide the following percentages of total (active plus reserve) Army forces:

Note: In this essay the term reserves is used in a generic sense. Reserves = U.S. Army National Guard, U.S. Army Reserve, U.S. Air Guard, U.S. Air Force Reserve, U.S. Naval Reserve, U.S. Marine Corps Reserve, U.S. Coast Guard Reserve, and Individual Ready Reserve. The primary focus of this essay is upon the Army reserve forces since they comprise the largest and most significant element of the U.S. reserve forces. The distinction between and among classes of reserves and types of reserve forces is almost Byzantine in its complexity and beyond the scope of this essay.

54% of all deployable forces
52% of all infantry and tank battalions
58% of all field artillery battalions
60% of all tactical support forces.[1]

These percentages belie any notion that the reserves are
not important to the nation's military capability. The
active forces today cannot fight for long without support
from the reserves, and they cannot fight for long with the
reserves in their present condition.

Commentators of late have fairly and accurately
described the parlous conditions of the reserves--short of
people, short of equipment, untrained and unready.[2]   There
have been numerous proposals to remedy these ills. The
adoption of these remedies has done little more in terms
of ultimate effectiveness than increase the yearly cost of
the reserve establishment, which will approach seven
billion dollars in the FY 1979 budget.

It is not likely that any efforts at revivication of
the reserves in their present form will succeed. In fact,
it may be just as well that they do not. For our concern
for remedying these ills should not mask the fundamental
problem of the reserves. The reserves are presently
organized and tasked to reinforce U.S. forces in Europe
in the event of war. The reserves are largely unable to
meet the readiness/deployment schedules which would be
necessary for them to have an impact on the initial battles
of the war. New concepts of organization might be able to
provide a significantly improved response capability in
certain areas of support, and suggestions to this end will
be made, but any strategy which depends on reserve combat
units to make a major contribution to the first battles is
seriously flawed. Active forces will have to bear the
initial brunt of combat and our capabilities and strategies
should explicitly recognize this fact. To support this
proposition, we need only examine the interrelationship
between the active forces and those reserve units tasked
to provide support to these active forces in the event
of war.

At the present time, the Army, and to a considerably
lesser degree the Air Force and Navy, is dependent upon
reserve forces to provide a very large proportion of the

[1]These percentages provided by Maj. Gen. Francis Green-
lief, USANG, Retired, Executive Vice President, U.S. National Guard Association, 23 March 1978.
[2]For a comprehensive analysis of U.S. reserve forces
and their many problems, see Martin Binkin, U.S. Reserve
Forces (Washington, D.C.: Brookings Institution, 1974).

backup, noncombat, support functions for the active divisions.
This is support without which these divisions cannot sustain
combat operations. Approximately 300,000 of the active Army's total support-force requirement is to be provided by
the reserves. The plan which supposedly integrates the active and reserve forces into a smooth-working team is called
the total force concept. This concept is based upon some de-
monstrably false assumptions concerning the readiness for
deployment of reserve forces in the event of mobilization.
These assumptions concern a high level of fill of personnel
and equipment in these units and the achievement and maintenance of peacetime training objectives. For the reserve
forces as a whole these assumptions are not valid today nor
have they been valid historically. Even if these assumptions were valid and the reserves could realize their peacetime readiness criteria, the concept of employing reserves
to reinforce Europe would most likely fail because of the
character of a likely attack on the central front and the
probable nature of the battle.

To illustrate the total force concept graphically, a
deployment sequence for an active division and its reserve
support units is portrayed below. It is a "best case" por-
trayal for the deployment of both the active and reserve
forces in that it is assumed that all units are at their
peacetime readiness goals and that the Soviets will not
interfere significantly in the deployment.

Deployment Sequence to Europe

M Day

Active Division	Prepare & fill	Deployment	Move to position	Ready for combat	
	1 week	3 weeks	1 week	Cumulative time 5 weeks	

Reserve Support Forces	Call-up & report	Fill	Train & pre- pare for de- ployment	Deploy- ment	Move to position	Ready to support
	2 weeks	1 week	6 weeks	3 weeks	1 week	Cumulative time 13 weeks

Note: This is a notionalized schedule. M Day is mobilization day and
decision to deploy day. Forces are deployed by sea. Deployment time
includes movement of personnel and equipment to port, loading and un-
loading, and transit time. "Fill" means to bring the unit to wartime
strength in personnel and to satisfy unit equipment shortages. Certain
active divisions can be deployed by air to prepositioned equipment.
This even earlier deployment exacerbates the present problem of insufficient support forces in the active force structure.

        This deployment sequence reveals the salient weakness
of present U.S. strategy for the reinforcement of Europe: the
need for sufficient warning time before the commencement of
hostilities. A minimum of five weeks will be required for
an active division transported by sea to be in position. A
minimum of thirteen weeks for reserve forces to deploy and
be functional.

        If one accepts General Haig's estimate of as little
as eight days' warning of probable Soviet attack as a
reasonable estimate,[3] then the relevance of U.S. based, sea-
deployed forces to at least the initial defense of Europe is
questionable. This is especially so for the reserve forces.
When the likelihood of very abbreviated warning is coupled
with the dramatically increased destructiveness of the modern
battlefield (total tank losses by the Arabs and the Israelis
in the three weeks of the October 1973 War were roughly
double the total number of tanks in the U.S. Army units
in Europe), the implication is that future battles will be
violent and relatively brief (wars may well be as protracted
as ever) and decided by those forces in the theater of
operations at the commencement of hostilities.[4]

        If this hypothesis is correct, then the justification
of reserve forces for the reinforcement of Europe against
Soviet attack is misguided at best and at worst perhaps
fatal to our objective to deter a conventional Soviet
attack since our strategies are based on false expectations
of reserve responsiveness.

        There are certain qualifications to these generaliza-
tions that should now be made. First, the inadequacies of
the reserve forces are not related to the dedication and
competence of individual reservists. There are many part-
time soldiers, sailors, and airmen in the reserve forces who
are the equal, in all respects, of those on active duty.
Second, as a general rule the elements of the air reserve
structure (Air Force, Army, Navy, and Marine Corps)--trans-
port, refueling, fighter, helicopter and attack squadrons
are at a much higher level of readiness and easier to deploy
rapidly than the remainder of the reserve forces. There are
also company-sized and specialized units within the Army
which are at a level of training readiness to permit early
deployment. (The staffing and operation of a military
hospital is in essentials little different from a civilian
hospital.)

[3]"Haig Lifts Estimate of NATO Alert Time," New York
Times, 15 September 1977, page A-10.
        [4]For a convincing scenario outlining a limited Soviet
attack on NATO with little warning, see General R. Close,
L'Europe sans Defense? (Brussels: Editions Art and Voyages,
Collection Inedits, 1976).

These caveats do not invalidate the initial proposition that present reserve forces are unable to accomplish
their stated principal military function, which is to provide
forces in a timely fashion for the defense of Western
Europe. Others might argue that the reserve forces serve
an essential function in meeting military requirements in
less than general war situations. The record to date of the
employment of reserves--Korea, the Berlin Crisis, and
Vietnam in less than general war situations is a dismal one.[5]
(Again, individual reservists, as distinct from reserve
units, have been valuable to the nation in meeting these
crises, especially in the Korean emergency.)

No amount of metaphysics on improved deployment procedure or increased training readiness programs can mask the
realities described above.[6] Further, without warning time
much greater than now anticipated, the United States cannot
hope to win a reinforcement race with the Soviet Union. It
is less than 700 miles from the Soviet Union to Frankfurt,
West Germany. All but the last 100 miles is under positive
Soviet control. Even if Soviet reserve forces were in
disarray equal to that of the United Staes reserve forces,
the advantages of geography would assure victory to the
Soviets in any race to reinforce. In the event of hostilities
with the Soviet Union in Central Europe, the United States
would be severely pressed to sustain the forces currently
in Germany, let alone augment these forces with major reinforcements from the United States from either the active or
the reserve forces. Without more warning time than anticipated, reinforcements cannot arrive soon enough to influence the outcome of the initial battles. The initial
battles would be decided within a week to ten days of the
initiation of hostilities.

[5]For an excellent summary of the history of reserve
call-ups, see Herman T. Boland, "The Reserves," Studies Prepared for the President's Commission on an All-Volunteer
Armed Force, Vol. 2 (Washington, D.C.: U.S. Government Printing Office, 1970).
[6]During the Vietnam war, the readiness of U.S. strategic reserve forces was a matter of great concern to the secretary of defense and the services. Every effort was made to
improve the readiness of the strategic reserve forces with
only slight result. One of the chronic deficiencies plaguing
readiness was a serious shortage of equipment. One of the
means used to remedy this equipment-shortage was an assumption,
explicit in a footnote on the monthly readiness report, of
instant redistribution of worldwide equipment assets, e.g.,
depot and war reserve stocks, in the event of mobilization.
Hence, the use of the term metaphysical is appropriate in
describing efforts to improve deployment capability during
that era.

With the reserve forces as they are today and as they are likely to remain without major reforms, the military posture of the United States almost surely would be improved by the elimination of the reserves and the money thus saved might be better spent on other defense needs.

Elimination of the reserves would provide immediate and direct benefit through the release of a conservatively estimated six billion dollars each year to meet other defense needs. For example, in six years those savings could finance almost the entire U.S. Navy's ship-construction program. The savings of four years would fund the original B-1 bomber program.

To an uncertain degree, elimination of the reserves would reduce the growing competition between active and reserve forces for manpower. Army reserve forces alone need 100,000 nonprior service personnel each year to maintain its ranks. Active Army yearly requirements for nonprior service personnel are currently in the 120,000 to 140,000 range.

Of perhaps greater importance than the benefits described above would be the unavoidable necessity for the United States to build its strategies solely upon the capabilities of active forces. Strategies based on this reality are far more likely to succeed than strategies based on assumptions of the rapid availability of reserve forces.

There are three principal reasons given for retaining the reserves. First, the reserves provide the country with an essential military capability at a cost less than equivalent active forces. In theory this is true, but in fact it is not so, especially in light of the demands placed upon U.S. forces by the nature of modern warfare. Second, the reserves provide forces to the states for civil disturbance and disaster emergencies. This is true, but equally effective forces for these purposes can be provided with much less expensive organizations. Third, the reserve forces provide an important nexus between society and the active forces. This is also true, but it should be remembered that despite protestations to the contrary, the active Army and its leaders with few exceptions have a veiled disdain for the value of the reserve forces. This disdain puts in question the value of maintaining this "connection" between the civilian-soldier and his regular counterpart. Whatever military and social values one assigns to the reserves, they hardly sum up to make a case for keeping them under present conditions.

There is a case for the reserves, a strong case, provided that reforms in reserve organization and missions are accomplished and are based upon realistic assessments of the capabilities of reserves. The remainder of this paper is devoted to the consideration of proposals for a "new" reserve, a new reserve in terms of mission and organization.

The nation's reserve forces should be organized for three missions:

1. Augment and reconstitute the active forces which will have undergone severe losses regardless of the outcome of hostilities.

2. Provide the organization and talent for training the citizen Army, Navy and Air Force which would be created.

3. Provide local forces for state authorities in the event of civil disorder or disaster. In the event of a nuclear attack provide with the active forces the basis for civil order and organization for the reconstruction of vital services.

A closer look at these three missions will show how the reserve structure can be rationalized to provide a real and substantial contribution to our national security.

In the event of short-notice hostilities in Europe (or anywhere else for that matter), the most urgent demand will be for replacements for combat losses. Daily losses for units in active combat can be conservatively estimated to be between 5% and 10% of the force engaged. Losses for the U.S. Army in Europe could easily reach 5,000 per day.[7] These losses do not occur evenly through the force. They are concentrated in the combat arms--infantry, armor, and artillery, and especially among the infantry. These losses need to be replaced promptly or the units will quickly become ineffective. Under the circumstances assumed throughout this paper (short warning, 30-day war) the only source for these replacements will be the active Army. A few might come directly from the training center, but most will come from active Army units. Drawing on active units for initial replacements is essentially the only alternative the Army would have at that time. Although there exists within the reserve structure a pool of individual replacements called the Individual Ready Reserve (IRR), which is largely comprised of

[7]Loss estimates must be speculative. Losses must include not only combat casualties but also losses to accidents and illness which can be expected to increase during hostilities. Actual losses would depend upon the intensity of the attack and the degree to which U.S. forces were forewarned and dispersed. The 5,000 estimate of losses is slightly less than 3% of the total number of Army personnel stationed in Germany.

prior-service personnel, the IRR is not sufficiently respon-
sive (present notification procedures are almost totally
ineffective) to the first 30-day needs of any of the services. There are also problems in the IRR of skills densities
(not enough of the high-demand skills such as infantry and
armor) and individual military proficiency.

Much can be done to improve the IRR, but its primary
function should be to fill personnel shortages in active
forces based in the United States, not the direct replacement
of combat losses, and secondarily, it can be used to fill
personnel shortages among mobilized reserve forces. Some
thoughts on how to improve the IRR will be presented in the
next section.

U.S.-based forces depend upon fixed facilities and
civilian industry to provide what might be called "housekeeping" support. Utilities, civil engineering, hospitals,
warehousing, telephone, and maintenance activities are
essentially fixed. An Army in the field needs the same
kinds of support and must depend on Army support units to
provide it. Ideally, for all but the most immediately deploying active forces which would depend upon active support
units, the reserve support elements should be able to deploy
either concurrently or immediately following the active
forces that they support. This cannot be done at present
largely because of the length of time necessary to alert
individual reservists, to fill units to strength, and to
complete training. Means to reduce this time will be
discussed later.

It can be anticipated that a major expansion of the
nation's military forces will commence upon mobilization.
To accomplish this expansion smoothly and expeditiously involves many activities beyond the scope of this paper,
initiation of conscription and industrial mobilization, for
example. One central function will be the training of
individuals to man new units in the expanding force structure
and to replace casualties. There is little elasticity in
the active military's training structure to meet these
surge requirements.

The rapid development of an expanded training base is
a function ideally suited to the reserve forces. Currently
within the reserves there are twelve training divisions with
precisely this responsibility. Their function upon mobilization would be to train all conscripts in basic military
skills and to provide advanced individual training in the
combat skills. Experience with these divisions has been
generally excellent. It is likely that these training divisions are the most cost-effective organizations within the
reserves. The training-division concept probably can be

expanded to contribute significantly more to the goal of
rapid expansion of forces than is true at present.

Disaster-assistance responsibilities are fragmented
among a number of governmental agencies: the Executive Office of the President, HUD, the Army Corps of Engineers, the
Department of Defense (Civil Defense), and others. The
coordination among these agencies is inevitably poor. The
Carter administration is looking at ways to improve these
programs. It is suggested here that the reserve forces be
given this responsibility. State National Guard units are
frequently called to service by state governors to provide
law and order and other assistance, and their services are
vital in this respect, as evidenced by their employment in
the Middle West and New England during the winter of 1978.

The experience gained in meeting natural disasters
would be of value in the event of a nuclear attack on
the United States. The military organizations of the United
States, both active and reserve, would probably be the only
national organizations capable of implementing the complex
tasks associated with rebuilding the nation. The civil-disas-
ter mission would also give vitality and meaning to the
reserve function. There is presently an air of unreality
about the reserves and their missions.

It is time to be more specific about how a reorganized
reserve could accomplish the three missions defined above.
The first mission involves reconstitution and augmentation
of the active forces. With the assumption that combat-
loss replacements would come from the active forces, active
units would rapidly lose effectiveness until these shortages
had been filled. In addition, there would be a need for
support units to support the active forces.

The IRR (Individual Ready Reserve) pool has been until
recently the principal source for these replacements.
Until the end of conscription the IRR pool was kept full by
the relatively high turnover of personnel associated with the
draft. The total military obligation for either a draftee
or enlistee is six years. His obligation to the reserves,
IRR, or other organized reserve component is five years less
his active-duty service. (The sixth year is spent in the
standby reserves.) Implicit in this organization of the IRR
as an element of the reserves was an assumption of indefinite
conscription with its two years of active duty and four years
of reserve obligation.

The reduction of the size of the active forces coupled
with longer enlistments (3 or 4 years are the norm) has reduced the IRR to the point where it is unable to meet wartime
requirements. It is forecast that by 1982 the IRR will be
short 300,000 personnel to meet M-Day to M + 180 requirements

just for the Army. Even if the IRR were at desired
strength levels, it would remain unwieldly and of value only
in a gross sense. First, it is difficult to call up the
IRR. The services do not have current addresses of individuals within the IRR. Individual members of the IRR do not
have mobilization instructions and thus cannot be mobilized
by general announcements through the press or radio.
Second, there is no program to maintain military skills,
many of which are highly perishable (such as a tank gunner)
or which become technologically obsolete through the introduction of new weapons systems. Third, its only source of
membership is prior-service personnel or personnel from the
reserves; that is, one cannot enlist   in the IRR. What
is to be done? Initially, the services will need a current
inventory of the skills and condition of the IRR and the
present addresses of its members. The next step is to give
everyone a mobilization assignment so he can be mobilized
by general broadcast. This will require legislation with
sanctions for those who do not keep their parent services
aware of their present addresses and current circumstances.

        This first step will make the present IRR more useful
and available. It will do nothing to increase its size or to
maintain or improve its skills.

        At any time the IRR is the best source of experienced
personnel, for this month's new Individual Ready Reservist
was last month's trained, active-duty soldier or sailor.
To put this in some perspective, the U.S. Army discharges
approximately 15,000 people each month who then enter the
IRR. Of this number approximately 30% are in skills designated as combat (the surge-demand skills needed at the
outset of hostilities). These individuals plus others
holding critical skills need to be personally identified and
at the time of discharge offered an opportunity and an
incentive to maintain their military skills while members
of the IRR. Though not all so invited would be interested
and not all those interested could be accommodated for geographical and other reasons, possibly as many as 50% of
those eligible might participate.

        To see how this might work, let us follow an individ-
ual, an Army tank gunner, who has agreed to participate in a
skills-maintenance program. This individual would be advised
of the military facility, active or reserve, nearest his home
which has the facilities to provide him the requisite training support. This support would consist of programmed instructional material, reference manuals, TV instructional tapes,
and, in the case of a tank gunner, probably a tank turret
simulator. Some of this material would be given or loaned
for home use, the remainder would be available at his conven-

ience, nights and weekends included. To test and encourage
the maintenance of these skills, the individual would be
required to take a skill test appropriate to his skill level
three times a year. Successful completion of each skills
test would be rewarded by a $300 tax-free payment from the
government (the amount could be increased depending upon the
criticality of the skill). Further, this tank gunner will be
offered the opportunity for two weeks of full time training
(including weapons firing) sometime during the year for which
he would be paid $1,000 above expenses.

The program would be voluntary; the individual would
belong to no military organization; there would be no
required number of drill periods; no uniforms to be worn and
no haircut regulations. There would be no perquisites or
other benefits. Once the obligatory period of service in
the IRR is completed, the individual would be offered the
opportunity to extend his membership in the IRR for several
more years (age 35 is probably a good upper limit) under the
same terms or perhaps with a slightly higher financial
incentive (the tax-free payments can be expected to become
more appealing as the individual moves into higher tax brack-
ets). When it is realized that there are only approximately
2,500 tank gunners in the entire U.S. Army in Europe, the
value of participation by only 2,000 to 3,000 personnel in
a program such as outlined above is apparent.

It should not be difficult to devise similar skill-
maintenance programs for other critical skills. Even the
complex skills of the infantryman are amenable to such a
program. Participation by 50,000 individuals of all services
in such programs would cost a small fraction (2% to 3%) of
the present reserve structure costs.[8]

Whether the system described above, or some other
system, will indeed provide 50,000 or more trained personnel
available for immediate call-up is not known. It is clear
that the present system cannot. It is time to search for
other means to meet this important requirement.

It is economically unwise and militarily unnecessary
to maintain all of the support forces in the active structure
that would be needed in the event of war. How many units of
what kind that can be placed in the reserve structure is
dependent upon the deployment timetable of the active forces,
and the concept of logistic support within the active forces,

[8]Cost estimates, even with the most sophisticated
analysis, are subject to a wide range of error. Cost estimates throughout this paper are educated guesses, but are
felt to be reasonable approximations.

and the availability of reserve units upon mobilization.
This relationship was partially displayed graphically at
the beginning of this paper. The military organization for
combat and the underlying concepts of logistic support are
not at issue here and are beyond the scope of this paper. For
the purposes of this paper these relationships are accepted
as given.

The challenge of all reserve units is the challenge
of converting loosely organized, geographically separated,
partially trained units into cohesive, trained, functioning
organizations. This challenge exists at all levels of the
reserve structure, but it becomes increasingly difficult
as the organizations become larger and more complex. For
example, bringing an infantry division to a functioning level
of combat readiness takes more time than realizing the same
goal for an infantry company. This problem is greatest when
the organization's primary function involves the use of
unique military skills--combat skills--and least when the
military function is similar to equivalent civilian functions, such as medical, transportation, communications, and
the like.

The support units involved in the initial augmentation
of the active forces will fall, by and large, into the
civilian-equivalent category. These units, broadly defined
as logistic units, include in addition to those mentioned
above supply, maintenance, engineering, and administrative
units. The skills necessary to man these units exists in
great abundance (in terms of demand) in American society.
There are doctors, nurses, and radiologists. There are
bulldozer operators and electronic repairmen by tens of
thousands. There are computer programmers, diesel mechanics,
air conditioning repair men, carpenters, and accountants.
All of these skills exist within the present reserve structure, and yet a conservative estimate of the time necessary
to bring these people, already partially trained in military
matters and organized in military units, from civilian life
to deployment readiness is 40 to 60 days. When one reflects
that the German army attacked Belgium on 4 August 1914 less
than three days after the declaration of mobilization (4:00
p.m., 1 August) and was within 20 miles of Paris on 30 August; when one reflects that the Israelis can add 200,000
personnel to their armed forces in less than 48 hours, then
one must have serious reservations concerning our reserve
system.

Without changing the present organizational structure
of these units, significant improvements in readiness can
be achieved for these early deploying units through the
adoption of the following procedures.

    1. Maintain a current inventory, reserve wide, by
unit, of current unit skill shortages. This will assist
in matching skills within the IRR with skill shortages in
units.

    2. A small cadre of active officers and enlisted
personnel would be attached to each unit at the time of
deployment to provide administrative and technical training
and support until such time as the unit is able to provide
these functions for itself.

    A cadre for a company would be no more than 4 to 6
people. A cadre for a battalion would be no more than 25
to 30. Those personnel who now comprise the reserve advisors
can be organized and augmented to accomplish this.

    3. Unit sets of equipment can be assembled from
current depot stocks and packaged and prepared for immediate
deployment.

    4. A coordinating and directive headquarters with
the sole mission of monitoring the training and status and
deployment of these units should be established.

    The ideas mentioned above are not especially novel.
The only thing notable is that these or similar proposals
have not already been adopted.

    The second mission proposed for the reserve forces
is to provide the organization and talent for training the
citizen Army, Navy and Air Force which would be needed in the
event of extended hostilities. As mentioned, there are 12
reserve training divisions whose function is to provide for
the Army trained individuals as either fillers or replacements
to existing units or fillers for newly created units.

    "Existing units" in the reserve structure, in addi-
tion to those intended to augment the active forces, are
organized on the assumption that in peacetime these units
can be maintained at a level of strength and training so that
in the event of mobilization the addition of trained fillers
from the IRR or the training base plus additional unit training would result in a combat-ready organization in from 3 to
4 months. These "existing units" include eight National
Guard divisions and numerous other units of brigade and
battalion size. All of these units would inevitably have
conflicting demands for people of certain skills and for
equipment that is short. Units scheduled for deployment
under certain schedules will have to be replaced by others.
Nondeploying units will be raided for men and equipment.
There will be chaos and confusion. Nothing will be as planned
The inevitable shake-out of personnel which has occurred with
every previous mobilization is likely to happen again. Some

people will suddenly be found to be too old or too infirm
for their responsibilities. Others will be too "vital"
to other aspects of the defense effort. And, lastly, too
many will be found to be incompetent.[9]

These are realities. Even if through some magic of
administration and motivation all of these problems could be
overcome (and they can be minimized for a small number of
logistic support units as discussed earlier), there may be
an insuperable barrier for the combat units. This barrier
has been called the "sophistication barrier" by Martin
Edmonds.[10] Considering the cost and complexity of training
regular forces and the argument by the regular establishment
that two-year draftees cannot be adequately trained to
fulfill military duties, it is difficult to conceive of how
reserve units could achieve more than a low level of training
readiness under the limited training regime required of
reserve units (48 weekly drill periods, two weeks of active
training each year). Much of this time is wasted and aptly
described by the ordinary soldier as "fumble time:" time
spent checking roll, having inspections, issuing and returning equipment, and passing out the latest exhortations from
higher echelons.

If the expectations placed on "existing units" are
inherently unreal, then it is time to consider alternatives.[11]
A more realistic and useful organization for the reserves
would be an organization which could take the personnel
completing individual training and train them as a unit.
The concept, the cadre concept, is a valid one and has been
employed by military organizations worldwide as an efficient
means for rapidly expanding forces. The cadre for a division
would be between 3,000 and 4,000 personnel. The cost of
maintaining and training a cadre divison in peacetime would
be much less than the current costs of training and maintaining one of the present reserve divisions, even in their
present parlous state. A conservative estimate of the costs
for a cadre division would be about one-fifth that of a
reserve division. The savings would come not only from a
generally proportionate reduction in manpower costs but also
from not operating expensive equipment. Peacetime training
for a cadre division would consist primarily of a close asso-

[9]Boland, The President's Commission, pp. IV-2-16.
[10]Roger A. Beaumont and Martin Edmonds, eds., War in
the Next Decade (Lexington: University of Kentucky Press,
1974), p. 44.
[11]For a most imaginative set of proposals intended to
make U.S. and NATO reserve forces more useful, see Steven L.
Canby, "European Mobilization, U.S. and NATO Reserves," Armed
Forces and Society, 4, no. 2 (Winter 1978).

ciation with like active units. The active unit would serve
as a tutor for the reserve unit. In addition, there would
be instructional programs tailored to the problems of assim-
ilating large numbers of fillers into an organization. It
should be pointed out that the active Army operated essentially a similar program on a much smaller scale until
1962. This program was titled the Overseas Unit Replacement
Program. An active cadre accepted graduates from the
training base, conducted unit training from squad through
battle group level, and then deployed overseas as a unit.
The program was a great success and was abandoned because
of the pressures of the increasing United States commitment
in Vietnam.

     Units so constituted should have a basic combat
capability within four to six months after receiving fillers,
from ten months to a year following mobilization. This may
seem to be an excessive period of time. It isn't. The
last time the U.S. Army created a division from scratch to
go to war was in 1966 when the 9th Infantry Division was
activated. From activation to deployment to Vietnam took
nearly a year. It would be unrealistic to expect that any
reserve organization could create an equivalent division out
of whole cloth any faster. Battalion- and brigade-sized
units could be made ready sooner and could be added to existing divisions to increase their combat power. The number
and kinds of cadre organizations within the reserves would be
tailored according to the estimated strategic requirements,
the availability of manpower within a given period, and the
quantity of equipment available.

     The third mission for the reserves--the provision of
local forces to state authorities in the event of civil
disorder or disaster, or in the event of nuclear attack, to
provide with the active forces the basis for civil order and
an organization for the reconstruction of vital services--is
a mission which is a direct descendant of the traditional
militia function. It can be described as a home defense
mission. The need for military forces to quell civil disorder and to assist in the recovery from natural disasters
requires no justification or demonstration.

     In time of war numerous communication, power, indus-
trial, and governmental facilities will need security. It
would be most appropriate for the National Guard to assume
the civil defense responsibilities of a state. All of these
tasks are amenable to accomplishment through part-time participation by citizen soldiers. Assistance in recovery from
nuclear attack would be a logical and natural extension of
these functions.

     Many will argue that the political power of the reserve
forces, especially that of the National Guard, will effective-

ly block any major reforms. They will argue that reform
can only be made at the margin. Certainly that has been
the fate of reforms proposed in recent years. Today
circumstances are different, and it is necessary to address
these issues again.

For years conscription kept the ranks of the reserve
forces filled by providing a less painful alternative than
serving on active duty. The reserves are now atrophying and
proposals to bring them back to life are little more than
palliatives.

Even if it were possible to bring the reserves back
to life, there remains the "sophistication barrier." Modern
military organizations, technically and doctrinally, are
too complex for part-time soldiers. Once it was possible to
beat ploughshares into swords and turn plowmen into sharpshooters. Our defense now demands far more than swords and
sharpshooters.

Lastly, the dramatic increase in Soviet capabilities
to launch a major attack in Central Europe on short notice
undercuts any strategic concepts that depend on rapid reinforcement from the reserves.

Since it is not possible for U.S. reserve forces to
play any significant role in the defense against a sudden
Soviet attack,[12] the United States should consider the
shifting to the reserve forces of our NATO allies many of
the functions that could be performed by in-place reserve
forces. Two such functions that can be readily performed
by reserve elements of other countries would be engineering
and transportation.

To illustrate with a specific example of how NATO
reserve forces could expedite the arrival of U.S. forces,
we need only consider the status of prepositioned equipment
earmarked for U.S. forces to be flown to Europe. This equipment is kept in humidity-controlled storage sites generally
along the Mannheim-Kaiserslautern autobahn. The process
of moving personnel from the arrival airfields to these
depots and then to dispersal areas is complicated, time
consuming, and, because of congestion, vulnerable to air
attack. Three-thousand German reservists trained in driving
American vehicles could move an entire division's equipment
into selected dispersal areas in less than a week. U.S.
troops would then move directly to their vehicles and should

[12]There are a number of reserve organizations, as
mentioned earlier, that would be able upon mobilization to
quite promptly assist the active forces. The value of the
reserves must be considered in their entirety and in relation to their strategic mission.

be able to fight within 24 hours. The five to seven days
saved by this procedure could be vital to a successful
defense.

        A host of other functions can be transferred to
European reserve forces. The United States has a legitimate
interest in the reserve capabilities of our NATO allies.
NATO's reserves, like ours, have been generally neglected.
The United States should attempt to bring a reserve program
with the NATO allies that is mutually supporting. This would
have not only important military consequences but would also
be of great political signficance in symbolizing NATO solidarity and determination.

        The nation's military strategies and the structures
and missions of the active and reserve forces are seriously
out of balance. To bring these elements into proper balance
will require new perspectives and new assessments of the
reciprocal relationships between forces and strategies.
The nation needs reserves. They are vital to our security.

MUDDLING THROUGH WON'T DO

Robert Leider

On the surface, the all-volunteer force appears to be a
success. It has not shrunk to Andorran size. It has not
turned all black or all illiterate. Its increased cost--
estimated at $3 billion per year by the General Accounting
Office--is not much more than Uncle Sam pays for pushing an
interstate highway through a residential neighborhood or
an agricultural subsidy. And, best of all, the military
still wear uniforms and march in parades.

All Is Well--Or Is It?

Of the scores of predictions and forecasts that were made
in five stormy years of all-volunteer-force debates, a few
actually came true but with less beneficial and less ominous
consequences than had been prophesied. Most fell wide of
the mark or never materialized.

In strength, the all-volunteer force seems capable of
fielding one defender for every one hundred Americans--a
figure that may be more closely allied to the ability to
recruit and pay than to any real security need, but still
an impressive figure.

Grouped by mental profile or years of school attendance,
the volunteers, in the aggregate, compare reasonably well
with yesterday's draftees.

Among the four services, the Air Force found it the
easiest to meet recruiting goals, with the Navy but one small
step behind. The Army and the Marine Corps, always less
popular, had to work harder for their manpower, engage in
some flackery and foolishness, and squeeze their recruiters.
But they, too, generally reached their objectives, though
with a fewer number of high school graduates than the
services might have preferred.

The forecast that came the closest to the truth is the
decline in Reserve strength without the nourishing nipple

of the draft. It is now a fact. What is less clear is
how much concern one should attach to this development.

Its significance for state governors who want to deal
with floods, blizzards, and looting is beyond doubt.
Governors may have to reach a greater accommodation with
the effects of natural disaster and human villainy.

There is less certainty about what a shrinking Reserve
means to the execution of NATO reinforcement plans. Even
at full strength, the Reserves suffered from perpetual
reorganization woes and chronic unreadiness. There was,
moreover, a silent but persistent skepticism about the
motivation of a force that drew large numbers of people who
felt more comfortable with the remote chance of a call-up
in the distant future than with the sureness of immediate
service. Personnel strength and capability are not synon-
ymous concepts. And yesterday's numerically hefty but
unready and unmotivated forces may have been neither more
capable nor less of carrying off an effective reinforcement
than today's reduced and unbalanced components.

Other predictions made in all solemnity during the
AVF debate proved to be mere exercises in theory or emotion.
The elaborate elasticity calculations which demonstrated
that incremental increases in pay would stimulate propor-
tional increases in enlistments, considering prevailing
wage levels and unemployment rates, turned out to be in
error. The theorists had excluded too many chunks of
reality from their equations. They had considered the
military in the aggregate, as though riflemen and aircraft
mechanics, gunnery mates and clerks were, for statistical
manipulation, interchangeable entities. They overestimated
the importance of pay as a career determinant. And they
overlooked the competitive influence of governmental programs that furnish youth with training and education,
placement and jobs, without asking for anything in return.

The forecasts of great monetary savings that would be
achieved through decreased turnover never materialized.
Here, the prognosticators did not anticipate that a change
in the recruiting base and the abandonment of the draft's
screening machinery would shift the need for sifting to
the services. The chaff that once fell out on the way to
the Armed Forces Examining and Induction Station now makes
it into uniform and is not found out until basic training
and beyond. In consequence, 400,000 plus accessions--
150,000 more than predicted--must be pumped into the
military every year to keep the strength reservoir at the
2 million mark.

Then there were the emotional broadsides. Continuation of the draft will allow the President to bypass

Congress in his quest for foreign adventures; while the
all-volunteer force would exert pressure on him to find
and start wars so that the mercenaries could advance in
rank and encounter loot and glory. The less said about
these arguments, the better. They seem terribly dated
today, rooted more in the rhetoric of the Vietnam War than
in the reality of America.

Finally, the threatened four-alarm blaze of an all-
black military turned out to be an ashtray fire.

Can we then say that all is well? Can we draw comfort
from the fact that the pendulum swings of prediction, to
unheard of benefits or stark disaster, not having occurred,
left the services much as they were? That the numbers which
testify to the all-volunteer force's quantity and quality
remain in a reassuring range? Shouldn't we put aside our
concern over military manpower and concentrate, instead, on
what is said to be the real national security problem: the
imbalance in military equipment, and go on an inventing,
developing, and buying spree?

We can--if we want to follow a hazardous course. The
happy surface characteristics of the all-volunteer force,
despite the optimistic pronouncements which they elicit,
conceal more than they reveal. They do not warn us of a
rapidly shrinking demographic accession base. They do not
reflect the proliferation of uncoordinated government programs that provide aid, assistance, and inducements to young
people, just because they are young. They gloss over underlying attitudinal, social, structural, and functional
changes--even changes in strategic and tactical concepts--
that tend to separate the military more and more from what
it believes and professes itself to be. And they afford us
little cause to remove control of military manpower matters
from the expert numbers manipulators who are the cause of
growing problems. Their power, position, and credibility
seem secure. An unbroken record of faulty predictions,
erroneous conclusions, and expensive results has not
loosened their hold on the field. Their faith in inappropriate techniques remains unshaken, and their sense of
problem formulation is such as to exclude real issues from
surfacing and debate.

Each of these trends, taken singly, can cause trouble
ahead. Collectively, and in synergistic reinforcement,
they spell disaster.

A Declining Base

Nineteen fifty-seven was the peak year for baby production
in the United States: 4,308,000. The four million plus

figure held for seven more years. But by 1965, parental
priorities began to shift. In that year 3,760,358 babies
were born. And by 1973 only 3,141,000 new Americans managed
to navigate between the Scylla and Charybdis of pills and
vasectomies, abortions and sterilizations. The elementary
school closings that are now sweeping the country are but
harbingers of the closing of divisions, wings, and fleets.

The Congressional Budget Office, clouding its crystal
ball with a futile relationship between military manpower
supply and unemployment rates, predicts an annual shortfall
of 95,000 accessions by 1985--not yet the worst year in
terms of young people supply. It is a shaky figure, derived
from faulty associations pioneered by the Gates Commission,
but it could be right, though for different reasons than
the CBO economists considered. Here is why: Of the 1.7
million young men turning eighteen in 1985, one million will
be physically and mentally qualified for military service.
Of that one million, 400,000 (at the present rate) will go
on to college and technical schools. The remaining 600,000
are high school graduates or drop-outs with acceptable mental
profiles (I through III). These 600,000 constitute the
primary recruiting pool. The services will want better
than one out of every two members of that pool. But they
are facing stiff competition.

Jobs

As the members of the plentiful baby years move upward on
the career ladder, there may not be enough applicants to
fill the vacancies which they leave behind. Youth unemployment, except for that hard core of unemployables, may
become a phenomenon of the past. And while youth unemployment never was the primary determinant of enlistments--the
Gates and CBO economists to the contrary--it provided a
respectable assist. The 1985 recruiter will not have the
benefit of that assist.

Education

Length of schooling may swing upward again, reversing a
present trend. The universities, colleges, commuter
colleges, community colleges, and technical schools built
to accommodate the graduates of the baby boom will not shut
their doors and turn themselves into condominiums because
of a decline in the student population. Rather, we should
expect an all-out marketing offensive to gather in learners.
There will be inducements for attendance, a multiplication
of attractive, easy-to-pass courses, the invention of
certification criteria for fields that hitherto required no
academic preparation, and collaborative programs with

employers to adjust educational prerequisites upwards to
emphasize selected courses and length of academic exposure
as conditions of being hired. The impact on our recruiter?
Any 1% increase in postsecondary school attendance will
remove 10,000 prospects from the primary pool. Given the
efforts of schools to keep their classrooms and dormitories
occupied and given the continuing expansion in federal
assistance programs for higher education, a 10% or 15%
increase in the stay-in-school rate is not out of the question.

Competitive Government Programs

Then there are the government programs designed to help
young people become adults. By any rule of experience,
these programs should gather momentum in inverse proportion
to the size of the population served. There are the Job
Corps, Peace Corps, CETA grants, impact aid, Youth Opportunity Acts, basic education opportunity grants, supplementary
educational opportunity grants, work-study programs, guaran-
teed student loans, direct student loans, tax credits for
job creation, programs geared to regional or local unemployment percentages, and counter-cyclical programs. Each of
the two major incentives used in military recruiting--job
training and education--has a government program counterpart
that will help youngsters gain their personal objectives
without asking them to stand at attention, obey their elders,
trim their hair, wash their feet, work long hours, relocate
to strange places where no shakes and burgers can be found,
or expose themselves to physical dangers. These programs
are not limited to the poor. They serve middle-income
families and even the rich in the form of tax relief. They
are flexible programs. Any decline in the client population
can be rapidly offset by changes in eligibility, broadened
benefits, and softened criteria.

     The poor recruiter, fishing for prospects in his small
and evaporating pool, must put up with the nets and lures
of the competing government programs, right by his side,
overharvesting the little that is left.

     And what is left? That 600,000-man pool, now partially
emptied by employment, shrunk by an added 100,000 to 150,000
who decided to go on to college, and drained some more by
any of a dozen major competitor programs, has become a pool
with magic properties. Each little fish that can be persuaded
to join a service may have to fill not one but several
uniformed vacancies.

     Thus, the days are numbered for the happy quantity
figures of the all-volunteer force. Four more years, to
repeat a well-known slogan, of adequate supplies; increasing

shortages thereafter. What then? Naturally, there will
be cries to recruit women if we cannot get men, to reach
for the dumb if we cannot get the smart, and to accept the
lame if we cannot get the healthy. But more of that later.

Rampant Vocationalism

The public and, unfortunately, many analysts see but the
outside of military service, and the military's exterior
facade has not changed. The pictures are familiar: the
uniforms and the bands; the steel-helmeted soldier pulling
the lanyard; the sailor carrying his sea bag across the
gangplank; the pilot climbing from his cockpit. It could
be the late show or World War II, except that the aircraft
are faster, the bombs are bigger, and missiles have joined
the arsenal.

But behind the trusted exteriors, there are fundamental
changes. Attitudinal and structural transformations are
occurring, and traditional strategies and concepts of
force employment are being replaced. The changes reach so
deep as to make a shambles of all perceptions of what the
term military conveys. Even the military's self-image of
heroism, sacrifice, and the centrality of combat at close
quarters no longer fits reality.

In the attitudinal area, for one, there is the steady
movement away from military professionalism to vocationalism.
Professor Charles C. Moskos describes it well. It is the
offspring of an unfortunate marriage between the military
tendency to get things neatly organized, tagged, and stowed
away, so that the commander can tell at one glance that all
hands are ready and prepared for action, and the value
system of the civilian job analyst whose point of reference
begins with positions, and not people. Each position must
be classified, described, dissected, costed out, justified,
evaluated for its contribution, and fitted into a subsystem
that serves a larger system. A number is then assigned to
the position and a body found to wear that number.

It began with the design of occupational specialty
structures, and should have ended there. But an effort
was made to achieve a numerical match among positions, people,
and training requirements. Computers that could play the
match game were brought in. Positions became the given
element of the program, people the variable. Each position
was characterized with a uniqueness of specialization, as
though it encompassed the duties of a brain surgeon. Only
those possessing the highly detailed prerequisites and
having gone through the prescribed training programs were
allowed to occupy it. This rigidity proved too much for
small computers. Larger machines were installed that were

up to the job. They could provide instant printouts of
excesses and shortages, mismatches and imbalances, and
trigger instant corrections by ordering turbulent and dis-
ruptive reclassification and termination actions.

Then the financial analysts entered the picture. Dollar
values were assigned to training programs and cash bonuses
offered for enlistments and reenlistments in fields considered to have shortages or high replacement training costs.

To top it all off, a cradle-to-grave skills testing
and validation program was invented that spelled the
difference between retention or release, advancement or
stagnation.

Before long, a complex vocational structure had come
into being that, based on its computerized requirements,
classified, tested, trained, promoted, rejected, retrained,
reclassified, transferred, and separated people; while
people responded in their own way, seeking to pick the most
advantageous path through the structure--preferably by
effort and hard work, but also by end-runs and law suits,
should these offer the only way.

It happened without a policy change or a policy
announcement. Ten or fifteen years ago, a man, when asked
for his job, responded, "I am a soldier, sir, but also a
line repairman." Today, the elements in the reply have
been reversed. The vocation is now central, the profession
of secondary import. Our man is now a line repairman who
incidentally, happens to be in the Army.

The all-volunteer force has given added impetus to the
trend. By intensely emphasizing the skill training and jobs
available in the services, it has institutionalized the
value shift.

In consequence, the majority of the force--the enlisted
members and younger officers--subscribe to a value system
different from that of the senior officers. A few parades
and military spectacles can no longer bridge the gap between
the two. The majority view them as annoyances and inter-
ruptions--as something that must be put up with. The symbols
which these functions represent--pride, loyalty, esprit,
dedication, discipline, instant response to orders--are no
longer understood because they have no counterpart in the
daily work experience or carry any impact on assignment,
advancement, special pays, or retention.

Enter the Ladies

A second challenge to the traditional concept of "military"

comes from the integration of women into the armed forces.
By the early eighties, more than 200,000 women will wear
the uniform and perform duties in all fields except those
defined as combat.

But what is combat? And how does one pinpoint parti-
cipants or predict who will be involved in the shooting?
It is not as clean-cut as in the theater where only union-
card-carrying stage hands are permitted to move the scenery.
Directors, actors, dancers, and producers must keep their
hands off the props--else they provoke a strike.

The official view of combat is little more than an
application of past wars to future situations. It is made
up, in large part, of senior officers' reminiscences of
youthful glories. It emphasizes close encounters of the
dangerous kind, which are obviously on the decline, and
minimizes the widely scattered damage that enemies can
inflict on each other by means of the greater mobility of
units and the longer range and larger destruction radii of
weapons. The battlefield has become a war zone.

In applying this definition to their own situation,
the services have become embroiled in a metaphysical and
theological self-analysis that might have been of credit
to a medieval monastic.

The Army may have thought that it could make an easy
distinction between combat and noncombat, but not for long.
Keep women out of combat units--the infantry, armor, artillery,
the Army said. On closer examination, however, it was noted
that combat units contain soldiers who are not combat
specialists. There are cooks, clerks, and supply people in
infantry battalions. What to do now? Let women be cooks,
clerks, and supply people--but only when the positions are
assigned to noncombat units? Such a decision might pose
serious implications for recruiting male cooks and clerks.
A second, equally ornery problem was uncovered. Are there
only combat units in the combat zone? Is there a cleanly
defined front line, where two sides struggle fiercely in
sight and touch of each other, while duties become less
dangerous and more vocational and further one moves to the
rear? If this definition holds, how far forward can a
women be assigned? Can she hold a mechanic's job in a
division maintenance battalion, which is rear, but not be
permitted to go forward with a repair team to fix a dis-
abled tank where it broke down on site, near the front line?
Must a male mechanic do that job? Are security duties in
a rear area that is threatened by guerrillas, long-range
patrols, and helicopter assault teams combat? Will units
located there resemble besieged medieval towns, with the
men on the walls and the women safely behind the fortifica-
tions? For that matter, will the concept of combat be

limited to offensive acts, but exclude the defense?

How will the Navy adjust to the definition? Will it
draw distinctions between ship and shore, between combat
and noncombat vessels, or between combat and noncombat
positions aboard ship? Will only jobs that may require
repelling cutlass-swinging boarding parties be defined as
combat?

What about the Air Force? Will fighters and inter-
ceptors be "no-no's," while patrol and reconnaissance
aircraft are deemed safe for women? Or will the distinction
be made by crew assignment? The tail gunner must be a man
while the navigator can be a woman?

The issues are as complex as they are arbitrary and
artificial. Their solution, as currently contemplated,
evokes a union card maze of "go's" and "no-go's," "do's"
and "don'ts." Special restrictions, no doubt, in the form
of numbers will be added to occupational codes, delineating
when a position or even a task within the position must be
performed by men. The man-job matching system, already
almost impossible to balance, will sink even deeper into
the morass of unmanageability.

Finally, will men raise the hue and cry of discrimin-
ation--protesting that they are directed to take infinitely
greater risks than women, while holding down identical jobs,
being classified in the same grade and skill, and drawing
the same pay?

But even more important, the gyrations to define combat
have forced the services to swallow large parts of their
self-image and concede that many of their elements neither
engage in heroics nor face particular hardships and risks.
Under the evolving definition, the combat enclave has become
embarrassingly small. While its immediate purpose may be
to create an all-male club, in the longer run its lack
of size will raise serious questions about what sociologists
call the military institution's "uniqueness" and "legitimacy."
In other words, why must so many be decked out in the trap-
pings of a dangerous profession, when so few are exposed to
danger? Is the arrival of women but the first step in whole-
sale civilianization?

The assignment of women to "safe" duties is but one
problem. Another problem arises from the fact that women
are by no means interchangeable with men, though both may
carry the same occupational coding. A whole new range of
personnel policies will have to be designed to cope with
the conflicting aspirations and career development requirements of uniformed husband-wife teams; with the needs of

single-parent families; with attritions that may come at
different reasons; and with difficult adjustment problems.

A third problem for which the services are ill-prepared
is their sudden plunge into the emotional-political arena
where women battle with each other over their role in society.
It's the feminine versus the feminist, the right-to-lifer
versus the abortionist, the total woman versus the total
libber. Regardless of who wins this battle, if victory of
any sort is possible, the services are bound to lose. Any
policies which they adopt will raise echoes in the public
arena, bring boos and cheers, and suffer unwanted, but
mandated, changes.

The only winners in the "womanization" of the Armed
Forces are the numbers manipulators. Valves are being
opened to a large personnel reservoir that holds the promise
of keeping the accession pipes full even when the flow from
the male pool begins its inevitable decline.

Can Pigeons Fire Missiles?

Changing strategic concepts and, to a lesser degree, over-
analytical approaches to tactical warfare pose a third
challenge to what is traditionally military.

The land-based leg of deterrence depends on highly
sophisticated command and control equipment--satellites,
over-the-horizon radars, global positioning systems--and
hardened and survivable silos. Components are either
unmanned or heavily sheltered. It is not people who move,
expose themselves, search, and fight, but equipment and
signals that do the moving, exposing, searching, and fighting.

Employment concepts and design of the deterrent are
already in civilian hands. Maintenance is usually performed
by civilian engineers. Entire operating parts of the system
have been contracted to civilian firms. The remaining
duties, assigned to the military, lack any association with
bravery and dash. They do not require exposure to hardships,
danger, and discomforts. They do not call for prolonged
family separations. All that is asked of the military members is that they demonstrate mental stability and have
dispositions that won't be soured by boredom. In a startling
paradox, the requirement for uniformed military and the
duties which they perform ends when war actually begins.

The sea-based deterrent, like the land-based, is linked
to surveillance and command control and communications systems with civilian characteristics and heavy civilian
participation in design, operation, and maintenance. The

crews, on the other hand, retain a greater association
with traditional military requirements than the men inside
the silos. Large measures of discipline and dedication
are still in demand for submarine duty, and hardships, risks,
and danger are very much present.

Tactical Warfare: A Game for Analysts

Even the holy inner sanctum of tactical warfare has been
invaded by civilian thought. Analysts from the business
colleges rather than military from the war colleges are
shaping the force structures and employment concepts of
tactical troops. If a chess analogy can be used, the shift
in thinking has centered all attention on the pieces owned
by each player--their value and number. The moves, on the
other hand, possibly because they cannot be as easily computerized and quantified, are assigned to limbo. Under
analyst rules of warfare, the player with eight pawns will
always defeat the player who possess but seven.

Analysis thrives on military balances, in terms of
pieces, the discovery of asymmetries, and the case for
erasing them. The direction it sets calls for the development, procurement, and issue of equipment with the narrowly
defined capability to match, neutralize, or remove the enemy's
counterpart capability, so that the two sides of the ledger,
down to the last decimal point, remain in balance. The
balancing fad is not limited to weapons. It encompasses the
entire panoply of command and control devices, communications,
electronic warfare, electronic countermeasures, and counter
countermeasures. There is a tit for every tat, and a tat
for every tit.

The outcome of this trend--which would be most dangerous
to our security had not our principal potential enemy selected
to play the same game--is the accumulation of finely tooled
combat equipment, highly accurate, very destructive, and
totally useless for any purpose other than shattering its
mirror image, counterpart capability. The real possibility
exists of extremely short exchanges that, in their intensity,
leave the two sides disarmed and the war zone a littered
junkyard of destroyed, smoking equipment shells.

Should the struggle continue beyond this first exchange,
it can take only two forms. It can go the primitive, sling-
shot, bows and arrows route for which there is no planning.
Or it can escalate to the nuclear level. That, of course
would be the supreme--and final--irony; for analysts value
general-purpose forces, and justify them, precisely for
their ability to provide an alternative to nuclear war.

What drops out of the analysts' war are the tactical

dimensions of mobility, terrain, and time; and, even more
important, the human dimensions of stamina, guts, motivation,
ingenuity, improvisation, imagination, and other valued
attributes of the traditional military. The analysts' war
does not conceive of men in combat and how, by virtue of
their determination, they can affect the outcome. It can
consider only equipment combat. The human contribution is
subordinated to the equipment and defined in mechanistic
terms: operator and procedural skills that follow prescribed
and detailed sequences laid out in the operating and assembly
instructions.

But more than just military capabilities and qualities
have been dropped from the conduct of tactical war. Entire
military units have been removed from participation because
they added nothing to the "military balance" formulas. It
happened this way: To add to the measurable elements of the
balance, without spending any money, large chunks of support
services--the troops that furnish maintenance, supply, and
transportation, called "the tail" in analyst lingo--were
converted into "teeth" that could be clamped onto the combat
weight on our side of the scale. Since logistical requirements did not decrease, the slack was taken up by civilian-
izing support duties. Some civilian specialists, known as
technical representatives, found themselves assigned all
the way forward, even on combat ships.

Thus, warfare itself--the ultimate justification of
the military on which rests its claim to uniqueness and
expertise--no longer belongs exclusively to the uniformed
forces. It is shaped and supported to an ever greater
degree by civilian thought and civilian participation.

The Retreat of the Military

The draft was highly valued for exposing the military to a
civilian presence; while the end of the draft was mourned
because it would deprive the military of this benign
influence and let it revert to its natural, antidemocratic,
Prussian rigidity.

The fact is that even without the draft, since World
War II the military door has been wide open to all things
civilian. Like a conglomerate going beserk, the military
has joined every fad and trend that appeared to have a
technological, technocratic, or pseudoscientific foundation,
and offered up its own domain for experimentation and eventual occupation.

To manage its troops, the military imported personnel
experts schooled in stonewalling unions while providing
executives with exotic perks and deferred compensation

packages. The outcome, as already noted, has been the
growth of rampant vocationalism, spiced with the budding
seeds of unionism.

Strategic and tactical thought were readily transferred
to civilian experts who prided themselves on their ability
to attach numbers to all things and present the numbers in
alternative arrangements for the gratification of top
decision-makers. Although here the military seemed, on
occasion, stung by this abdication and fought back by creating
uniformed think tanks to counter civilian dominance, the
efforts were short-lived and ineffective, with the output
of the think tanks ignored and the military thinkers re-
assigned to other duties for purposes of career development.
The outcome here, as also noted earlier, has been the
enthronement of quantifiable capabilities--an approach that
may be feasible with an enemy who thinks in like terms, but
fails miserably, as in Vietnam, where the enemy eschewed
the rules by which the graduates of the Harvard Business
School play.

A sizable piece of military terrain was lost through
an excessive fascination with computers and "systems"
which were allowed to pervade almost the entire uniformed
structure, from personnel to maintenance, from supply to
transportation, from accounting to budgeting, and from
welfare to morale. The direct outcome has not been an
improvement in management but the surrender of all management functions to people who understand computer applications.

Of more concern are the indirect costs. Computers--
what can be done with them and how they are used--operate
in opposition to values that mark the military profession.
Command, and the ability to control and direct, is important;
but computers tend to shift the authority ever upward to
the highest level that receives the print-out. A sense of
morale and readiness, based on direct observation, experience, and intuition, is important; but computers tend to
value only what can be measured, while their minions, in
good faith, distort problems so as to fit them into a
quantifiable mold. Keeping informed and, based on one's
knowledge, influencing the action, is important; but
computers tend to exclude from decision-making all those
who are not trained in machine language or have access to
outputs and terminals. Finally, flexibility is important;
but computers impose absolute rigidity. Changes in soft-
ware or hardware are immensely expensive--so expensive in
fact that even inappropriate applications must be retained,
and allowed to govern, rather than write off the huge
sums that brought them into being.

The growing pressure to integrate women in the military
has led the military to search out and mark an all-male

club known as "combat." But through its own lack of self-
understanding, the military produced a definition of combat
based on World War II confrontations as seen through the
rose-tinted glasses of fond memories. In a nutshell, this
definition said that no part written for John Wayne should
ever be played by a woman. The price of establishing this
exclusive, minuscule enclave has been the consignment of
all other military functions to an amorphous realm where
the arguments that justified the presence of women could
be just as easily adapted to justify the assignment of
civilians.

That lack of self-understanding, of not knowing where
to draw the line, has carried over to the encouragement
of programs that are completely antithetical to military
values. Take the self-awareness fad. Pseudoreligion,
transcendental meditation, heightened consciousness, bio-
rhythms, and what not have found a supportive reception on
military installations--almost a welcome designed to
demonstrate to all who care how "with-it," contemporary,
and modern the military really is. The elementary fact
that it is the military's job to build units which require
the individual to subordinate his personal preferences to
the team mission was totally forgotten. Meanwhile, self-
fulfillment and self-gratification were declared "in."

In a similar misunderstanding, the military has
supported and encouraged group awareness along racial,
sexual, or life-style lines. With great zeal and a "can-do"
attitude that went far beyond mandated requirements or the
size of the problem that was to be cured, formal programs
were invented and instituted that built and fostered
individual loyalties to the group--be it black, Hispano,
native American, woman, homosexual, vegetarian, single
parent, or Moonie--and helped advance an overriding interest
in the group's collective status in the military. The fact
that these programs, too, worked at cross purposes with
unit building was never taken into account. The poor
battalion commander was bombarded with directives and programs that required him to fragment his organization. It
became infinitely more important to feed the soldier ethnic
food in the chow line than make him believe that he was
a member of the best platoon, in the best company, in the
best battalion, in the best brigade, in the best division,
of the best damned Army in the world.

Occasionally young officers are puzzled by the intrusion
of civilian practice on military values. They will write
articles for military journals in which they attempt to
sort out the relationships among "command," "leadership,"
and "management." Through tortuous reasoning, they will
usually prove that the military "command" is still preeminent,
reigning over the civilian "management." The power and

authority that they associate with command, however, seldom
conveys more than the right to tell a soldier to button his
pockets.

And that is where the military is today. With most of
its territory abandoned to civilian practice, it has chosen
to make its last stands at the barber chair and on the parade
ground. It continues to exercise eminent authority over the
design, composition, and wearing of the uniform and those
parts of the soldier, sailor, and airman that are not covered
by cloth, such as the head and the hair growing from it.
Here, iron-clad rules have been imposed that emanate from the
top commanders. These rules are defended with great ferocity.
No quarter will be given. It is a fight to the last man.
Infidelity and moral dereliction may be forgiven, but not an
untrimmed sideburn. That is a challenge to constitutional
authority. An equal degree of control and high-level interest
is exercised over ceremonies and protocol, movements and
honors, and on which foot to give the preparatory command,
"to the rear."

The military, in effect, has become a guardian of
traditions that appear unrelated to everyday activities. But
rather than commemorate these traditions on an appropriate
day, once a year, such as the Fourth of July, most military
energy is now expended on imposing them every day. Restructuring military life so that traditions, symbols, and duties
regain their connection and reinforce one another has not
entered anybody's mind.

The Manpower Plumbers

The "fix" for all the problems capsuled in the preceding
paragraphs is to focus on the quantity of military manpower,
as expressed by force size, and on the quality, as measured
by years of school attendance or mental profile.

Two schools of fixers work on this numbers match. Both
are deeply entrenched in the upper echelons of the Department of Defense, the responsible executive agencies, the
congressional committees, the Congressional Budget Office,
and in their umbilically linked think tanks.

School One, of a slight, right-leaning bend, advocates
free-market forces for securing and retaining accessions.
"Pay enough," their credo reads, "and you will get all the
troops you need." Their operating theory is not that simple,
of course. It is grounded in econometric measures and
elasticity calculations which liken recruitment success to prevailing wages and unemployment levels on a region-by-region
basis. From these curves formulas are derived that are said
to predict--but never do--the drawing power of incremental
increases in pay.

School Two leans slightly to the left. It believes
that the country is threatened more by inequality and lack
of opportunity than an external enemy. If there must be a
military, its main function should be the creation of employment and career chances for groups that hitherto were
denied their fair share of the pie. School Two subscribes
to social manipulation and focuses on the manpower pool. If
you can't get male high school graduates, of certain physical
characteristics, who also know how to read and write, their
reasoning goes, then drop the educational prerequisite. This
will add thousands to the pool. It will also help the disadvantaged gain an education. Then tamper with height and
weight standards. Swell the pool with the tall and short,
fat and thin. In this manner, the military gets its recruits
and the recruits get overdue medical attention and care.
Create more opportunities for women. By this all young women
can join the pool. It also opens up the nation's largest
employer to the ambitions of career women. Should all these
approaches fail, attack the size of the manpower requirement.
By substituting civilians, the need for military recruits is
diminished. And, of course, fewer citizens will be exposed
to the harsh, undemocratic ways of the uniform. Better still,
redefine security needs or the number of wars in which the
United States may fight simultaneously, and the manpower
requirement can be lowered even more.

Once the accessions have entered military service, they
are routed by a second set of manpower plumbers into an
elaborate pipe and valve arrangement of Rube Goldbergian
invention and complexity. Flows are increased, decreased, or
turned off on the basis of primary and secondary occupational
specialties, career content versus noncareer content, grade
limitations, quality measures, mental and physical profiles,
sex, decision points, bonuses, top six ratios, tour lengths,
prerequisites, validations, test scores, regular versus
reserve status, base year of commissioning, expected termination of service, disciplinary records, and what have you.
The gadgetry, with the artificial imbalances which it produces,
may provide an intellectual game challenge to the operators
who control the flows; for those caught in the pipes the
process creates turmoil, turbulence, confusion, insecurity,
and dissatisfaction.

There is still a third group of plumbers who are
charged with defending expenditures. They operate in
direct opposition to the first two groups, while using the
same machinery. Their job is to snip off all the carrots
that the incentive manipulators are dangling in front of
the troops. They turn off benefit valves, thin out the
flow, change qualifications or eligibility criteria, or
even introduce new concepts such as having individuals
share in the cost of their fringes. The result of these
manipulations is even more turbulence, insecurity, and

dissatisfaction plus the evocation of outright resentment. Dollars may be saved in the targeted programs; but invariably more dollars than were saved must be added to the programs that suffer when unhappiness lowers recruiting, retention, and performance goals and leads to court challenges and unionism.

One thing the two schools and three sets of plumbers share: complete faith in numbers, in manipulation, and in theory. Theory is allowed to dominate procedures, no matter that reality tends to disprove it once or twice a day.

The British experience with the volunteer force provides a superb preview of what can and will happen here. Theorists, wedded to the same econometric and manipulative shibboleths as ours, have been in charge of the British conversion and giving it policy direction. In the process, they have attempted every gimmick and incentive that is contemplated by United States personnel experts: changes in enlistment age, in enlistment lengths, in bonuses, in the pay structure, the pay format, and the pay levels. No gimmick has achieved the hoped-for and predicted effects. Rather, the size of the force had to be decreased, following successive White Paper studies. Costs, meanwhile, have gone up in inverse proportion to force size. The invariable byproducts of econometric engineering--social, human, organizational, and value problems--made their appearance. And the experts who unwittingly evoked these problems, lacking the knowledge, techniques, and skills to understand or solve them, reacted as expected, with pathetic, buck-passing cries for more leadership recruitment, identification, and training.

Who Needs the Uniform?

Obviously, we cannot maintain the size of our present forces unless we wish to return to the draft or impose a form of national service. Diminishing demographics rule out a voluntary arrangement of two million armed troops that must be replenished by 400,000 plus accessions per year.

And, just as obviously, we have blurred the military character of our forces. One can no longer say, with great clarity, that here is the line that separates the civilian from the military. Elements of both are on either side of the line. The mixture applies not only to support and operational functions but to management and employment concepts as well.

The mixture is unhealthy. The military, on the civilian side, add to costs. They are, moreover, disgruntled and confused because they cannot equate the requirement of the uniform, and what it conveys, with the nature of their

nonmilitary duties. Their dissatisfaction is contagious
and tends to infect the military who perform true military
duties. The civilian presence on the military side of the
line adds to the disease. By injecting faulty and inappropriate theories and procedures, it corrodes and wears away
the necessary uniqueness of the military, which is its
greatest strength.

The overriding question which we must answer in the
next two years is not who can be inveigled to wear the
uniform, through pay or valve manipulation or games with
sex and standards, but who still needs the uniform? And
once that question is answered, we must sort out the deck
and place civilian presence and thought on one stack and
military presence and thought on the other.

There have been efforts in the past to identify the
jobs which require military incumbents. Usually, these
efforts were part of civilianization programs that took a
position-by-position approach. Each position, then, would
become a miniskirmish. The military defenders would raise
the issues of deployability, rotation base requirements,
and combat. Eventually, some positions were vanquished
and occupied by civilians, but never as many as leaders of
civilianization had announced as their objective on the
eve of battle.

A second approach has been the contracting out of
functions--helicopter maintenance, kitchen police, some
security tasks. The struggle here, more often than not,
has pitted career civil service and wage board employees
against contractors, with one group of civilians replacing
another as the outcome.

A third approach has centered on the definition of
combat duties. The purpose here has been the creation of
job opportunities for women. The approach has resulted in
the replacement of male troops by female. Its value is
that it has identified many positions that could as easily
be filled by civilians.

The Power Company Model

A more profitable approach for sorting out the civilian-
military mix would not start at the bottom, with positions,
but at the top, with the big picture, and address entire
functions. The process might begin with an examination of
other organizations that serve the public and how such
organizations are staffed to deliver reliable, uninterrupted
service.

A power company is an excellent model. It must produce

electricity, in the quantities needed, around the clock.
Were its service to fail, even for a relatively short time,
unspeakable chaos would result.

The typical power company is manned by four distinct
groupings of personnel. It is important to note at the
outset that while all four groups contribute to the workings of the company, not all contribute to the uninterrupted
delivery of electricity.

First, there is the managerial-professional-technical
element. It includes top management; the long-range planners
who anticipate future area power needs; the rate setters
who must devise charge structures and defend them before
the public service commissions; the energy specialists who
must balance fuel needs with fuel availability; the government policy experts who must consider the impact of federal
and state energy and environmental programs on present and
future company operations; and the financial, procurement,
R&D, real estate, personnel, advertising, marketing, and
public relations managers. This is a workaholic element
that puts in 60 to 70 hours per week at the office,
brings work home, and occasionally leaves home for inspec-
tion trips or professional conferences. The group's
commitment and dedication are divided between the need to
keep the juice flowing and a desire to achieve the maximum
return on investment allowed by the rate commission.

Second, there is the routine service-support element,
charged with maintaining internal records, external billings
and collections, the processing of connections, disconnections,
and new installations, the handling of customer inquiries
and complaints, and so on. This is an eight-to-five element.
Members of this group, unlike the first, can function effectively without a sense of identification with the company
or commitment to its goals and social purposes. Such
factors as pay, working conditions, accessibility to public
transport or parking are probably the most important job
satisfiers.

A third group staffs the monitoring and control net-
work. This is an around-the-clock, seven days-per-week
function. It regulates fuel flows and electricity production,
handles interchanges with other systems, detects breaks
or interruptions in service, and directs emergency actions
to restore service. Dedication and reliability are important
elements in carrying out this function. There has to be
an absolute mastery of procedures that are spelled out in
great detail, and some judgment in selecting the procedures
that must be followed. The group, in its duties, resembles
the military who are assigned to strategic support functions.

The fourth group encompasses the maintenance crews.

These are the soldiers of the power company who will go out
and restore service at any time of day, in any neighborhood,
no matter how disreputable, during any kind of weather, be
it windstorm or blizzard. Their work exposes them to considerable hardships and physical dangers. There is no shift
or eight-hour limit. They must stay on the job until it is
done. Maintenance crews operate not only in their own
service area, but also in neighboring areas that were badly
hit by icestorms, floods, or other disasters. The crews
take pride in their skills, in the importance of their jobs,
in the dangers that they face. They consider themselves
the most important link in furnishing uninterrupted service.
Their elitism and the nature of their work bring them very
close to the true military. The fact that they are union-
ized merely adds to their group solidarity.

     There are four lessons that can be drawn from this
model:

     1. While all members of the power company contribute
to the functioning of the organization, not all members are
directly involved in delivering its vital service.

     2. A sense of identification with the company and its
purpose is important for the people who give the organization
its direction and are responsible for uninterrupted service.
The people engaged in routine support and organizational
maintenance, on the other hand, can discharge their tasks
effectively without developing a psychic dimension.

     3. Not all members of the organization must be
available for round-the-clock operations or for immediate
service under adverse conditions.

     4. There is little mobility among the four groups
of employees. Organization members are valued for their
expertise in their chosen field, not for their familiarity
with and direct experience in every company job.

     What is the value of these lessons for the Department
of Defense? Simply this: the power company has found much
cleaner lines for grouping people and their attributes with
the duties that they perform. Within the Department of
Defense these lines are blurred. Consider that:

     1. Here, too, all members contribute to the function-
ing of the organization, but not all are involved in the
direct delivery of its service. But both civilians and
military, as individuals and in groups, are located in
jobs that relate to the maintenance of the organization and
jobs that make up the service delivery element.

     2. Some members of the Department of Defense require

the psychic dimension of identification with the organization, mission, and higher purpose to discharge their
assignments; others do not. But here, too, civilian and
military elements are dispersed throughout the two categories.

3. Some members of the department, but not all, must
be available for immediate service. Once more, distinctions
are unclear with civilians and military found in both the
deployable and nondeployable groups.

4. Finally, the military component of the department,
unlike the power company, has great faith in job rotation.
In the course of a career, a military member may serve with
elements that deliver the department's service, and then
with elements that maintain the organization. For three
years he may require a sense of greater purpose to give
him strength, and in the next three years be plunged into
an eight-to-five environment. He may serve with a deployable component and, on his next tour, with a fixed activity.

This blurring of functions has benefited neither the
civilian component of the department nor the military. It
tends to wear away distinctions down to the lowest common
denominator level. A regrouping is in order.

For one, it will be necessary to distinguish philosophically (and not by job analysis) between civilian and military
attributes. The latter need to be defined in the traditional
terms of discipline, devotion to duty, loyalty, and the
willingness to endure hardships and family separations and
face physical dangers. These attributes must be coupled to
the belief that pride, esprit, endurance, skills, imagination,
and innovation can be built into units and can contribute
more to success than high scores on computerized readiness
reports.

Once the philosophical distinctions are understood,
the main dividing line can be drawn between fixed activities
and deployable activities. Fixed activities contribute
chiefly to the internal management and functioning of the
organization, while deployable activities deliver the
service. In this sense, fixed activities, which include
installations, bases, depots, communications stations, and
laboratories, are civilian in nature, while deployable
activities--the units, wings, and ships--are military.

If this grouping is to work, the military must abandon
the policy of individual replacements and shift to a unit-
replacement concept. Otherwise, uniformed members will
continue to be assigned to civilian activities in the interest of maintaining a skill rotation base.

A second demarkation line must be drawn through headquarters activities to separate control of deployable tasks--command, operations, planning, and doctrine--from control of fixed tasks such as financial management, R&D, procurement, contracting, property disposal, club management, public relations, congressional liaison, and the like.

The corollary measure here is to silence the argument that a military presence is needed on all staffs so that actions can be evaluated for their impact on combat. If this argument had merit, the president of the power company would weigh all his decisions for their effect on pole climbing. In fact, the discharge of fixed-activities tasks requires a unique expertise which the rapidly rotating military can never acquire; while the knowledge of combat, that can be injected, is often as dated as it is irrelevant. When it does become a factor, it usually tends to lean the staff project toward the last war, rather than the next one.

The result of the reshuffling: a major realignment in the staffing of functions. The 30% of the present uniformed strength, located in the fixed activities sector, would be converted to civilian positions; the band of influential civilian positions in the deployable sector would become military. The smaller, better-defined military that would emerge from the realignment can, in all probability, continue to be raised through voluntary means, even in the years when the baby-bust generation reaches young adulthood.

More important, the realignment restores a sense of consistency to philosophies, professionalism, the nature of staffing, and the duties assigned. It ends thirty years of blurring and fuzzing. Both sides of the house, civilian and military, as well as the department and the nation, should benefit from this cleaning up. The civilian sector, for its part, can capitalize on the continuity of its members and their academic and managerial expertise. The military side, purified and rejuvenated in its professional standards, its uniqueness once more cleanly delineated, can concentrate on what it does best: the delivery of service.

Contributors

GWYN HARRIES-JENKINS is a faculty member in the Department
of Adult Education at the University of Hull, England. He
is chairman of the British Inter-University Seminar on
Armed Forces and Society and vice-chairman of the Research
Committee on Armed Forces and Society of the International
Sociological Association. His previous publications include
The Military and the Problem of Legitimacy and The Army in
Victorian Society.

JOHN B. KEELEY is director of the research project The
Military in American Society, which is being conducted by
the Miller Center of Public Affairs of the University of
Virginia. He is a retired Army officer whose assignments
have included four years on the U.S. Naval War College
faculty, three years as an insturctor at the United States
Military Academy, command of an infantry battalion in
combat, and various high-level staff assignments in the
United States and abroad. He holds degrees from the United
States Military Academy and Princeton University.

CECILE LANDRUM is senior analyst in the Office of the
Assistant Chief of Staff, Studies and Analysis, Head-
quarters, United States Air Force. Prior to joining the
Air Force staff, she was a staff mamber of the Defense
Manpower Commission. She also served as a professional
staff member of the Senate Permanent Subcommittee on
Investigations, Government Operations. Mrs. Landrum came to
Washington, D.C., from Boston, where she was active in
Democratic politics and served on the personal staff of the
mayor of Boston, Kevin White.

ROBERT LEIDER is presently the president of Octameron
Associates. A former Army officer, he spent two years in
the United States Navy and twenty-five years in the Army.
He has held a variety of command and high-level staff
assignments. He is a frequent contributor to the New York
Times and military and foreign affairs journals. In 1973
he was the gold medalist of the United States Naval Institute's annual essay contest. He holds degrees from
Columbia and George Washington Universities.

CHARLES C. MOSKOS, JR., is professor of sociology at
Northwestern University. He is the author of The American
Enlisted Man and Peace Soldiers: The Sociology of a United
Nations Military Force. He is also editor of "Public
Opinion and the Military Establishment." He serves as vice
chairman of the Inter-University Seminar on Armed Forces and
Society.

WILLIAM P. SNYDER is an associate professor of political
science at Texas A&M University. A former Army officer,
he has had extensive staff and command experience, including
an assignment as an analyst in the Office of the Assistant
Secretary of Defense, Systems Analysis, and as a staff
officer in the Office of Emergency Preparedness, Executive
Office of the President. He has served as a faculty member
of the Department of Social Sciences at the United States
Military Academy and at the Army War College. He is the
author of The Politics of British Defense Policy: 1945-1962
and Case Studies in Military Systems Analysis. He holds a
bachelor of science degree from the United States Military
Academy and a doctorate of philosophy from Princeton University.